IN SEARCH

OF THE SELF

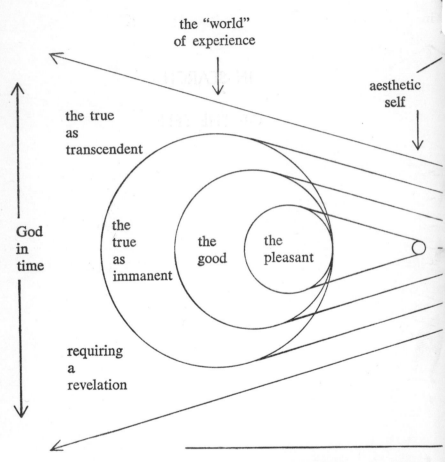

the "world"
of experience

aesthetic
self

the true
as
transcendent

God
in
time

the
true
as
immanent

the
good

the
pleasant

requiring
a
revelation

A SCHEMA OF THE

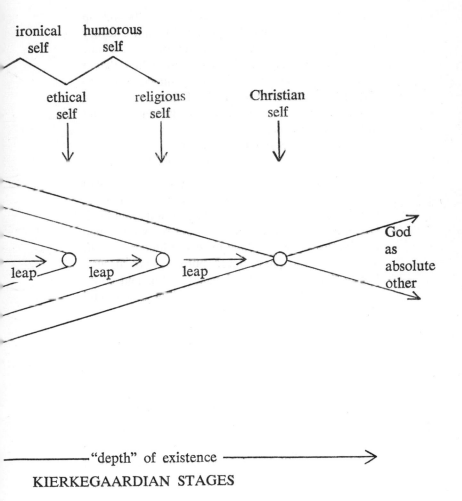

KIERKEGAARDIAN STAGES

With the category of 'the individual' is bound up any ethical importance I may have. If that category was right, if that category was in place, if I saw rightly at this point and understood rightly that it was my task (certainly not a pleasant nor a thankful one) to call attention to it, if that was the task given me to do. . .—in that case I stand fast and my works with me.

—Søren Kierkegaard
The Point of View, pp. 131-132

It is very dangerous to go into eternity with possibilities which one has oneself prevented from becoming realities. A possibility is a hint from God. One must follow it. . . . If God does not wish it then let him prevent it, but one must not hinder oneself. Trusting to God I have dared, but I was not successful; in that is to be found peace, calm, and confidence in God. I have not dared: that is a woeful thought, a torment in eternity.

—Søren Kierkegaard
Journals, No. 829

I hope with my writings to have achieved this much: to have left behind me so exact a description of Christianity and its relation to the world that a young man with enthusiasm and nobility of mind will be able to find in it a map of the conditions, as accurate as any topographical map by one of the well-known institutes. I have not had the help of such an author. The old doctors of the Church lacked one side, they did not know the world.

—Søren Kierkegaard
Journals, No. 849

IN SEARCH
OF THE SELF

The Individual in the Thought of

KIERKEGAARD

Libuse Lukas Miller

The King's Library

Muhlenberg Press   Philadelphia

© 1962 BY MUHLENBERG PRESS

Library of Congress Catalogue Card Number 61-10282

Printed in U.S.A.   UB896

To Howard and Edna Hong

for introducing me to S. K.

Preface

Now that the most important works of Kierkegaard have been translated into English, it is a little easier to write something about him without risking the misunderstanding that one is presenting the sum and substance of his thought, or at least expounding the most significant part of it. There stand the works themselves, in English, and the reader can easily resort to them to correct any such misapprehension and to achieve the balanced view. Or, so it would be in the ideal case. However, while it is generally agreed that a balanced view of Kierkegaard is desirable, one cannot but wonder how many people actually would take the trouble to read the thirty-odd works now available in English. I have found that to an astonishing degree, even after all that has been published about him, even in circles where such reading is supposed to be done, people know Kierkegaard only as a slogan. "The Absurd!" "The Leap in the Dark!" I do not claim to have any solution to this situation, and I here disclaim that this book presents the sum and substance of Kierkegaard, and I heartily recommend the reader to those thirty-odd works for the balanced view. After fourteen years of reading Kierkegaard, and reading about him, I have come to doubt that a balanced view of him could be placed between the covers of a single book.

I do not consider myself to be a disciple of Kierkegaard. In regard to him I feel rather like the surprised beneficiary of a distant relative's last will and testament. When I discovered Kierkegaard in 1944, my thinking had been along sympathetic lines, and then I found he had said it all so much better, a hundred years ago. This book was written then, in part to discharge a debt of gratitude, but also because I feel there is so much we can learn from him today, without becoming his disciples. And I feel this in particular with regard to his idea of "the individual." How it could enrich the present understanding of the nature of the individual here in America! For Americans are by tradition exponents of the individual, but there is something missing in our idea of what an individual is, and what he can become.

Kierkegaard was misunderstood by his contemporaries, and he suffered from that misunderstanding—a fact that makes him seem, to me at least, more human than if he had been haughtily indifferent to what they thought. In *The Journals* there are many places where he bemoans this misunderstanding, and one gets the impression that he would have loved a real fight with a worthy opponent. "In a big country I should have met with opposition, which I should have had to recognise; I should have had to fight outwardly."* But in little Denmark he had to suffer only the opposition of "all that is petty and wretched." He had to suffer from his contemporaries the petty meanness of envy, gossip, ridicule, and impudent curiosity in relation to himself as an "eccentric person"; in relation to his works he had to suffer the invincible ignorance of those who can't be bothered to read for themselves, yet presume to have an opinion on every subject, as all educated people in a modern state are expected to have.

It would be a hardy soul who would hazard a guess as to whether Kierkegaard is today more widely read and understood by the same kind of people who were his contemporaries in Copenhagen—not by dons and professors, but by those same ordinary educated people in a modern state who are expected to have an opinion on every subject. There is at least one entry in the *Journals* in which Kierkegaard shows a more realistic estimate of his author-reader relationship: "The expression 'an author's author' which I once used because it was unavoidable, and which was later adopted by several people, really denotes the something which I possess over and above the usual. I am really an author for authors; I have no direct relation to the public; no, as an author I make others productive. Therein lies my suffering, as long as this is not understood, for during that time the something in me which is over and above the usual becomes a minus instead of a plus."†

From this acknowledgement, that he was an author for authors, I have drawn some sustenance in justifying the writing of this book.

* *The Journals* of Søren Kierkegaard, ed. and trans. Alexander Dru (New York: Oxford University Press, 1938), No. 852, p. 276.
† *Ibid.*, No. 1006, p. 350.

As for the content of his works, I think that today we do Kierkegaard the least injustice when we simply try to learn what we can from him for ourselves, for our own tasks, and then leave the rest to history. And I hope he will forgive me for making a chart of the Kierkegaardian stages—for he could hardly be expected to approve of the manner in which we have all become chart-minded these days.

I am gratefully indebted to the Rev. Robert J. Page and the Rev. Charles J. Stoneburner for reading the manuscript and for giving me helpful suggestions.

LIBUSE LUKAS MILLER

Published Works of Kierkegaard

For a bird's eye view of the authorship and for the reader's convenience, this list of Kierkegaard's works in the order of their original publication is taken from the chronology in Alexander Dru's translation of selections from Kierkegaard's *Journals*. Asterisks signify that the work is now available in English.

1838 *From the papers of one still living,* 'published contrary to his will, by S.K.'

1841 *On the concept of Irony with particular reference to Socrates* (S. K.'s dissertation).

1843 *Either-Or*, edited by Victor Eremita.*
Two Edifying Discourses, S.K.*
Fear and Trembling, by Johannes de Silentio.*
Repetition, by Constantin Constantius.*
Three Edifying Discourses, by S. K.*
Four Edifying Discourses, by S. K.*

1844 *Two Edifying Discourses*, by S. K.*
Three Edifying Discourses, by S. K.*
Philosophical Fragments, or a Fragment of Philosophy, by Johannes Climacus, published by S. K.*
The Concept of Dread, by Vigilius Haufniensis.*
Prefaces, by Nicolaus Notabene.
Four Edifying Discourses, by S. K.*

1845 *Three Occasional Discourses*, by S. K.*
      Stages on the Road to Life, edited by Hilarius Bookbinder.*
      S. K.'s article in *The Fatherland* asking to be attacked by *The Corsair*.

1846 *Final Unscientific Postscript*, by Johannes Climacus, published by S. K.*
      A Literary Review, by S. K.*

1847 *The Book on Adler* completed in its first form.
      Edifying Discourses of Varied Tenor, by S.K.*
      The Works of Love, by S. K.*
      The Book on Adler completed in its third form.*

1848 *Christian Addresses*, by S. K.*
      The Crisis and a Crisis in the Life of an Actress, by Inter et Inter, appears as a supplement in *The Fatherland*.
      The Point of view for my Work as an Author 'as good as finished.' It was published by his brother in 1859.*

1849 *The Lilies of the Field and the Birds of the Air.*
      Second edition of *Either-Or.*
      Two Minor Ethico-Religious Essays, by H. H.*
      Sickness unto Death, by Anti-Climacus, published by S. K.*
      The High-Priest—The Publican—The Woman who was a Sinner: Three Discourses before Communion on Friday, by S. K.*

1850 *Training in Christianity*, by Anti-Climacus, published by S. K.*
      An Edifying Discourse.
      On my work as an author.
      Two Discourses at Communion on Friday.
      For Self-Examination.

1851-1852 *Judge for Yourself*, the second part of *For Self-examination*, published by his brother in 1876.*

1854 The article against Martensen, 'Was Bishop Mynster a witness to the truth?'*

1855 Articles arising out of the attack on Martensen.*
      Nos. 1-9 of *The Instant.*
(*Johannes Climacus, or, De Omnibus Dubitandum Est, and A Sermon.*
Apparently not published in Danish.)

Acknowledgments

For extensive quotations from Kierkegaard's writings, the author wishes to thank Oxford University Press *(The Journals,* "Two Notes About 'The Individual,' " *The Point of View, etc.),* Princeton University Press *(Concluding Unscientific Postscript, Philosophical Fragments, The Sickness unto Death, Either/Or, Fear and Trembling, The Concept of Dread),* and Harper and Bros. *(Purity of Heart).*

CONTENTS

1

How to Learn Something from Kierkegaard

1. The Giver and the Receiver

The life and authorship of Søren Kierkegaard, Denmark's second gift, after Hamlet, to the domain of existential reflection, poses a peculiar question to the successive generations of his readers, whether they have been enthralled or enraged by what they have found in his writings. When a man of such formidable' intellectual gifts, who obviously could have done something useful for society and could have supported himself in a respected profession, decides instead to spend his life educating himself in public through his writings, at his own expense, what is one to think? Either the man must be a supreme example of pompous asininity, one who imagines that his own education is of special importance to the world, or he must be primitively humble, one who imagines that his own education is of importance to the world, though only in the sense that every man's education in life is of importance to the world, to himself, and to God.

The lovers and haters of Kierkegaard will not hesitate too long over the answer to this question. For even the haters of Kierkegaard, if their hatred is based on firsthand acquaintance with his works rather than on academic hearsay, have to admit that here was a man who literally expended himself for a cause. More exactly, he thought that a higher power had decided that he was expendable. So he paid out his thought, his passion, his fortune,

[1] The designation "lovers and haters" (and this is the way his most understanding readers must be characterized) should not be confused with uncritical and critical readers of Kierkegaard. Criticism is always partly a labor of love, for one does not bother to criticize that which he finds intrinsically worthless. So the true lovers of Kierkegaard are his best critics. On the other hand, the true haters of Kierkegaard are not those who have misunderstood him (as if a little explanation could change their attitude) but those who have read him critically, understood him well, and then found that the need to defend a basically rationalistic or humanistic or intellectualistic attitude toward the human condition practically forces them, in all good conscience, to denounce him.

1

his personal relations, and his life's energy in the service of an idea, always at the expense of some more natural and more rewarding career that would have been possible for him. He was an exceptionally solitary man, a fact disturbing to his lovers and fortifying to his haters; but however they may variously explain his solitariness, they must regard the fact of his authorship as his breakthrough out of that solitariness, his own attempt to share whatever he had to give in the only way he could give it. What he gave in his writings comprised the results, in life and thought, of an "experiment" in Christianity conducted in the laboratory of a single soul by one who used himself both as guinea pig and as observer, an experiment relating to the question of what it means to become a Christian. Such a gift, like every gift, presupposes a receiver. Kierkegaard thought of himself as an exception in regard to what he must be prepared to give up and to undergo for the sake of learning truth, and in this feeling he was no different from any scientist or any artist who takes his work seriously. But he certainly did not think of himself as an exception as to his participation in what is essentially human and concerns every man as man. He assumed that if the question of what it means to become a Christian is of any importance at all, it is of equal importance to every man.

For the receiver, the essential thing about any gift is to accept it in the spirit in which it is offered. In this book it is assumed that to accept the gift of Kierkegaard in the spirit in which it is offered is to accept the entire authorship as an occasion for self-examination by the reader. Thus far in the reception of Kierkegaard's work by such reading public as he has had, it has generally been assumed that only the religious discourses are for self-examination, whereas the aesthetic, philosophical, and psychological works are for theological and philosophical reconstruction or for entertainment. Surely no great harm would be done if the nonsermonic works were taken to be for entertainment, since that would be playing into Kierkegaard's Socratic game as well as he could wish! But to take them solely as a point of departure for theoretical construction in philosophy and theology is, it seems to me, to sidetrack his purpose in a way that obscures his direct relevance to our own situation.

The books that have appeared in English about Kierkegaard have been largely of two kinds. The first is the presentation type, in which some abridgment, or summary, or interpretation, of the voluminous authorship has been attempted, for the benefit of the short-winded reader who has neither the time nor the inclination to go through a leisurely examination of the originals. This type of book performs a useful function. The second kind, of somewhat higher academic standing, might be called the Ph. D.-thesis-type, in which some philosophical or theological "position" of Kierkegaard has been abstracted, developed as a concept, and then criticized or compared with other concepts in the field, in order to prove some thesis for the writer. Such books as this also perform a useful function. They provide the writer with his doctoral degree,[2] and they make the reader think. However, everything depends on *what* they make the reader think. If they make the reader think that now he is in a position to pigeonhole Kierkegaard as a certain type of philosopher, theologian, Christian, or psychopathic case, the reader has probably learned something interesting *about* Kierkegaard, but he has not learned anything about himself *from* Kierkegaard. And it is his own fault, because he did not listen closely enough to the original works to catch the sound of his own name. For it seems to me that *all* of Kierkegaard's works try, in some way, to tell the reader something about himself, even the most "indirect communications," even the most abstract analyses, those works that tend to generate the Ph. D.-thesis-type of book.

It will be assumed here that enough of these two kinds of books about Kierkegaard have appeared so that a certain familiarity with the subject matter can be presupposed, and we can therefore proceed to this question: "What can we learn from Kierkegaard for our present situation?" Or, more specifically: "What can I learn about myself from what Kierkegaard went out of his way to tell *me*, the particular individual I happen to be?" It will be pointed out that the answers to these questions are necessarily different for

[2] I refrain at this point from growing suitably ironical on the subject of dons and professors. Kierkegaard fervently prayed that dons and professors would not lay a hand on his work, but in our time dons and professors have become so much more diffident and humble, and so on the defensive as intellectuals, that they are no longer, at least in this field, appropriate targets for sarcastic attacks.

different readers. That is certainly true beyond a certain point, but not to such an extent that discussion is useless among those who wish to learn something from Kierkegaard in this way. Kierkegaard's talent as poet and introspector enabled him to describe the states of human inwardness in such imaginatively appealing and yet psychologically apt terms that the reflective reader recognizes the descriptions as real possibilities present within himself in various degrees of strength and awareness. Such writing helps him as a guide helps us by holding a flashlight on our path when we go through the forest at night. We know that the path is there already—the flashlight does not create the path. But it helps us to see and name, and to choose or avoid, what actually lies in the path, and thus to move on. The paths through the forest may be different for different individuals, but they are not so different that they do not all exhibit some characteristics that distinguish them from, let us say, an express highway. Nor does this mean that we follow in Kierkegaard's own path when we make use of his light. Rather, like a visitor caught out at night, we borrow the Kierkegaardian flashlight, each to illuminate his own path through the forest on his way home.

2. *Needed: Clarity and Relevance*

The practical prerequisite for learning something from Kierkegaard in order to learn something about oneself is that one must gain a perspective on him which deliberately seeks to avoid certain easily accepted distortions of him. A powerful personality whose temperament, passion, wit, and private life invade all his writings (and enliven them) makes it difficult for his readers to avoid getting entangled with him in a personal relationship. Thus, the lovers and haters of Kierkegaard, although they understand him better than the indifferent readers, are constantly tempted to canonize him or condemn him wholesale because he is able to make them happy or angry, sympathetic or scornful, by the impact of his personality coming through his writings. The cure for this is not indifference, but aesthetic distance and historical perspective. Aesthetic distance is to the contemplation of life what objectivity is to scientific description. In this case it simply means that in order to make a fair or just estimation of such a complex phenomenon as

Kierkegaard's personality and authorship, one must be willing to suspend, postpone, or qualify the simple desire to approve or disapprove until as many as possible of the contributing elements have been allowed to play their part in the total picture he presents. For example, if we think we detect certain neurotic tendencies in his character, we should also look about to see how he himself understood them and dealt with them, before we rush to dismiss his work as the outpourings of a neurotic personality. Or, if we are offended by his supposed pessimism, we should be willing to give just as much attention to the possible external justification for his pessimism as to the ingrained melancholy he himself complained of, and perhaps we should also be willing to look for a word that would describe his attitude more correctly than the too-simple term "pessimism." On the other hand, if, for example, we rejoice in his attack on Hegel, we should not let this pleasurable sensation blot out the necessity for critical examination of his own use of the Hegelian terminology in conducting the attack, and also of the effect of this battle-terminology on his particular restatement of religious experience and Christian doctrine. In this way aesthetic distance can prevent the *lovers* of Kierkegaard from becoming his *disciples*—something for which he would give them no thanks— and it can prevent the haters of Kierkegaard from disposing of him as easily as they would like, by the method of blanket condemnation.

Historical perspective, on the other hand, has the function of bringing the relatively undistorted picture of Kierkegaard that we hope to achieve by aesthetic distance into a practical and challenging relationship with the modern reader. Historical perspective is particularly important in the case of Kierkegaard because he took history seriously enough to want to apply a corrective to the direction it was taking in his own time. He was a reformer rather than a philosopher. His point of departure was no set of philosophical axioms and his objective was no system of thought explaining everything, something to be judged by the ordinary philosophical rules of consistency and adequacy aside from any historical embodiments. Plato, Aristotle, or Aquinas could be judged in this way, but not Kierkegaard. His point of departure was the actual religious and philosophical situation of western

Europe and particularly Denmark in the first part of the nineteenth
century; and his objective was to expose the contradictions and
errors inherent in that particular situation in the light of a standard
which itself needed to be clarified in order to be applied, namely,
the Christian standard. His way of clarifying that standard was to
direct attention to the question of what it actually means to become
a Christian, and he did this in defiance of an age and a country in
which it was simply taken for granted that everyone already was
a Christian. Getting the proper historical perspective on Kierkegaard is therefore no simple matter, with such a controversial subject as what it means to become a Christian entering the picture.
One cannot gain this perspective on his ideas simply by listing the
historical influences that molded him. If Kierkegaard's ideas have
any relevance for the modern reader, it must be because his criticism of his historical situation has some relevance to our understanding of our own historical situation, and because his clarification
of the Christian standard has some relevance to our understanding of the same standard.

The historical situation and the standard are inseparable. Without the standard the situation cannot be judged, and in fact it does
not properly exist outside of the judging light that reveals it. And,
conversely, without the situation the standard does not get a
purchase on reality, but flails the air. The interaction between
situation and standard raises the question whether it is possible to
get the proper historical perspective on Kierkegaard if one does not
subscribe both to his analysis of his situation and to his interpretation of the standard by which it should be judged. A second
question it raises is whether one can really learn anything from
Kierkegaard if one does not subscribe, at least in principle, to the
validity of applying some renewed vision of the Christian standard
to history with the objective of criticizing and changing history—
the methodological principle of all reforming movements in
Christianity. What, for example, would a Marxist exegesis of history make out of Kierkegaard's critique of nineteenth century bourgeois culture, and what, for example, would an individual Marxist
make out of the Kierkegaardian plea for a restoration of individual
inwardness in the committed life? I raise this speculation only to
indicate that when there is a question of learning something from

Kierkegaard for our present situation, the basic presuppositions or ideological tenets with which we approach him cannot be ignored. But this is not the same as saying that only a Christian or a would-be Christian can learn anything from Kierkegaard. He was not an evangelist, he was a reformer, and a reformer's first task is to show that things are not as they should be. He did not ask his con-temporaries to become Christians, but only to acknowledge that they were not Christians and that what passed for Christianity in Christendom was for the most part a fraud, either an unconscious or a partly conscious fraud. Certainly a Marxist could learn from Kierkegaard, simply on the basis of a logical and philosophical analysis, the difference between Greek rationalism and the para-doxical New Testament faith, without subscribing to either of them, provided he could suspend his personal hostility to both long enough to follow the analysis to its conclusion. In the same way the Marxist could acknowledge the correctness of Kierke-gaard's indictment of his historical situation in the light of the Christian standard, even if he thought the standard was illusory and should not be applied. And the individual Marxist could even learn a little something about self-commitment and appropriation and singleness of mind, even though he would have to apply them to a different ideal. Similarly, humanists, atheists, rationalists, and the so-called liberal interpreters of the Christian standard can all learn something from Kierkegaard, even if he only clarifies their understanding of a direction in which they do not choose to go.

3. Kierkegaard's Thought and Faith

There are two factors involved in all of Kierkegaard's writing which it is helpful to keep separate in one's mind while analyzing or criticizing any of his ideas. These may be roughly distinguished as (1) the nature of his thought and (2) the nature of his commit-ment, or, even more abstractly, as his understanding and his faith. These factors correspond subjectively to the historical situ-ation and to the standard by which it is to be judged. For instance, if we disagree with Kierkegaard's attack on Romanticism, it makes a difference whether we disagree because we feel his interpretation of Romanticism (especially the specifically nineteenth century Romanticism he attacked) was wrong, or whether we disagree

because he defined the Christian standard so as to exclude Romanticism. In the first case we merely have to show where his understanding of Romanticism was mistaken in order to justify our
disagreement with his attack on it. In the second case, holding his
interpretation of Romanticism to be correct, we have to declare
our disagreement with an interpretation of the Christian teaching
on life, self, God, and history, which scores Romanticism as error,
and further, since we cannot have it both ways, we must be prepared to defend Romanticism in relation to what we believe the
Christian standard to be. The same holds for our reaction to his
attack on speculative idealism, his attack on the crowd or mass
over against the individual, and his attack on the institutional
Christianity of his day.

As soon as the reader distinguishes for himself whether it is the
situation being judged or the standard of judgment with which he
takes issue, he can no longer escape the responsibility to defend
either a different interpretation of the historical situation than
Kierkegaard's or a different conception of the Christian criterion of
judgment than that which he delineated. In this way the modern
reader of Kierkegaard gets drawn into an argument in which he
feels that something important is at stake, for the ground on which
he stands is constantly shifting back and forth between objective
analysis of history and subjective interpretation of standards, a
process calculated to unseat rigid preconceptions and to promote
re-examination of the reader's own basic attitudes and beliefs. The
uncertainty involved in this process constitutes the capacity for
being taught something, for if in any argument or discussion about
life we do not feel our basic convictions to be threatened or at least
questioned, we also do not learn anything, and we cease to respond
and to grow.

Kierkegaard was certainly not the first man to apply the Christian
standard to the criticism of history. His special talent was to do it
in such a way as to provoke the reader into involvement in the
issue, even against his will. He never asked the reader to agree
with him on the basis of the persuasiveness of arguments or rhet-
oric. He simply exposed certain inconsistencies of thought and
certain incongruities of behavior so as to leave the reader saddled
with them, having previously deprived him of all the usual ways of

shaking them off by referring to public opinion, to what the age demands, to human nature, and to the customs of the natives. However, had he done nothing but expose the inconsistencies and incongruities, he would have been merely a satirist, one who shows the discrepancy between the supposedly ideal and the presently real, with the assistance of irony and ridicule. That he was able to saddle the reader with responsibility and discomfort over the discrepancies was due to a factor other than logical analysis, namely, his psychological insight into the workings of the human spirit, or what we would now call his concept of man. It was with these psychological insights that he snared his readers to begin with. However much they might protest his criticism of history or denounce what they called his irrational interpretation of Christianity, if they recognized themselves in his description of the human situation, they at least had to stop and think on how this could be and on how these psychological insights were related to his other ideas, for example, to his more "severe" religious interpretations.

The modern reader is also snared by Kierkegaard's psychological insights (or his view of man, however we prefer to put it). Correspondingly, the person most likely to learn something from Kierkegaard is the individual who is interested in learning something about himself. Here is no question of proving or disproving some general theories of psychology by means of laboratory evidence, but simply a matter of recognizing inner facts about ourselves on the "nonscientific," everyday level. If a man describes to us a certain human trait, or an attitude or condition of mind, or a relationship of life, in such a way that we cannot help but recognize our own case in his description, we do not say that he has proved or disproved something; we simply say, "He is talking about me." Nor do we necessarily discover something absolutely new about ourselves in this way. It is the old familiar self which we have with us day and night that we always deal with, but in so far as that man is able to discriminate and name for us some of its constituent elements, the self becomes for us more clear and definite and even partly manageable, instead of being nebulous, undifferentiated and unarticulated, and always taking us by surprise.

Kierkegaard's concept of man was a compound of Socratic self-knowledge and the biblical view of man. Socratic self-knowledge properly pursued tells us not who we are but what we are composed of, and when it is properly Socratic, it leaves the question of who we are resting on the Socratic ignorance. The biblical view of man tells us who we are in no uncertain terms, but only if we believe the biblical revelation. And if we do believe what the biblical revelation tells us in respect to who we are, it has implications for what we are composed of, since we must be made of that which will permit us to be who the Bible says we are. A creature made in the image of the biblical God and intended for a father-and-son relationship with that same God is made of something different than a creature who excels the animals only by the possession of reason and may participate in the divine only through the possession of reason. Kierkegaard was well aware of the limitations of Socratic self-knowledge, and also of the peculiar circumstance that because of the introduction of Christianity into the world, self-knowledge has become aware of new constituents and new potentialities in the self, even where the Christian revelation is not believed. It is as if human nature changed wherever it encountered Christianity (even where the encounter is an unhappy one), so that the man who has rejected Christianity is not quite the same as the man who has never heard of Christianity. And even the man who has never made a conscious decision about Christianity is aware of states of mind and feeling implicit or explicit in the language and culture of the "Christianized" world that would have been impossible in the pre-Christian consciousness. Kierkegaard shows that paganism within Christianity is something different from paganism outside Christianity, for paganism within Christianity has lost its innocence, while at the same time it has gained in psychological depth.

As in the case of the criticism of history, in the case of Kierkegaard's psychological analysis the modern reader is helped by trying to distinguish his picture of the human situation from his interpretation of the Christian standard for man. But in this case it is even more difficult, and the reader will again be drawn into an argument in which he must either concede the truth of Kierkegaard's description and thus perhaps concede more than he would like concerning, for example, the Christian criterion of spiritual health, or he will be forced to defend some different description of human psychology and thus also be obliged to "explain away" the objectionable elements of the Kierkegaardian psychology. In any case he will be driven to self-examination, as well as to the realization that where moral and religious truths are concerned, one cannot have it both ways.

To sum up, the way to learn something from Kierkegaard is to approach him in a mood of willingness to be taught concerning oneself, one's historical situation, and one's own interpretation of the Christian criterion by which both of these may be judged. In this way the reader becomes a lover or hater of Kierkegaard according to whether he is drawn toward Christianity or repelled from it, by what he learns from Kierkegaard. This is exactly what he intended: to arouse attention in such a way as to make indifference impossible. But the reader should not become a disciple of Kierkegaard. If the reader learns anything about himself and about his relationship to Christianity, this fact becomes for him far more important than the fact that it was from Kierkegaard he learned it. And this too is what Kierkegaard intended. He wanted to force people to acknowledge certain facts about themselves and about Christianity, not in order to spread any new doctrine, but in order to leave them with this knowledge as a burden on their consciences.

4. Discarding the Irrelevancies

When we approach Kierkegaard in the mood of willingness to be taught and with the desire for self-knowledge, we not only become aware of ideas and insights in his prolific authorship which are relevant for ourselves and for our day, but by the same token we also discover that there are some things in his life and authorship that are irrelevant to us and should not concern us overmuch. It is these irrelevancies that are generally picked up and made much of by people who are anxious to dispose of him, in one way or another, so as to be able to ignore him.

First there is the form in which he chose to present his thought to the world, the series of pseudonymous "belles lettres," one might almost call them, accompanied by the series of religious discourses bordering on sermons. This form is certainly calculated to give a headache to any academic philosopher in search of a handy abstract of Kierkegaard's ideas to be used in classroom comparison and criticism. The form of his authorship has been used against Kierkegaard to show that he was really no philosopher at all—certainly not one to be taken with philosophical seriousness—because he so flaunted the demand for systematic coherence and systematic presentation of the various parts of a philosopher's thought. There certainly is something ironical and even comical about such a reproach being leveled against a man who proclaimed the bankruptcy of the academic philosophy of his day. In so far as philosophy is a speculation about the general nature of things, Kierkegaard hoped to teach men to stay away from it, if they were really concerned for their souls. He wanted to show his readers how the pursuit of this external, "indifferent" knowledge is able to make a man a stranger to life and to himself. His polemic was directed specifically against Hegel, but it holds equally well against all forms of abstract, impersonal knowledge about the world, such as the body of scientific knowledge itself, as well as the various pseudo-scientific generalizations about man and the world he lives in that are now being propagated under the banners of various "isms." What an irony it would have been if Kierkegaard's protest against abstract, impersonal systems had turned out to be just another abstract, impersonal system! As it is, the irony is turned against those who want to use the nonsystematic form of his authorship against him to detract from his value as a "serious" thinker. Apparently, they disapprove of a thinker who takes the form of his writing so seriously as to want to make it correspond to the content! Perhaps the best they can do is to dismiss him as a poet.

The second irrelevancy, from the standpoint of those who want to learn something from Kierkegaard, is the matter of his peculiar temperament, or altogether the question of his psychological make-up. In this case the would-be disposers assume the psychological "explaining-away" attitude, the only humane thing to do, after all, with such a sad case history as Kierkegaard's. They read what he has written, thinking only of him, not of themselves. Then they search out any and every biographical tidbit they can lay their hands on, every allusion and speculation concerning the events of his private life. And they have their reward—they find more than enough! Then they proceed to "explain away" what they consider to be the peculiar aspects of his thinking by referring them to some social maladjustment in his early childhood, some peculiar temperamental or even psychopathic trait in his emotional make-up, or some neurotic over-sensitivity in the reactions he displayed toward persons and events. According to this school of Kierkegaardian criticism, one could never learn anything from anyone who does not correspond to an imaginary composite picture of what statistically constitutes the "average" person. But, as we know, all the great people of history from whom we have been able to profit would have to be called abnormal in one way or another according to a standard that sets up the "average" man as exemplifying what is normal. If we are to pass any judgment on Kierkegaard's private life at all, it can be only in relation to what he himself thought and did about it, especially in relation to his own providential interpretation of what he had been called by God to do. The fact that he did not marry Regina is no more to be interpreted as a mandate for celibacy than is his melancholy disposition to be used as an excuse for a pessimistic interpretation of Christianity. Nor is his attack upon the Danish Church to be interpreted as a revolutionary desire to do away with ecclesiastical organization. All such interpretations are mechanical, undialectical, and unhistorical, and they show how little their proponents understand the Christian idea of a unique and unrepeatable life lived under the direct guidance of a divine calling, in relation to a specific personal-historical context. Just as one cannot use the method of abstraction and generalization in order to construct a system out of his thought, so one cannot use this method to draw lessons from his life as to whether one should be cheerful or melancholy, married or single, popular or unpopular, for the Church or against the Church, conservative or radical. What one *can* learn from his life is the way he himself set about to cope with it, that is, in a manner always determined by his God-relationship as he understood it; then one can apply the same to himself in regard to his own God-relationship. Other than that there is little to be learned from studying Kierkegaard's life, for the fact that a man is melancholy or that he has had an unhappy love affair is surely no remarkable occurrence in this world.

The prize irrelevancy, however, is the pious concern of those whose interest in Kierkegaard is summed up in this question: "But was he himself a Christian?" Kierkegaard never boasted that he was a Christian, or, on a comparative scale, that he was at least more of a Christian than some he could mention; nor did he seek to condemn any individual for being less Christian than himself. He knew that this was a matter between each man and God alone, who alone is in a position to tell who is really a Christian and who is not. He did claim, however, that he knew what it means to be a Christian, in contrast to what it means to be a pagan of the several varieties then current, including the religious pagan, and he emphasized the fact that knowing this is still something quite different from becoming a Christian. For example, in both *Philosophical Fragments* and *Concluding Unscientific Postscript* he posits an "author" who poses as a detached spectator, one that is intellectually curious to know what it means to be a Christian, without committing himself to becoming one. On this ground we can argue with Kierkegaard if we are prepared to defend a different idea of what it means to be a Christian, but not on the ground that he was or was not a Christian himself. The latter matter is really none of our business, no more than it is, when we go to church, to know whether the others collected there are any more or less Christian than we are. All that can be done *publicly* is to try to clarify the idea of what it means to be a Christian, and then let the idea judge the man (each for himself) who allows himself to be judged by it.

The moralistic criticism of Kierkegaard's private life, the fact that he did not have to earn money for his living, and his extravagance in spending his inherited money so that it would last as long as he did but no longer (thus subsidizing himself in his vocation as some generous but calculating Renaissance pope might have subsidized an artist)—these objections will really tell us nothing about whether or not he was a Christian. If we do want a hint about that, we should ask why any man would want to spend his one life trying to clarify the idea of what it means to be a Christian, finally losing his life attacking the established Christianity in the service of this idea. Surely it was a waste of breath and life unless he was in some sense committed to this idea as to the truth, though God alone could judge the nature of his commitment. Humanly speaking, there is no public way of defining a Christian except as one who in some way is committed to Christianity as the truth.

5. Kierkegaard's Importance Today

If Kierkegaard's idea of "the individual" is important for us today, it is because the present historical situation is one that demands a new beginning, and a new beginning apparently cannot be made without a new understanding of himself by the creature who is expected to make the new beginning. We are only a hundred years removed from Kierkegaard, but in that time the world has transformed itself—physically, with the rapidity of an adolescent, and spiritually, as it moved from what was probably its most naïvely enthusiastic and forward-looking golden age, through two startling wars, and into the opaqueness of the present period, when the very fact of human survival on this planet has become questionable, and even the value of such survival has become uncertain in the hearts of men. Pessimism and optimism have become equally irrelevant, for they both assume the existence of something precious which is either threatened or supported by whatever seems predictable in the surrounding conditions. But now it is just that "something precious" about which man is uncertain—what it is, and whether it is. At first glance it would seem that physical human survival might be the "something precious," but a moment's reflection shows how often life must be sacrificed to save life. Then civilization might suggest itself as the precious thing, but it is precisely the present civilization which has brought with it such evils and confusion as to rob life itself of meaning and make it impossible to decide whether the civilization deserves to survive, or whether its destruction should not be the prerequisite for a new beginning. Whether there will be a war which destroys all human life or at least the manner of living it that we now call civilization, or whether the manner of living that we now call civilization will survive precisely by the intensification of the evils that make it questionable and make man himself questionable—these alternatives come pretty much to the same thing. A criterion is needed to separate what deserves to survive from what deserves not to survive, and so finally the "something precious" is presented in the form of a set of abstract ideals, such as freedom, democracy, equality, security, society, the state, and so on, for the sake of which men are expected to live a meaningful life or die a meaningful death. Unfortunately, the same evils that make the civilization questionable make it impossible to get any agreement on what these abstractions mean. Concretely, they do not succeed in defining life, for the abstractions themselves need life to define them. They receive their pragmatic definitions from the variety of purposes and functions men actually live by, and thus they come to mean such different things to different men that far from becoming a criterion for judging the survival value of the civilization, they become a criterion for estimating the degree of the lack of any real communication or understanding among men. Even misunderstanding becomes too mild a word to use for this breakdown in communication.

A new beginning, if there is to be a new beginning, must therefore go backward into primitive self-awareness beyond the point where men depend on their relation to others, or on abstract concepts, for their understanding of themselves, to the place where each man is alone with himself, not necessarily understanding himself but understanding at least that he must begin with himself. Kierkegaard said that every man has essentially to do only with himself and with God; this is sometimes taken to be one of his anti-social statements, but it is really an attempt to remind people that a beginning can be made only where the beginning actually is, where each man always inescapably is, with himself—and with God—before he can be with anyone else in a human relationship.

A new beginning cannot be made simply by analyzing the evils of the present situation and recommending what in the situation needs to be changed. In our generation there is no lack of able diagnosticians who can trace the causes of the present impasse with great persuasiveness, considering the complexity of history, and who are even able to prescribe remedies both practical and reasonable. Such procedure is the only sensible thing to do in any historical situation that calls for a change. But such diagnosis and such prescription take for granted precisely the one thing which in our historical situation can no longer be taken for granted, namely, that men really know what they want. To press the often-used medical analogy into service, the doctors are helpless not so much because they don't know the disease but because the patient either has no idea of what it means to be healthy or, subconsciously, does not wish to be healthy. The temptation is great for those doctors who think they understand the disease to try to force the remedy on the patient against his will but for his own good. Christian diagnosticians succumb easily to this temptation, for their understanding of the disease is clear and the remedy obvious: all must become Christians. But this disease happens to be one in which the cure cannot work against the will of the patient, because the disease is *in* the will of the patient, so far down in the sources of the will that he does not recognize it as a disease, nor as being in the will. He is bombarded from all sides by reasonable arguments and reasonable threats. "If you want this kind of world, you must do thus and so. If you will not believe, or at least act as if you believe, such and such articles of faith, this is what will happen to you and your world." The arguments and threats are convincing enough, and perhaps bring many a convert into the official fold of the Church. Whether they constitute a new beginning, whether a new beginning can be made simply with arguments and threats, is another question.

Kierkegaard saw through the fallacy and futility of trying to urge the truth of Christianity in terms of the "results" it promises to produce in the future. "The truth," he said, speaking to "the individual," is the truth "which is edifying for thee." This statement again must not be interpreted in modern terms as an unsocial, arbitrary, and relativistic view of truth. It simply means that if the truth is not something which is able to grasp the man in his inmost self-awareness and there to "build him up" or stand him on his feet as a man so that he becomes more himself and more truly man than he was without that truth, then what good does it do to cajole or to browbeat him with "results" in history? How can a man care two cents for history if he does not realize and increase in his own being the meaning of what it is to be man, the creature that has history and is history? The effect of the browbeating technique, the arguments and threats, is that the man may very well accept Christianity, but for the wrong reasons. He accepts it out of fear of certain "results" and desire for others, and so he does not become a Christian after all, he does not come to a better understanding of himself, and he does not make a new beginning. And Christianity, or at least the Church, becomes that hypocritical and equivocal institution we know so well, that mask of many motives which is the body of Christ become an offense to the pure in heart. What is needed is more patience and more honesty and less hankering after results. The human spirit cannot be hurried or forced, even by the obviousness of the Christian diagnosis and the Christian remedy, if the cure is to be radical and not merely a symptom-dosing.

Today it is a sign of hope, as well as a recognition of the need for self-knowledge, that in several different fields of intellectual endeavor the interest is shifting from the supposed laws of nature to the mysterious ways of man. In the field of philosophy, existential studies, phenomenology, and the revival of some classical concepts of man represent a new humanistic emphasis that seems about to shoulder aside the endless repetitions of unnecessary justifications of science. In psychology, concern over man's acute, unsatisfied human needs, as these reveal themselves in clinical evidence rather than in psychological theories of behavior, has produced a sudden proliferation of the accommodating "depth" psychology. History and political science, shying away from, rather than refuting, current deterministic ideologies, show a certain humble willingness to reassess some traditional views of man and of human values that in the past were able to make some sense out of historical existence and political movements. And some modern literary criticism, in studying the creative process in man and searching for standards of literary achievement, is discovering that the supposed arbitrariness and incommunicability of the individual human inwardness may be due as much to literary incompetence, or to a misunderstanding of the function of literature, as to any insurmountable barriers among men. On a less intellectual level, big business, the naughty child of the industrial revolution, is making belated efforts to humanize industry, and the Church for its part is making a belated effort to let its language speak to the condition of men in terms of the needs they find in themselves. In such different ways man is cautiously re-examining the creature man, returning perhaps unconsciously to the Socratic starting point, but with something less than the Socratic simplicity and the Socratic faith in reason, now no longer possible. For modern man has a certain guilty knowledge of his own possibilities implicit in the objective evidence of what he has been doing for the past twenty-five hundred years, evidence which cannot be simply ignored or written off the books by any new attempt at self-knowledge, as if history had never happened. At the same time, he has the power of a new kind of knowledge, scientific and technical knowledge, about which, paradoxically, there is no disagreement whatever, even among those most violently opposed in their views of man. Kierkegaard saw already in the middle of the nineteenth century, at a time when scientific knowledge had reached nowhere near its present proportions, that it would corrupt man, not because it was intrinsically evil, but because the power in it would seduce him away from the awareness of limitation, and because the objectivity of it would anaesthetize his ethical and religious sensibility. He pointed out, at a time when scarcely anyone suspected the need for a new beginning, the direction in which men must go in order to make a new beginning, in both their understanding of themselves and their understanding of Christianity—the inward direction.

6. The Problem of Terminology

Lastly, in the matter of trying to learn something from Kierke-gaard, it is best to admit from the outset that his use of the Hegelian terminology presents a real difficulty. Evading this issue will only tempt us to dispose of his thinking by means of the familiar accusation that he "out-Hegeled Hegel." He surely did that; he fought Hegel on Hegel's own ground with Hegel's own terminology—a case of fighting fire with fire. But he strained and stretched and cracked and broke it in the process, filling it full of contradictions and paradoxes which, in another terminology, might not seem either so glaring or so violent. And yet by this very feat he managed to call attention to the difference between that which can be adequately expressed in abstract thought, namely, some philosophical understanding of the world, and that which cannot be adequately expressed in such a manner, namely, the personal, individual existence to which ethico-religious truth is addressed.

Perhaps a personal confession would be in order here. When I first began reading Kierkegaard, my own philosophical position was anti-idealistic, radically empiricist, and inclined toward positivism, a quite "natural" philosophical outlook for one who had been milk-fed and reared in the natural sciences. I considered Hegel's system to be a prime example of how, by manipulating pure abstractions, one could build step by step an intricate structure of ideas, seemingly consistent and logically airtight, which, however, somehow carried one further and further away from reality the more imposing it became and which finally approached fantasy when "nature" and "history" were supposed to be deducible from it or somehow "explained" by it. Therefore, Kierkegaard's attacks on Hegel, his jokes and barbs, his sly digs and sarcastic asides, were sweet music to my ears. I revelled in them. But when I read further in the Kierkegaardian authorship and saw that he had no intention of abandoning this battle-terminology even when the attack on Hegel was not the immediate issue, I became not a little puzzled. As all Kierkegaard readers surely do at some time, I tried to classify him as a philosopher. But how can you classify as an idealistic philosopher a man who uses the old familiar idealistic vocabulary only to oppose and overturn the old familiar idealistic tenets? It seemed to me that Kierkegaard somewhat stubbornly used the traditional idealist's terms to support and emphasize what I believe to be the essentials of a traditionally empirical and realistic position: that existence precedes essence; that the world does not depend on our ideas about it in order to be what it is; that knowledge is an approximation process; that the rational is only one aspect of the real; that the world is not a poor imitation of pre-existing heavenly essences but is simply the *given*, to which our thought must try to conform as best it can. All these ideas were congenial enough to me, but I found quite exasperating their reiteration in the terms of a vocabulary so uncongenial to them.

Now, after many more years of Kierkegaard reading, I feel rather more resigned about it. I know that there are writers on Kierkegaard, especially those of the Roman Catholic parish, who feel that if only Kierkegaard had been familiar with the body of Thomistic thought he would have found a more congenial intellectual framework for his own ideas, and a better ground from which to launch the attack on Hegel.[3] I rather suspect, however, that Kierkegaard would have been as much repelled by the "body" of the Thomistic *summas*—those huge paragraph-grinding machines running smoothly according to the question-and-answer progression, in slavish obedience to the form of metaphysical realism engineered by Aristotle—as he was by the Hegelian paragraph-machine.

I do not believe we should be too hard on Kierkegaard for his choice of weapons in the fight against Hegel. The issue is, after all, not simply that between a realistic and an idealistic metaphysic. For it is quite possible, as Kierkegaard clearly saw, to build up on the basis of a realistic metaphysic a huge body of objective knowledge—the endlessly accumulating information supplied by all the separate sciences—which, if accorded exclusive attention and emphasis, would be just as lethal to the inner development of subjectivity or selfhood as are the world-historical panoramas and the infinite idea-vistas of Hegel. What Kierkegaard required was a psychological vocabulary that would permit him to describe the inner transformations of selfhood (the self's pilgrimage through existence), and there simply was no science of psychology worthy of the name to supply him with such a vocabulary in the period in which he was writing. The psychology of his day was either embedded in idealistic philosophy, or was just beginning to try to be a natural science, that is, just beginning the long process of reducing man to the status of matter, and mind to the physiology of the nervous system, in what later came to be known as "psychology without a soul." It is hardly to be expected that this latter line of development would supply Kierkegaard with a congenial vocabulary; nevertheless, he was aware of it. For he writes in the *Journals:*

All such scientific methods become particularly dangerous and pernicious when they encroach upon the spiritual field. Plants, animals, and stars may be handled in that way, but to handle the spirit of man in such a fashion is blasphemy which only weakens moral and religious passion. . . .
Materialistic physiology is comic (that anyone should believe that the way to find the spirit which gives life is to put to death); the more

[3] See especially, James Collins, *The Mind of Kierkegaard* (Chicago: Regnery, 1953), chap. VIII.

modern, spiritual physiology though cleverer is mere sophistry. It admits that it cannot explain the miracle [how consciousness arises from unconsciousness], and yet it wants to go on; it becomes more and more voluminous and the volumes deal with this that and the other thing, all of which is most curious and interesting—but nevertheless does not explain the miracle. . . .

We learn from this sophistical physiology that 'the *key* to the knowledge of the conscious life of the soul lies in the unconscious' (Carus). But what precisely does the key mean if the transition from unconsciousness to consciousness is not explained? The transition is a leap (which answers to marvelling) which no key can open. . . .

And so physiology spreads out over the kingdom of plants and animals showing more and more analogies which are not really analogies, since man is qualitatively different from plants and animals.[4]

Idealism, then, supplied Kierkegaard with a vocabulary which at least recognized that "man is qualitatively different from plants and animals," and at the same time placed him in the tradition of European thought that goes all the way back to Socrates, in which human nature rather than nonhuman nature is considered to be the proper goal of wisdom. I believe, then, that we must simply tolerate Kierkegaard's use of the Hegelian vocabulary in order to learn what he had to say about human nature. How his insights are to be understood in terms of contemporary thinking— in terms, let us say, of the several varieties of analytic psychology, or philosophical anthropology, or phenomenology, or theory of value—is another matter, one that can be attempted only piece by piece, at the relevant points in the subject matter. This attempt will involve taking the repeated risk of "translating" Kierkegaard out of Hegelian. That this is a risky procedure, far more risky than it was to have translated Kierkegaard out of Danish into English, I have no doubt. But now that the first risk has been taken with fair success (and I am told that we have in English some of the best translations of Kierkegaard available in any language) I believe it is no less necessary to take this second risk, if Kierkegaard's contribution to the knowledge of the human individual is to receive the wide understanding it deserves.

For Kierkegaard did not merely oppose Hegel's speculative system of philosophy. He presented the reader with an alternative. To Hegel's "phenomenology of spirit," and to every philosophical

⁴ *Journals*, No. 617, pp. 182-184, *passim*.

attempt to demonstrate the *appearances* of spirit, in nature, history, and culture (a task he declared impossible in view of the conditions of existence), he opposed what can only be termed, with reservations, the *ontology* of spirit, a description of what spirit is in its inner reality, and what it means to be a human existent in the process of becoming spirit—for spirit is just that factor in the human constitution that never permits pure being, only becoming. We have no term in general currency today to designate this attempt, only the archaic word "pneumatology." Modern psychology of personality, and, from the negative, pathological standpoint, psychoanalysis, both attempt something of the kind in their several jargons, yet Kierkegaard's effort can hardly be evaluated merely as psychology. Spirit is more than mind and body together, although it is detectable only as an orientation of the total mind-body complex, an active orientation, never static. Kierkegaard's attempt can be called an ontology of spirit only with the reservation that the very nature of spirit precludes any static, finished "being," whose ontic "nature" might be fixed and frozen in definitions.

In the chapters that follow, which are primarily concerned with Kierkegaard's delineation of the human existent's pilgrimage through existence, I have again and again taken the risk of translating his Hegelian terms into the several vocabularies of more recent ways of talking about human nature. But, in order to reduce the risk as much as possible, I have also included generous quotations of Kierkegaard's own words, so that the reader may judge for himself if I have gone too far, or not far enough, or if I have taken unjustifiable liberties. I see no other way out, and I can only hope to persuade the reader that the rewards of attacking the Hegelian obstacle outweigh the difficulties and justify taking the risks. For I am convinced that Kierkegaard has a specific contribution to make to our own attempts to understand the specifically human, namely, what it means to be neither subhuman nor superhuman but human as God would educate man to be, and what a wealth of possibilities this entails. And I am convinced that if we are willing to learn from Kierkegaard on this score we shall advance our own ideas to greater precision and richness.

II

Portrait of the Intellectual as a Rich Young Man

1. The "Saviors of Religion"

It is easier for a camel to go through the eye of a needle than for an intellectual to enter the kingdom of God. Who, then, can be saved? With men it is impossible, but not with God; for all things are possible with God. Let us allow this paraphrase of the story of the rich young man[1] to serve as the overarching theme as we try briefly to connect Kierkegaard's historical situation with our own.

It is a telling commentary on our historical situation that we now have to look back upon the nineteenth century as upon one of the Golden Ages of mankind. These ages, as Toynbee tells us, occur only when the civilization of which they are the flowering is already on the decline. And only now, with some historical hindsight, can we recognize in Kierkegaard the lonely prophetic voice of one who foresaw and analyzed several of the hidden, incipient dangers that lay ahead of his age. Kierkegaard was like a warning signal set out in the middle of the nineteenth century, a bell buoy in the middle of an apparently danger-free channel, to call attention to the difficult terrain below the surface. But of course he was ignored, because there was something so confident and affirmative in the atmosphere of that time that men saw only clear sailing ahead. In fact, it seemed to many of the leaders of the nineteenth century that Europe had almost achieved, or was well on its way toward achieving, another great synthesis of thought and conduct, of philosophy and religion, of practical institutions and ideal values, an achievement that would take the place of the famous Medieval Synthesis which had been destroyed by the Renaissance and the Reformation together, leaving Europe torn by religious wars, political revolutions, and intellectual doubts.

We can better appreciate Kierkegaard's unique position if we

[1] Mark 10:17-27, Luke 18:18-27.

24

recollect that philosophical thought in the nineteenth century considered itself to be in a period of religious reconstruction, rather than demolition. However, to understand why religious reconstruction was needed, we must go back two centuries earlier, in order to discover what had happened to the two great liberating insights of the Reformation for whose sake the split with Rome had taken place. The great liberating insight of Luther, justification by faith alone, became formalized even within his lifetime to mean a forensic justification on the basis of believing correct doctrine; the great liberating insight of Calvin, the absolute sovereignty of God, became reduced to the doctrine of the double predestination, and the problem of right conduct in accordance therewith. In both cases, a legalistic interpretation of "correct doctrine" became the touchstone of salvation, and so the following century, the seventeenth, devoted itself to the defining, codifying, and enforcing of correct doctrine and became what is now called the period of Protestant scholasticism, or the Protestant *orthodoxy*. The word "orthodoxy" became much more appropriately applied to Protestantism than to Catholicism, for the latter retained, in addition to correct doctrine, an almost equal emphasis on individual conduct and the religious life (as was to be expected if salvation must be earned).

Against the Protestant orthodoxy there eventually arose two movements of protest, the pietistic movement and the rationalistic attack. The pietistic movement did not, by and large, attack the doctrines of orthodoxy. It merely shifted the emphasis from doctrine to life, and made the touchstone of salvation the inner experience of the believer, followed by conduct witnessing to regeneration by the Holy Spirit. It was a partial return to Catholic piety, in so far as the latter was not tied up with the institutional aspect of the Roman Church. Rationalism, on the other hand, attacked the doctrines of orthodoxy directly, those of both the Protestant and the Catholic orthodoxy. It was a revival of the humanism of the Renaissance, which had never really died out but which had, under cover of the noise of doctrinal clashes, quietly begun to devote itself to the study of nature, thereby laying the foundations of modern science.

The initial attack of rationalism on the Protestant orthodoxy was not conceived as an attack at all, but as a boring from within which desired to demonstrate at one and the same time both the reasonableness of the Christian religion (when properly interpreted) and the all-sufficiency of human reason for determining what is right and what is true. Thus, the early Deists were mostly supernaturalists who believed that it was quite reasonable for revelation to authenticate itself by means of miracles. But as soon as it could be shown that Christianity was quite reasonable even without miracles, these fell by the wayside, as did one after another of the traditional doctrines, which the Rationalists tried first to rehabilitate, then finally discarded as unnecessary. Their criterion of necessity, however, was always the promotion of civic virtue and the good society, so that little by little it became evident that the Rationalists really wanted to use Christianity as a means of producing a rational ordering of society on the basis of ideals still retained from the Gospels, rather than to interpret Christian doctrine as a system of truths recommending itself to the minds of rational men.

The Enlightenment fostered the first actual attack of rationalism against Christianity itself as being both unnecessary to the good society and unacceptable to reason, and hence a superstition to be destroyed, the sooner the better. Here began the real religion of reason, which naturally appropriated science as its guide and brought about the first real crisis in religion since the founding of Christianity by stating categorically that man could be either religious or rational, but not both.

The next series of reactions took place in relation to this crisis in which not just Christianity but all religiousness of any kind was at stake. This second, milder, and more critical form of rationalism, especially in the form of German Idealism, tried to overcome the narrow, hasty, and polemical rationalism of the Enlightenment, and especially to mitigate the dry utilitarianism and materialism into which it seemed to issue in practical life. Thus, when Kierkegaard came on the scene, the intellectual situation of western Europe was one that might be described as the second wave of reaction after the Reformation, the reaction against the reaction against that consolidation of doctrine known as the Protestant orthodoxy. The first reaction had been radical, iconoclastic, and intellectually hostile toward religion; the second reaction was conservative, reconstructive, and conciliatory toward religion.

What had happened in philosophy was that the Newtonian World-Machine, the picture of the universe as an infinite collection of particles endlessly combining and separating, colliding and rebounding, according to fixed mathematical rules, proved so hard to take that philosophic minds decided instead to take a second look at reason itself. They hoped to find, almost literally, an "escape hatch" in the very structure of reason itself by means of which the human soul could somehow elude the moral and spiritual meaninglessness of the scientific picture, and hoped to rescue from that picture at least some scraps and vestiges of the soul's "eternal values." Kant was the man who supplied the escape hatch, at least for the moral self and its values. His famous negation of the power of reason to reach to things-in-themselves, because of its imprisonment in its a priori categories for understanding appearances (except in the one case of the moral thing-in-itself which everyone knows directly because he has it within, or is it, himself) —this was to be the escape hatch. As he himself admitted, he had to "destroy reason to make room for faith."

But the Kantian agnosticism in its turn proved hard to live with. Kant's critiques, to be sure, destroyed the certainty with which reason claimed to lay hold of all of reality according to the naïve realism of the scientists. But tremendous sophistication of mind was required to convince oneself that the marvelous structure of the universe that science was uncovering must be called "mere appearances." Appearances of what? Of invisible, unknowable things-in-themselves? But if invisible and unknowable, how could they succeed in removing the curse, the intellectual obstacle, of the discrepancy between the new scientific and the old traditional Christian world-pictures? From the starry heavens above to the moral law within there seemed to be no direct transition—rather, a complete hiatus. For surely it was no help to call the former the phenomenon (or appearance to us under the forms of reason) of the latter, the noumenon. Kant himself had the courage to maintain the noumenal status of the moral self in the teeth of this hiatus, but his successors were not such hardy souls. They found in the Kantian agnosticism with respect to "things-in-themselves" either a reduction of knowledge to pure description or a carte blanche for speculation. For either one could argue that if things-in-themselves are unknowable they can be safely ignored (as did the later phenomenologists), or one could argue that if knowledge is only of phenomena, nothing can prevent each philosopher from making his own best guess at the identity of the noumenon which shows itself to us in this way.

Speculative idealism and aesthetic romanticism were the movements that resulted, immediately after Kant, from this German philosophical guessing game. Both asserted the prior reality and rights of the human self or spirit over against the nonself, or the material world. Thus in their common antimaterialism, both considered that they were capable of saving religion and especially of saving it as a possibility for the nineteenth century intellectual. Speculative idealism assured the intellectual that his own thinking self, the conceptualizing spirit (not merely his moral conscience), was the real thing-in-itself, and that through this every individual finite spirit was immediately grounded in the Absolute. The Absolute was the Infinite Spirit that expressed itself both through the finite selves and through the so-called objective world, which it created for itself as an "other" to be overcome or to enable it to come to consciousness of itself. Fichte and Schelling emphasized the creative role of the individual spirit in bringing the outside world into reality, whereas Hegel emphasized the self-activity of the Absolute Spirit which was behind both the finite selves and the material reality. This self-activity of the Absolute consisted of the eternal self-enrichment of the Absolute through the constant creating and overcoming of opposition. By applying the dynamic dialectic of thesis-antithesis-synthesis to all of nature and history, one could explain and justify everything that existed and everything that happened. Even religion, even Christianity could in this manner be explained and justified. This was how speculative idealism intended to save religion, by making it one of the many self-objectifications of the Absolute Spirit, necessary to the eternal enrichment thereof.

Aesthetic romanticism, on the other hand, took the Kantian "impossibility of knowing the world as it is for itself" to mean that this objective reality was not *worth* knowing. True wisdom and fulfilment were not to be found in knowledge at all, but must be sought in the realm of feeling, intuition, imagination, and mood. The human self was never meant to be a recording instrument for objective knowledge, except in the minimal sense in which this is necessary for survival. The human self was meant to be the locus of the passions and moods of the world spirit. This world-feeling, world-suffering, world-enjoying function of the self was based on the self's mystical unity with nature and with other selves, something which every sensitive person could experience immediately, but which thought could not demonstrate or even conceptualize, since the attempt to do that would destroy the precious immediacy which gave the experience its authenticity and its worth. Only creations of the artistic imagination could hope to embody and convey such experience, and so the romantics, holding these premises, quite naturally turned from philosophy and science to literature and the arts.

In the sphere of religion, the romantic outlook not only seemed to be in accord with the pietistic shift of emphasis from doctrine to life, from believing dogmas to experiencing the presence of the Holy Spirit, but it also seemed to provide religion with an independent ground of validity which would remove religion entirely out of the range of attacks by science. On this ground, the whole argument between certain religious doctrines and the new empirical evidences could be waved aside as a ridiculous misunderstanding of the meaning and function of true religion. Schleiermacher was the man who "saved religion" for the modern mind on this basis, and that this was consciously his purpose is indicated by the title of one of his works, *Discourse on Religion Directed Toward its Cultured Despisers*. He saved religion by giving it a new ground of validity in the feelings of man, making true religion entirely independent of both theoretical doctrines and empirical observations. The essence of religion was man's feeling of dependence on, and union with, something greater than himself; to this feeling or awareness all the essential attitudes and practices of religion could be traced. The traditional dogmas of the Church were nothing but the attempts of religious men to express their religious feelings in theoretical, that is, theological and cosmological, terms—an effort that on the grounds of Schleiermacher's philosophy must be considered a mistake. Nevertheless, we can still get meaning out of these dogmas—but only by imagining our way back into the original feelings they were intended to express, not by applying logical or factual criteria to the dogmas themselves. Unfortunately for the dogmas of the Christian Church, Schleiermacher's idea of this "something" on which man feels dependent was of it as nothing but the totality of the universe itself. His theology therefore resulted in a type of emotional pantheism with moral overtones that accorded very well with aesthetic romanticism, but was quite alien to the awesome, compelling, and transfiguring religious feelings that the traditional dogmas of the Church seemed to express.

Thus, when Kierkegaard came on the scene, the two dominant idealistic philosophies of western Europe were both busily "saving religion," that is, saving it as a possibility for the intellectual. Himself an intellectual and a man of intense poetic sensibilities, he could appreciate their efforts. But his upbringing by his father in the "strictest" form of Christianity, his dialectical skill, and his propensity toward irony enabled him to see that this effort was vain, partly because its very posing of the problem was reversed. For if Christianity was the truth (and if it was not, why bother with it at all?) the real problem was not to save religion as a possibility for the intellectual, but to save the intellectual as a possibility for Christianity. More specifically, he saw that his own task would have to be first of all to save Christianity *from* the philosophers, from both the speculative idealists and the romanticists, who in their desire to save religion were rapidly changing Christianity into something quite incapable of saving anybody, and then to show what the proper function of the intellect is in the sphere of religion, so that, with God's help, even an intellectual might be saved.

2. The Capitulation of the "Saviors"

The subsequent development of speculative idealism and aesthetic romanticism reflects the irony of history. Both of them capitulated, but not to the Kierkegaardian attack. They capitulated to the intellectual dominance of empirical science, which had the effect of reducing speculation to irrelevance and romanticism to impotence.

Speculative idealism was the last attempt of the human mind to remain in control of the knowledge situation, to attain a godlike knowledge of the universe. Its starting point was not to ask if this kind of knowledge were possible, but rather to ask what kind of a world it must be in which such knowledge would be possible, answering its own question thus: why, the kind of world in which the real is the rational and the rational is the real. To which brilliant conclusion Kierkegaard answered: bravo! but let us not confuse such a world with *this* world, lest we forget that we are men. "If Hegel had written the whole of his logic and then said, in the preface, that it was merely an experiment in thought in which he had even begged the question in many places, then he would certainly have been the greatest thinker who had ever lived. As it is he is merely comic."[2]

From the experiments in the laboratories of the several sciences came a kind of knowledge that made Hegel's identification of his "experiment in thought" with the world we live in seem not even "comic," but merely irrelevant. Empirical science did not bother to ask the speculative philosopher whether he would be pleased to call its findings rational or not. It simply weighed and measured, inferred, theorized, implied, and measured again, and the results it reported turned out to be something quite different from what even the clearest-headed logician could have deduced from the necessary principles of reason or even from the dialectical operation of the Absolute Spirit in history. Dressed in the charming new "humility before the facts," empirical science quietly thumbed its nose at metaphysics and vindicated itself before men by performing technological wonders.

It is not altogether certain that, were he alive today, Kierkegaard would rejoice at the ignominious defeat of speculative philosophy by empirical science. Academic philosophy retreated abashed, dropped the word "spirit" from its vocabulary, and in every way tried not to say anything that would be offensive to science. But the speculative interest remained. It concentrated its efforts on constructing a patchwork panorama of the world out of the data supplied by the several sciences, using as metaphysical metaphors for the "whole show" certain concepts suggested by the several

[2] *Journals*, No. 497, p. 134.

sciences themselves: mechanism, evolution, growth, organism, adaptation, Gestalt, process, emergence, and others. However, in the old speculative idealism, although it may have falsified man's position in existence and exaggerated his cognitive powers, the speculative interest had not lost sight of the speculator, *the self that wants to know,* for whose benefit the knowledge-panorama is exhibited. In the new panorama based on the new assorted bits of assembled empirical knowledge, it became increasingly vague and even slightly improper to talk about the knower, the cognizing self, for the new metaphysical metaphors left no room for him in the picture. The criticism leveled by Kierkegaard against Hegelianism, that it made men "forget" what it means to exist, to be a self in existence, would now be even more forceful against the speculative interest that conforms itself to empirical science, because it has lost the concept entirely while claiming to deal with the sole reality that could be known. Except as an emotionally colorless recorder and logical sifter of sense data, as something that must be presupposed for the enterprise, the self has no intellectual standing in the picture of the world presented by empirical science.

Now the curious thing is that the meaning of the self became equally attenuated in the subsequent development of aesthetic romanticism since the Romantic Age. From being the mystical bearer of the moods and passions of the world spirit, presenting a picture that seemed to imply some kind of unity or harmony underlying the diversity of individual selves, the ego became increasingly the battleground on which competing drives and interests fought for supremacy. The artists and poets of the romantic movement wanted to express "themselves," but strictly speaking they had no selves, only fragments. One after another, the various possibilities or aspects of human selfhood that were being neglected or offended by the objective order of things (as presented by the scientific picture of the universe and the industrial orientation of society), were taken up as battle cries, with increasing arbitrariness and subjectivism as the revolt took on the character of a fight for survival. In the ensuing anarchy it became more and more difficult to grasp intellectually the idea of what a self might be, and hence more difficult for the intellectual to understand himself.

Contemporary myth-makers came to the rescue. Physiologists identified the self with a large ganglion in the nervous system, for undoubtedly a moderate tap on the head could deprive even the stoutest romantic of *his* precious self. Freud called it the libidinal urge, foredoomed to frustration for the benefit of civilized life. Marx called it the worker deprived of his tools. It was also called the will to power, to freedom, to immolation, to creation, to death, to sheer life and growth at the expense of other life. The human self was becoming most evidently the no-man's-land "where ignorant armies clash by night."

We in the middle of the twentieth century surely must ask ourselves how it was that this solitary, cryptic Dane was able to see through the incapacity of romanticism to "save religion" for the intellectual, an insight which enabled him to envision and almost to foretell the eventual spiritual corruption and moral capitulation of the intellectual under the avalanche of scientific knowledge. And we have to ask this question in some wonderment at the fact that he saw it so early in the game—quite a few years before the despair inherent in romanticism had worked itself out into the cultural atmosphere. As the nineteenth century moved into the twentieth, sensitive novelists and poets began to protest more and more vehemently against the way in which the scientific attitude toward everything was ruining man spiritually and ruining society morally. One thinks here of Yeats with his "holy hatred" of science, his calling on the old heroes of Ireland for help, and his taking refuge in a private theosophy. Or one thinks of D. H. Lawrence, with his intellectual's revolt against intellect and his longing for a physiological religion of the dark mysteries of the body. Or of Mallarmé, with his aristocratic bitterness against the "educated" mob (so like Kierkegaard's against the "crowd"), the democratic mob that presumed to "learn" poetry in school as if it were a science, in order to dictate to the poets what they should write. And one thinks of all the English romantic poets—everywhere there was protest, plenty of protest, and some weak, fumbling, or defiant attempts to restore a religious vision to a society gone utterly secular, technological, Philistine, and this-world-utopian. Yet all these protests sounded like the last, piteous outcries of dying fighters in a lost cause. The protesting poets had nothing to offer except their moans, their noble desperation, their occasional self-irony, their lonely defeat, and their self-pity.

In contrast to the romantic impotence, the protest of Kierkegaard against the corruption of the intellectual by science is something much more stern, severe, even sarcastic, and therefore much more bracing. This was because Kierkegaard had an alternative, a positive task, to offer in place of all this effeminate, aesthetic bemoaning of past religious visions and feelings now obliterated by science. It was the task of self-knowledge and self-activity, undertaken not as some kind of escape into a private world but as every man's simple duty in the matter of what it means simply to be human. *Who I am and what I ought to do*— these were the eternally obligatory matters for every man as man to be concerned with, and, in bringing them once more to the attention of his contemporaries, Kierkegaard was not inventing any new thing, but merely pointing to the great "X," the great unknown in the scientific picture of reality that science itself could not discover there and therefore conveniently ignored. But not by star-gazing or by atom-smashing, or even by history-explaining, could these questions about the self be answered. They had never got answered in this way in the past, nor would they ever get answered by this means in the future. Only by the individual self's inward activity—by the hard way of choice, decision, resolution, responsibility, commitment, obedience, and action—would they get even partially answered. Only by the self working out its salvation in fear and trembling.

With all this work to be done, this interior task waiting for each and every man and woman, Kierkegaard wasted no pity on the intellectual of his day, even the most sensitive poetic individual (such as he was himself)—and we can be sure that he would have wasted no pity on the intellectual of today, even though, regarded as a rich young man, the intellectual has now acquired the standing of a tycoon. The amazing thing is that Kierkegaard saw quite clearly what was happening to the intellectual when he was as yet only comfortably rich, not as yet really starving from the discomfiture of the Midas touch as many are today. Kierkegaard spoke to him like a stern but well-meaning Dutch uncle, saying in effect: my dear young man, you are suffering from too much knowledge, spiritual immaturity, and no passion worthy of the name.

3. The Need To Act Decisively

How is it possible to suffer from too much knowledge? If the knowledge is factual, fragmentary, and cumulative (as all scientific knowledge is), we run, sooner than we think, into the old problem of not being able to see the forest for the trees. Or, to change the figure, we run into the jigsaw puzzle effect. A thousand-piece jigsaw puzzle is more difficult to put together than a hundred-piece puzzle, even if the picture on the puzzle is the same. It takes longer to do, and we play with it for the very reason that it is a greater challenge and a better time-killer than the hundred-piece puzzle. But suppose it is really the picture itself we are after because the picture happens to be a map we need to guide us in action. It would then seem that there are advantages to the hundred-piece puzzle, for the sooner we get it together, the sooner we can start on our way. In Kierkegaard's day it was the "still unfinished" system of Hegel that promised to give the over-all picture, now it is the "still unfinished" empirical science that promises the same. But neither of them take account of the fact that the more details included, the harder it is to get the total picture. In the sciences, the whole enterprise turned out to be much more complicated than anyone had anticipated, so that, instead of making it easier, science was making it harder and harder to get any over-all picture. And of course it is for the intellectual that science makes things harder, for he is the one best equipped to see the details—the many, many pieces that must be fitted together before the picture is clear.

The too-much-knowledge from which the intellectual suffers today is the fragmentary but reliable information about the structure and the operation of the actual world that keeps pouring in from the several sciences, augmented by the shifting though plausible speculations about the totality that issue now and then from the more hardy philosopher. That there is this knowledge available, that it keeps accumulating, that the system or totality, the panoramic view, keeps having to be readjusted in order to take account of the most recently discovered facts—this always unfinished state of affairs is the very element which constitutes the psychological atmosphere of our time, maintaining the intellectual in a constant state of suspense, always undecided, always waiting. We can imagine our intellectual stretched out comfortably in his library easy-chair, the books of his inheritance stacked on the floor and bulging the shelves; he sits there reading and waiting, reading and waiting. What is he waiting for? For the telephone at his elbow to ring. He is expecting a call which will inform him of the latest theory, the most recent discovery, the newest obsolescence in opinion, the newest new understanding. He feels vaguely that sometime he must get out of that chair and *do* something, but then again he knows he cannot act intelligently until he receives the next call. For what if in the meantime . . . ?

Now this paralysis before incomplete information, which expects more and more "understanding" as the answer to the human question, is what Kierkegaard means when he speaks of spiritual immaturity—something of which Socrates, with far less erudition than a present-day high school senior, could not be accused.

The majority of men in every generation, even those who, as it is described, devote themselves to thinking (dons and the like), live and die under the impression that life is simply a matter of understanding more and more, and that if it were granted to them to live longer, that life would continue to be one long continuous growth in understanding. How many of them ever experience the maturity of discovering that there comes a critical moment where everything is reversed, after which the point becomes to understand more and more that there is something which cannot be understood.

That is Socratic ignorance, and that is what the philosophy of our times requires as a corrective.[3]

In other words, as far as this external knowledge is concerned, spiritual maturity consists of discovering that the over-all picture on the puzzle is not a map but a mystery, and that this is so whether the puzzle is put together out of a few pieces or thousands.

And yet, surely, to be a rational being means to act in accordance with one's reflection, in accordance with having thought through the various possibilities. The intellectual is quite right to say that he cannot act intelligently until he knows what all the possibilities are. But what are *all* the possibilities in relation to the

---

[3] *Journals*, No. 962, p. 330.

mystery which is the over-all picture? How can one act rationally in relation to the totality? And it is just this acting in relation to the totality that Kierkegaard means when he talks of "acting decisively, infinitely." This situation, the fact that a rational being, with all his powers of reflection, must act in relation to a totality which to his reflection remains an "equilibrium of possibilities" (that is, a mystery), is what Kierkegaard calls *absurd*. In the following excerpt, it is neither man nor reason nor the totality, but the *situation,* that is called absurd.

If I really have powers of reflection and am in a situation in which I have to act decisively—what then? My powers of reflection will show me exactly as many possibilities *pro* as *contra*. The meaning of which is that I, like all men, shall be pleased to observe that there is a providence, guidance, a God, and that my powers of reflection, or those of any man, only enable one to learn and become aware of that fact; that here, if I may so express myself, is where one pays the turnpike money. Now what is it that I have come up against? The *absurd*. And what is the *absurd*? It is, as may quite easily be seen, that I, a rational being, must act in a case where my reason, my powers of reflection, tell me: you can just as well do the one thing as the other, that is to say where my reason and reflection say: you cannot act—and yet here is where I have to act. But that is the case every time I have to act really decisively; because I am then caught up in an infinite passion, and that is just where the incongruity between action and reflection becomes evident. In the routine of everyday I do not notice the secret of reflection, and so imagine that I am acting upon reflection in spite of the fact that nothing is more impossible— because reflection is the equilibrium of possibilities.

The absurd, or to act by virtue of the absurd, is to act upon faith, trusting in God. It is perfectly simple. I must act, but reflection has closed the road, so I take one of the possibilities and turn to God saying: This is what I do, bless my actions, I cannot do otherwise because I am brought to a standstill by my powers of reflection.[4]

It should be observed that it is only thanks to passion—an infinite passion, or the passion of the infinite—that the "rational man" actually breaks out of this absurd impasse and into action. Whether or not he "believes" in a providence that somehow covers and blesses his act, he has to act, if he is to act at all, as though he did. If the modern paralyzed intellectual would only think through his situation with passion, realize its futility and absurdity, and

⁴ *Journals*, No. 871, p. 291.

recognize that in the matter of finding out who he is and what he ought to do, he is no better off with all his knowledge than were the ancients, he would find the anger of protest. He would get out of that chair in sheer disgust, like a lover fed up with waiting for a call from his lady, and would regain the initiative by taking it. But alas, our intellectual is so debilitated by his prolonged indecision and procrastination and by his indolent lounging in that chair, that he no longer has the energy and the passion to make a move; he doesn't care enough.

It is useless to present ever more elaborate and convincing reconciliations of science and religion to the intellectual, for he has forgotten what it means to live as a human being must live, and therefore the problems dealt with by religion do not properly exist for him at all. He needs to be made to see the situation he has got himself into, and then be goaded, ridiculed, stung, or shamed into a desire to get out of it at all costs. Socratically, if we want to help him, we must begin with him where he is, paralyzed by his intellect, but proceed in such a way as to help him use his intellect to overcome the paralysis, not to make his situation worse by giving him more of what he has too much of, namely, more objective knowledge, more cumulative information about the world. Kierkegaard deals with this in the *Concluding Unscientific Postscript* under the heading, "How the Subjectivity of the Individual must be Qualified in Order that the Problem may Exist for him."[5] If the less Hegelian term "selfhood" is used in place of "subjectivity," it is evident that the first thing that must be done to break the spell is to draw the intellectual's fascinated gaze away from the mountain range of facts, the natural and world-historical panorama, and to force that gaze to come to rest upon himself and dwell there.

It is surprising how much force and cleverness the intellectual employs to resist such a shift of attention. He is willing enough to discuss the latest theory on any subject, and to discuss it with graciousness and humility before the facts. He will perhaps even discuss with considerable erudition the latest findings of psycho-

---

[5] *Concluding Unscientific Postscript*, trans. D. F. Swenson and Walter Lowrie (American-Scandinavian Foundation; Princeton, N. J.: Princeton University Press, 1941), p. 115.

analysis on the integration of personality through increased self-knowledge, will even visit a psychoanalyst and entertain his friends with amusing accounts of what an interesting case he himself turned out to be. But let it be suggested that self-knowledge is every man's most primitive duty and responsibility, that not to be always engaged in increasing one's self-knowledge is blameworthy in the most elementary sense (like not bothering to control one's temper or one's bowels in public, or not observing the minimum courtesies of social life), and right away the intellectual is on the defensive. He takes this suggestion as "personal," and therefore insulting. About this attitude Kierkegaard remarks in the *Journals,* "A curious usage: 'personal' in the sense of an offensive remark. We are so far from everything personal (and yet that is the whole mystery of life), that something personal, talking personally to a person is being 'personal' *i.e.* insulting."[6]

If the intellectual thinks of the personal as somehow insulting, it must be because he has something to hide, and what he has to hide are evasions and lies that he unconsciously or half-consciously lives by, instinctively defending them as "nobody's business." But somebody has to make it his business to insist that he face his own lies and evasions if he is ever to come to self-knowledge. This can be done, Kierkegaard claims, by the *manner* in which the problems are presented to him. And if it comes to a question of deliberating the truth of Christianity, the wrong way to go about it is to build up a "case for Christianity" by piling up all the accumulated evidence one can assemble from history, philosophy, morality, culture, and so forth, for this evidence may be true enough, or as true as any other evidence of this type, but its cumulative and probabilistic nature gives the intellectual exactly that loophole he needs in order to avoid coming to a decision. Behind these "probabilities" he can conceal from himself the fact that he is not prepared to make any changes in himself such as would be necessary should he "accept" the truth of Christianity, or rather such as would make his "acceptance" of the truth of Christianity a true acceptance.

Hence we do not here raise the question of the truth of Christianity in the sense that when this has been determined, the subject is assumed

* *Journals,* No. 863, p. 280.

ready and willing to accept it. No, the question is as to the mode of
the subject's acceptance; and it must be regarded as an illusion rooted
in the demoralization which remains ignorant of the subjective nature
of the decision, or as an evasion springing from the disingenuousness
which seeks to shirk the decision by an objective mode of approach,
wherein there can in all eternity be no decision, to assume that the
transition from something objective to the subjective acceptance is a
direct transition, following upon the objective deliberation as a matter
of course.[7]

To those intellectuals in the nineteenth century who objected to
Christianity because of its alleged conflict with science it would
have been proper and probably helpful (though fairly nasty) to
have said: "Do you mean to say that on the day this conflict is
removed you stand ready to start in on becoming another St. Paul,
another St. Francis, another John Wesley?" For when the question
is put this way it becomes evident that something other than
intellect determines the desire to evade decision and action.

As soon as decision and action appear, we are in the realm of
ethics, whether we wish to call it by that name or not. Or, more
exactly, as soon as a self acts in accordance with a decision (and a
nondecisive action is not really the action of a self but the response
of a passive awareness to the pushes and thrusts of nonhuman
nature, for example, to the body or the external environment), the
self finds that its action and the decision which produced it have,
willy-nilly, ethical implications and presuppositions. This is a simple
consequence of the fact that man as agent is not in the position of
the knight in the fable who was able to get on his horse and ride
off in all directions. Modern physics has its Principle of Exclusion
—and existential philosophy would do well to formulate an analogous principle of exclusion for ethics, to describe the situation of
man whereby one action excludes the possibility of other actions,
forever and irrevocably. "The Road Not Taken" is the road one
can never come back to, at least not as the same self that once
stood before it. The ethical principle of exclusion is what lends to
human action the quality of seriousness, the pathos of risk, falli-
bility, and guilt. Kierkegaard pointed out that all seriousness is
first of all ethical seriousness, because it is only in action that
something is risked, that is, only then that the self one wishes to

[7] *Postscript*, pp. 115-116.

be is risked, that life itself in so far as it is meaningful is risked. Aesthetically, contemplatively, abstractly, it is easy enough to do the horse-trick, to be half-a-dozen different imagined selves at once or to deliberate endlessly over the merits of the many fascinating possibilities. Ethically, that is, in action, existence takes over; one becomes what one has done, or ceases to be a "one."

4. Futile Quests for the Ethical

The intellectual of modern times also resembles the rich young man in the Bible in that his question, "What must I do to be saved?" lacks the requisite seriousness. The rich young man, however, was a considerably developed personality ethically. Compared with him the intellectual of today is a babe in the ethical woods. The young man had kept the commandments from his youth up, and yet he knew that this did not make him perfect, that he must still do "something," that he must do the particular thing that was demanded of him as his special task. On this occasion the demand was "Go, sell what you have, and give to the poor . . . and come, follow me." And the young man went away sorrowful, because he was impressed by large quantities. But the intellectual cannot give his intellect away. Presumably the wealth that the rich young man was asked to give away would have been helpful to the poor, but it is not certain that the intellect, considered as riches, would be an unqualified blessing, even if it could be given to the poor. It is enough of a problem for those who possess it, and, since they really cannot give it away, they must learn to live with it and take care how they use it.

Like the rich young man, the intellectual of modern times seems much impressed by large quantities and by the quantitative factor as it shows itself in history. Kierkegaard shows how this fact inevitably seduces the intellectual away from his ethical task and actually obstructs his ethical development. For there is something about the ethical that is jealous for its own quality and will not be impressed by quantity, so that if a person managed to perform the most prodigious deeds but did them without ethical motivation, they would count for nothing in the eyes of ethics. (For example, when a millionaire today gives half of his money to charity in order to avoid the income tax, we do not compare him favorably with the rich young man in the Bible, who at least felt that riches were a responsibility; nor do we feel that the millionaire has understood better the renunciation that Jesus demanded.)

It is for this reason that Ethics looks upon all world-historical knowledge with a degree of suspicion, because it may so easily become a snare, a demoralizing aesthetic diversion for the knowing subject, in so far as the distinction between what does or does not have historical significance obeys a quantitative dialectic. As a consequence of this fact, the absolute ethical distinction between good and evil tends for the historical survey to be neutralized in the aesthetic-metaphysical determination of the great and significant, to which category the bad has equal admittance with the good.[8]

After all, doesn't history immortalize, because of the big splash they make, its villains as much as its heroes? But even the desire to be an important villain is quite beyond the individual's control. Whether or not an action becomes historically significant is determined by factors other than its ethical motivation: accident, prevailing opinion, the complex crisscrossing of impersonal forces, indifference, misunderstanding, and so on.

Neither by willing the good with all his strength, nor by satanic obduracy in willing what is evil, can a human being be assured of historical significance. Even in the case of misfortune the principle holds, that it is necessary to be fortunate in order that one's misfortune may obtain world-historical significance. How then does an individual acquire historical significance? By means of what from the ethical point of view is accidental. But Ethics regards as unethical the transition by which an individual renounces the ethical quality in order to try his fortune, longingly, wishingly, and so forth, in the quantitative and non-ethical.[9]

The present century has become less optimistic about the nature or the foreseeable outcome of the historical process, but it shows by its very ethical despair, especially its despair of what the individual can do, that it, too, understands the ethical only in terms of its historical significance. The modern intellectual, statistically well-informed about the billions that populate the earth and conduct their lives without consulting him and even in total ignorance of his existence, is ethically paralyzed from the start because he can-

[8] *Postscript*, p. 120.
[9] *Postscript*, p. 120.

not see, even under the most favorable conditions, how what the individual does can matter much in the total picture. "This is possibly the reason why the contemporary age is seized with discontent when it confronts the necessity of action, because it has been spoiled by the habit of contemplation; and from this proceed, perhaps, the many sterile attempts to count for more than one by socially clubbing together, hoping thus numerically to overawe the spirit of history." [10]

The intellectual is spoiled by the habit of contemplating large-scale, statistical phenomena. He anticipates the result of the action he might have taken, calculates its small chances of making any great stir in history, and loses his ethical enthusiasm before he has begun—or else he cautiously and tentatively joins some organized movement. For he is such a selfless fellow that he hardly knows what a self is or what it might mean to develop himself ethically. At the same time that he resolves on an action, he declares, " 'I will this, but I also will that my efforts should prove to be of benefit to other men; for let me tell you, I am a very benevolent fellow, and anxious to do good to others, even to the extent of improving the whole human race.' " [11] The habit of large-scale contemplation spoils his ethical discernment, for the longer he contemplates history and the longer the part of history that he contemplates, the less certain, or the more equivocal, the ethical itself becomes for him. The quantitative dialectic operating in history combines with the impossibility of determining motivation in history to make the ethical ambiguous, as far as any mere human being can hope to discover it there. Of course, for God it is a little different.

For God, the apprehension of the historical is interpenetrated by His knowledge of the inmost secrets of conscience, alike in the greatest and in the humblest. If a human being seeks to occupy this standpoint he is a fool; if he refrains from such an attempt, he will have to content himself with a survey of the more prominent items, and this is precisely what makes the quantitative the deciding factor in the selection. That the ethical is present in the historical process, as it is everywhere where God is, is not on this account denied. But it is denied that the finite spirit can see it there in truth; and it must be reckoned a piece of presumption to attempt to see it there, a reckless venture which may readily end by the observer losing the ethical in himself.[12]

[10] *Postscript*, pp. 120-121.   [11] *Ibid.*, p. 124.   [12] *Ibid.*, pp. 126-127.

The ethical is in the man himself first of all, or it is nowhere. To look for it in history when one has not found it in oneself is to confess to the confusion of not having a self, for the ethical and the self arise together, as it were in the same breath, the same spirit. The eternal validity of the ethical resides in the eternal validity of the self, and conversely. Without the self, without freedom, responsibility, choice, self-relatedness, and self-consistency, the ethical disappears. Without the ethical as the eternally valid choice between good and evil, a choice which is the task given to the self by existence itself, the self disappears; it leads a subversive existence as a mere possibility enslaved by internal and external compulsions, immersed in one of the forms of despair.

The very fact that the ethical is by no means obviously displayed in history gives rise to the temptation to look for it with a spyglass or a microscope, to subject more and more data to more minute investigation—or the temptation to call for a prophet. The nineteenth century studied history and discovered anthropology, which revealed that in various times and places the ethical has been understood in various ways. From this it deduced that either the ethical is an illusion or it is relative to time—that is, it is something that the individual must wait for a prophet of his own "age" to discover and report. On this phenomenon Kierkegaard heaps his scorn:

. . . to let the ethical become something which it needs a prophet to discover, a man with a world-historical outlook upon world-history— that is indeed a rare and ingeniously comical conceit. Happy nineteenth century! If no such prophet arises, we can all enjoy a holiday, for in that case no one knows what the ethical is. It is already droll enough that the ethical is so lightly regarded that instruction in it is by preference left to divinity students and village school masters; it is ridiculous enough for one to say that the ethical has not yet been found, but still has to be discovered. And yet, it would not be a wholly insane notion if he meant that it was to be discovered by means of the self-penetration of the individual in himself and his God-relationship. But that a prophet should be needed for the purpose, a world-historical swashbuckler, who by means of a deep eye and a blue eye, by means of a knowledge of universal history, perhaps also by reading coffee grounds and laying out the cards, is to discover the ethical; that is to say (for this is the modern catchword of the demoralized ethic), what it is the age demands: this is in a double manner to create a confusion for which the lover of laughter must always be deeply indebted to the wise men of our time. . . . What the most stupid human being, deriving his instruction from a reformatory, can understand, has with the assistance of the professorial wisdom been transformed and improved so as to become this genuinely speculative profundity.[13]

5. To "Kneel Again Unto the Dead"

To summarize, the modern intellectual is like the rich young man in the Bible in that it is precisely his riches, his intellect, that stand in the way of his salvation. And in some ways his case is more pitiable than that of the rich young man, for he can no longer even ask, "What must I do to be saved?" because, thanks to the culture's intellectual development, all parts of this question, the "must," the "I," the "do," and the "be saved," have become meaningless for him. His persistence in the intellectual quest, however, his very flirting with world-historical panoramas, betrays his need to find an answer for the question that he cannot even properly ask. Brought up in the remnants of a religious tradition he cannot appropriate, he is no better equipped by his overdeveloped intellect to reject it unequivocally for some new and different faith than he is to embrace it with the allegiance it demands. *Ni chair ni poisson,* neither believer or resolute unbeliever, his case is accurately described in a poem by Allen Tate:

> This is the day His hour of life draws near,
> Let me get ready from head to foot for it
> Most handily with eyes to pick the year
> For small feed to reward a feathered wit.
> Some men would see it an epiphany
> At ease, at food and drink, others at chase
> Yet I, stung lassitude, with ecstasy
> Unspent argue the season's difficult case
>
> So: Man, dull critter of enormous head,
> What would he look at in the coiling sky?
> But I must kneel again unto the Dead
> While Christmas bells of paper white and red,
> Figured with boys and girls spilt from a sled,
> Ring out the silence I am nourished by.[14]

[13] *Postscript*, pp. 129, 130.
[14] "Sonnets at Christmas," I, *Poems 1922-1947* (New York: Scribner's, 1948).

Here is the paralyzed intellectual, "dull critter of enormous head," helplessly, nervously, casting about for anything, "with eyes to pick the year for small feed," unable even to ask the right question ("What would he look at in the coiling sky?"), slowly starving to death spiritually, "with ecstasy unspent." For the silence he is nourished by cannot be mistaken for any blissful mystical silence filled with a divine presence. It is the empty silence rung out by paper bells, with even the design on the paper conveying the ominous threat of undoing, the boys and girls spilt from a sled.

"But I must kneel again unto the Dead." Here is the hopeful point of departure for a new beginning, as far as a Kierkegaardian understanding of existence is concerned. Never mind if Christ seems Dead—that is really almost a historical accident, the accident of having been born into an age of intellectual exploration comparable to the age of Columbus and Magellan, whose explorations also did not solve the perennial human questions. The important thing, the hopeful thing, is for the intellectual to kneel, and on his knees to realize that in the matter of one's relationship to the divine, the possession of special capacities is no recommendation to God, who will simply scale the tasks accordingly— and to discover that on their knees all are equal in the only true equality, the equality of all before God.

Kierkegaard, himself an intellectual of such outstanding capacities that this fact almost cut him off from all of his contemporaries, could not come to terms with Christianity on any other basis. Either Christianity is for all or it is nonsense, and the philosophers, by turning it into a speculative profundity for the brainy, were rapidly turning it into nonsense. That he really worried about this difficulty is shown in one of the longer entries in the *Journals:*

There is one difficulty, where simplicity is concerned, which has often recurred to my mind. Imagine, for a moment, a young man, a student for example; he falls ill, cannot do anything, suffers spiritually. Had I to comfort him—oh, and how willingly would I not do so—I should say: consider now, your life is unquestionably as important and significant in the eyes of God as that of the man who astonishes the world and transforms it by his ideas. But consider further, in order really to rest in that elevation of thought: does it not require a powerful brain, considerable powers of mind? In that case we are just where we were before.

But immediately he goes on to say,

And yet I cannot abandon the thought that every man, absolutely every man, however simple he is, however much he may suffer, can nevertheless grasp the highest, namely religion, I cannot forget that. If that is not so, then Christianity is really nonsense. To me it is frightful to see the thoughtlessness with which philosophers and the like make use of difference-categories such as genius, talent, etc., in religion. They do not suspect that in that case religion is finished and done with. I have only had one consolation, the blessed consolation of knowing something which can bring comfort, and blessedly comfort every man, absolutely every man. Take away that comfort and I can't be bothered to live, I should have the spleen.

And again:

Think of the highest of all things, think of Christ—only imagine that he came into the world in order to save a few really clever people, for the others could not understand him. Horrible, disgusting! No human suffering repelled him, nor any limitations—but the society of clever people, that would certainly have repelled him.[15]

The problem of getting the intellectual through the needle's eye is first of all then the problem of preventing his intellect from issuing in mere cleverness, by turning it away from vain speculation to the seriousness of the human situation of existence considered as an unavoidable predicament in which all men without exception are universally and individually involved. Only from such employment of his intellect can the intellectual become aware of his own condition in such a way that the question of salvation can once more mean something to him. In the matter of becoming a Christian, the modern intellectual needs first of all to learn how to ask the question about his salvation properly, and only then can it make sense to give him the Christian answer.

[15] *Journals*, No. 1031, pp. 361-362.

III

Kierkegaard's 'Individual': The Single Person

1. Defining the Category

Not everyone has it in him to be an intellectual, but according to Kierkegaard every man has it in him to be an individual, and to become more and more completely an individual. Man's biological basis is given, so that as far as his physical body is concerned, there is no escape for man from existing in the form of an individual. Whoever does not find himself with an individual body is a biological mistake, like Siamese twins or a two-headed calf. So the physical substrate is there, as a hint from nature, but now it is a question of what the body's owner will do with the fact that as soon as he finds himself at all, he finds himself as an individual. Kierkegaard stretched the meaning of the term individual far beyond its biological and psychological significance, so that what he meant by "the individual" is perhaps better expressed by what we would now call "the single person." Since no one is born as a single person, but only as the possibility of becoming one, the term must always be used (as Kierkegaard uses "the individual") in the sense of a simultaneous being and becoming—a goal in the process of realization, always threatened with potential and partially actual nonrealization.

Before we examine Kierkegaard's use of the category of the individual in his polemics, let us look at some of the Kierkegaardian meanings underlying the term "single person." The "single" means alone, in the sense of apart from others, a condition recognized early in life as a bodily separateness, later on also as a psychological separateness. I *alone* can eat with this body, sense with these organs, think and feel with this mind. And "single" also means alone before God: I *alone* become aware of God, whatever my ideas of him may be. Even if millions of others subscribe to my ideas, it is as a single person that I exist before God holding these popular ideas. For Kierkegaard, *everyone* exists before God in this aloneness, even when he denies God completely or has the most erroneous conceptions of God in his mind. There is something prior to all desires and conceptions about it before which man, willy-nilly, exists. And it is just the blessedness and the burden, the privilege and the task, of being the single person, that he may become aware of the fact that in this aloneness he exists before God.

The "single" in single person also means unified, integrated, ordered around a central purpose, single-minded. In this sense the single person is contrasted with the scatterbrained, the dissipated, the pulled-in-all-directions person, the conflict-divided, or even the schizoid personality. "Purity of heart," which is to will one thing, namely, the good for its own sake, gives us the ideal ethical individual. His opposite number is the satanic or demonic individual, who single-mindedly wills the evil for its own sake. Thus the divided or the dissipated person is never demonic, though he may be "possessed," that is, partially in the power of evil. A single person oriented in the wrong direction is required for the demonic individual to be properly identified. But whether one becomes "pure in heart" or demonic is never decided by accident or circumstance alone. Hence, there is responsibility. The single person is the responsible individual.

Finally, the single person also has the meaning of the singular person, the unique, concrete particularity which each individual finds himself to be as a matter of fact. Speaking ideally and abstractly, we can understand easily enough that the individual ought to "realize the universal through the particular." But how is this to be done in actuality by a concrete, particular person, without either devaluating the particular, or else transgressing against the universal by claiming to be the exceptional? In this question are to be found many of the problems and temptations of the ethical sphere, and, as we shall see later, the ethical sphere must be transcended precisely because, in the Christian view, the individual is always both the universal *and* the exceptional. That is Kierkegaard's meaning when he says that "the individual" is *above* the race, that he is not a specimen in the way every animal is an individual specimen of the class or species to which he belongs, which is *above* the animal in the order of universality.

How often have I shown that fundamentally Hegel makes men into heathens, *into a race of animals gifted with reason.* For in the animal world 'the individual' is always less important than the race. But it is the peculiarity of the human race that just because the individual is created in the image of God 'the individual' is above the race.

This can be wrongly understood and terribly misused: *concedo.* But that is Christianity. And *that* is where the battle must be fought.[1]

Christianity accentuates the individual, by permitting him a relationship with the divine that is both universal and exceptional. Such is the personal relationship to Christ, which gives each concrete, particular individual a "calling," a providential task above and beyond the call of "duty," which is the universal. This providential task is not only his *duty,* it is *his* duty. So the Kierkegaardian individual is the single person understood as the unique, concrete, particular wholeness who is above the race, because through him the race as mere universality transcends itself, but who, as a matter of fact, even the humblest individual can be, and can strive more and more to become.

2. *The Nature of the Eternal in Man*

The aspect of Hegelianism which most of all incited Kierkegaard against it was the fact that it threatened to extinguish the possibility of anyone's being and becoming the individual in all of the above senses of the single person. Of course, it did not threaten the biological or the psychological individual; rather, it threatened his further understanding of himself as an individual in ethical and religious terms. Tremendous blows had to be struck at this philosophy, because it had become so entrenched that even the so-called ordinary man in the street, formerly protected against sophistry by illiteracy, was prattling about the world-historical significance of this and that, about mediation, and about what the age demands. Individual responsibility, the feeling that one is accountable for what one is and does and becomes, was fast disappearing from the world as all men struck the pose of contemplation from the standpoint of eternity, whereby the Absolute contemplates itself in the mirror of itself which is history. For if everything that happens now, today, and everything that will hap-

---

[1] *Journals,* No. 1050, p. 370.

pen tomorrow is already "explained" and "justified" from the standpoint of this higher contemplation, man's constitution as a creature who must face the future and make decisions for which he is responsible simply disappears. The very notion that an absolute idea marches through history and "moves" individuals, without their having any say as to whether they will allow themselves to be moved, reduces the individual to a puppet operated by an ideology and makes an accountable action almost incomprehensible. Decision is not just difficult but illusory, when, whatever a man decides and whatever he does in accordance with his decision, the Hegelian System stands by with a ready explanation of why *it had to be so*—or at least with a guarantee that such an explanation will be forthcoming as soon as a more perfect understanding of the Absolute Reason is achieved.

If the real is the rational, and the rational is the real, anything that happens for which a rational explanation can be found is thereby justified, which means that in the Absolute Reason everything is justified; so good-bye to the responsibility of man, and good-bye to the reality of the disjunctions in life that face him, such as true and false, good and evil. The very title of Kierkegaard's opening piece of his literary production, *Either/Or*, was a blow against this abstract or panoramic contemplation from above the plane of existence, for it reminded people that either/or exists, that it is something real for man, and that to be a man means to see and to deal with innumerable either/ors one after another in real life, not to contemplate both-and from the sky.

One reason no one listened to Kierkegaard was that it seemed much easier to listen to the soothing abstractions of the system builder. Men were delighted to be relieved of the responsibility of being men, beings who are required to make responsible decisions on which the nature of the future depends. Better to relax and let yourself be just one more abstraction among other abstractions comprising the panorama of world-history. All you had to do was to sit around in a dreamy, speculative trance, while you waited for the master-logicians at the System Headquarters to fit that particular little abstraction that was you into the king-sized, monster abstraction which was the universe. And of course it was no wonder that everyone was a Christian, some even more than that, for the

System had "taken care" of Christianity and gone beyond it, so
that the intellectuals of the day, at any rate, could hope to do better
than Jesus, while admitting that he had done very well for his day.

The prime mover of the Hegelian System, the dynamic that made
it run, was the famous dialectic of thesis, antithesis, and synthesis.
Mediation was the process whereby thesis and antithesis, after
being clearly distinguished and opposed, were raised up into a new
unity in the synthesis. But this was a purely contemplative act,
since in actual life the oppositions, if true and not illusory to begin
with, remained as before. Psychologically, Hegelianism provided a
method of escape from the contradictions of life, by removing the
essential subject, the *thinking* ego, to a sphere, *contemplation,*
where he could not be upset or harmed by the contradictions.
This process is somewhat similar to the one by which the oriental
religions try to rescue man from the irrationality and pain of
temporal and material existence, although with them it is more a
volitional than an intellectual act which disarms or cancels the
contradictions. In this distinction Kierkegaard would probably
have sided with the oriental religions against Hegel, for he believed
that a volitional act (such as is the Buddhist suppression of desire)
changes something in reality, changes the individual, whereas a
purely intellectual act changes nothing.

At any rate, something about the Hegelian mediation (now you
see it, now you don't; now the contradictions are real, now they
are erased, suspended, *aufgehoben*) certainly smacked to Kierkegaard of leger-de-main or of magic tricks performed with mirrors.
He was too much of a realist to swallow that—to believe that a
man could stand with his two feet planted in contradiction, while
with his mighty brain he spirited the contradictions away just by
thinking the right thoughts. And so he kept reminding people
facetiously that although for God in heaven it was at least conceivable to try such a stunt, when a man, an existing individual,
tried it, he only made himself ridiculous.

In Kierkegaard's view, dialectical thinking was the reaction
of the integral spirit to contradiction, a method for detecting and
tracking down the real oppositions in life—not, however, for the
purpose of escaping from them into another realm, but precisely
for the purpose of struggling with them in order to find one's real

self in the struggle, by grounding oneself in a deeper layer of existence. Dialectics enabled the self to penetrate deeper into that very existence in which the contradictions showed themselves, thereby establishing the essential unity of the spirit with itself and with something beyond existence—in other words, thereby bringing to self-consciousness the eternal in man.

Apparently for Kierkegaard the mere ability and desire to contemplate the whole of reality from above was not to be identified with the eternal in man. On the contrary, for him this characteristic of man was more like a refined temptation, which the true eternal in man had to face, see through, and resist. Thus, he warns against the alluring deceptiveness of the moment of contemplation:

Alas, contemplation and the moment of contemplation, in spite of all their clarity, readily conceal a deception; because the moment of contemplation has something in common with the falsified eternity. It is a foreshortening that is necessary in order that the contemplation may take place. It must foreshorten time a good deal. Indeed it must actually call the senses and thoughts away from time in order that they may complete themselves in a spurious eternal well-roundedness. It is here as when an artist sketches a country. The sketch cannot be as big as the country. It must be infinitely smaller; but on that account it also becomes all the easier for the observer to scan the outlines of that country. And yet it may well happen to the observer, if suddenly he were actually set down in that country where the many, many miles really exist and are valid, that he would be unable to recognize the country, or to make any sense of it, or as a traveler, to find his way about in it. . . . His knowledge has indeed been a sense-deception.[2]

This calm yet cautionary passage from one of the religious discourses reveals more clearly than much of his polemics what the basic difference between Kierkegaard and Hegel was. It was fundamentally a disagreement over the nature of the eternal in man. For Hegel, the ability and desire to contemplate from above was the true eternal in man. It was actually the self-communion of Absolute Thought, through the medium of all the finite thinking selves. By participating in this infinite thought of the Absolute Reason, the finite thinking self realized whatever of eternity was in it to be realized. No greater destiny than this could be in store for man, and no greater transcendence of the world could be achieved by

[2] *Purity of Heart* Is to Will One Thing, trans. Douglas V. Steere (rev. ed.; New York: Harpers, 1948), pp. 91-92.

him than this purely mental capacity for viewing from above the
world in the abstract. But for Kierkegaard this whole process of
participating in the eternal by means of abstract thought contained
a deception. It resulted in that foreshortening of time and in that
spurious well-roundedness (as in the artist's sketch) which characterizes a falsified eternity—and what consolation is there to be
found in an eternity that is both false and deceitful, no matter how
sure you can be of participating in it? In other words, Kierkegaard
simply mistrusted the power of human, all-too-human, abstraction
to "read off" the mind of God. "My thoughts are not your
thoughts," God had said, and Kierkegaard never forgot. To be
sure, abstract thought had its uses—it was something like a map
which made it "easier for the observer to scan the outlines" of the
land. But not even the most avid cartographer would in his right
mind suggest that a man should build his house, plant his trees,
and cultivate his vegetables on a map. Life is infinitely more rich
than thought, and if there is any eternal validity in man it must reflect that richness, at least as a sort of direction open to the future,
an inexhaustibility, a possibility of transcendence.

For Kierkegaard, the eternal in man was more like a possibility
of transcendence within each man—not, however, an inevitable
growth, but an almost miraculous irruption, intensification, and
purification of the spiritual dimension in man, which, by means of
the mysterious incrementation of discrete, qualitative changes
(decisions), brought the man all the way from the state of a squalling
infant to the state of the Christian individual existing before God.
It was the God-relationship that for Kierkegaard was the eternal
in man; and, as he showed, this relationship could pass through
many stages and qualitative degrees, but it was not dependent on
the power of abstract thought to read off the mind of God in
external events. And for this fact man should be eternally grateful
to his maker. For what if the relationship did depend on abstract
thought? Then the poor man would be lost in a desert indeed!
But fortunately for him this is not the case, though many men do
not make that wonderful discovery for themselves, even in a lifetime of searching. "If an Arab in the desert were suddenly to discover a spring in his tent, and so would always be able to have
water in abundance, how fortunate he would consider himself—so

too when a man who *qua* physical being is always turned toward the outside, thinking that his happiness lies outside him, finally turns inward and discovers that the source is within him; not to mention his discovering that the source is his relation to God." [3]

3. The Source of the Ethical in Man

In view of the fact that the ethical was so important to Kierkegaard's individual ("the beginning of all seriousness"), we should try to trace Kierkegaard's relationship to Kant, for after all Kant did try to rescue the ethical from science, by putting the "ought" into a category of its own. In the process we might also elucidate some of Kierkegaard's epistemological notions. Certainly it would seem that Kierkegaard would agree with Kant in giving a noumenal, not merely a phenomenal, status to the selfhood of man. Kant, however, thought that the ground and wellspring of the self must remain unknowable in the theoretical realm and can be known by us only in the practical realm, through the categorical imperative. But for Kierkegaard the whole object and purpose of selfhood was to come to that kind of self-knowledge and self-transformation which in the Christian terminology is called salvation, a state which presupposes some kind of knowledge about the relationship of God and man (the nature of this knowledge is not the issue here) that goes well beyond the merely rational demand that a rational person should act so that his maxim may be willed to be a universal law. After all, why be a rational person at all, especially when the attempt to be one merely saddles one with innumerable obligations? Kant himself never could answer that question, except by repeating the appeal to reason: reason itself demands that we be as rational as we can.

As for the theoretical realm, Kierkegaard thought that the real problem with respect to knowledge was not *whether* things-in-themselves can be known, but, rather, *which* things-in-themselves existence will allow man to be agnostic about, and which on the contrary it will force him to make assumptions about, just by the very act of his existing. Agnosticism with respect to those things-in-themselves represented by the phenomena in the objective world might well be what the prudent intellectual will settle for, when

[3] *Journals*, No. 995, p. 346.

once he sees the structure and limitations of reason. It is an attitude he can take up just because it will make no difference, either to himself or to the objective things-in-themselves, whether he knows them or not, loves them or hates them, creates or destroys them, since "in-themselves" they are by definition unrelated to him. For this reason Kierkegaard calls this kind of knowledge "indifferent." But it is quite otherwise when a man attempts to take up the attitude of agnosticism with respect to the self, and specifically his own self. For only by a self-deception can he pretend that it makes no difference to him whether he knows himself or not, loves himself or hates himself, preserves himself or destroys himself. Agnosticism with respect to the self would also be fatal for his development as a self, for it would provide him with a perpetual excuse for not examining the implications of his acts. No knowledge, no implications. And yet a self is so constructed and so situated in life that as soon as it acts, it acts "as if" something or other were true, both about itself and the world. So it is a question of whether the self is willing to face the implications of its acts, especially when these are likely to be far from pleasant, or whether it will use the many distractions that life offers to prevent this, or whether it will use the escape hatch of agnosticism which the clever intellect offers.

If then we were to insist with Kant that man can know nothing about the noumenal self except the demands of the categorical imperative, we would be arresting the self-knowledge of man just as it is starting out, having only just now escaped from the bondage of the self in the aesthetic stage, or hedonism. In Kierkegaard's terminology, we would be arresting the spiritual development of man at the ethical stage, and really just on the threshold of that. Kierkegaard would also disagree with Kant that through the categorical imperative reason gives laws to itself and is therefore autonomous. Here is what he has to say about autonomy in one of the few journal entries that contain a direct reference to Kant:

Real self-reduplication without a third factor, which is outside and compels one, is an impossibility and makes any such existence into an illusion or an experiment.
    Kant held that man was his own law (autonomy) *i.e.* bound himself under the law which he gave himself. In a deeper sense that means to say: lawlessness or experimentation. It is no harder than the thwacks which Sancho Panza applied to his own bottom. I can no

more be really stricter in A than I am, or than I wish myself to be in B. There must be some compulsion, if it is to be a serious matter. If I am not bound by anything higher than myself, and if I am to bind myself, where am I to acquire the severity as A by which, as B, I am to be bound, so long as A and B are the same.

This can be seen best of all in religious matters. The transformation which really lies in changing from immediacy to spirituality, that mortification is not serious, becomes in fact an illusion, a form of experimentation if there is not some third and compelling factor, which is not the individual himself.

That, too, is why all outstanding individualities, the real 'instruments,' are compelled.

Not only is the law which I give myself as maximum not a law; but there is a law which is given to me by one higher than I. And not only that; but the lawgiver takes the liberty of joining in at the same time in the character of educator, and applies the compulsion.[4]

If God is not the law-giver, the author of the moral law, it is illusion to call it a law, for it is then after all a refined matter of convenience, felicity, or utility, contrived according to reason's ability to detect contradiction and to foresee consequences. I act according to a maxim I could easily wish to become a universal law, and at once find myself in the position of qualifying it by saying, "that is, if only everyone were as good and righteous as I am." But if God is the lawgiver and the educator, there can be no such resting on one's moral laurels, for, ironically, it is just our rational righteousness that shows itself to be "filthy rags" before His holiness and His righteousness. And so the God-given moral law, even when rationally calculated according to Kant's rule, becomes not reason glorying in its own autonomy and freedom but "the schoolmaster." "Providence is no friend of that effeminate attitude whereby a man wishes to play at being autodidact, when there lives at the same time a teacher so outstanding as our Lord, to whom he can turn." [5]

It is interesting to note that Kierkegaard differed from Kant not only in his views of the moral law within, but also in the matter of the feelings aroused in him by the starry heavens above. Let us listen to Kant's own words in this famous passage:

[4] *Journals*, No. 1041, pp. 364-365.
[5] *Journals*, No. 1041, p. 365.

The first [the wonder of the starred heaven] begins with the place I occupy in the external world of sense, and expands the connection in which I find myself into the incalculable vastness of worlds upon worlds, of systems within systems, over endless ages of their periodic motion, their beginnings and perpetuation. The second [the wonder of the moral law within] starts from my invisible self, from my personality, and depicts me as in a world possessing true infinitude which can be sensed only by the intellect. . . . The first view of a numberless quantity of worlds destroys my importance, so to speak, since I am an *animal-like being* who must return its matter from whence it came to the planet (a mere speck in the universe), after having been endowed with vital energy for a short time, one does not know how. The second view raises my value infinitely, as an *intelligence*, through my personality; for in this personality the moral law reveals a life independent of animality and even of the entire world of sense. This is true at least as far as one can infer from the purposeful determination of my existence according to this law. This [determination] is not restricted to the conditions and limits of this life, but radiates into the infinite.[6]

What impressed Kant about the heavens was their sheer size, which reduced man to a speck of almost nothing, and their absolute determination by laws operating inflexibly through all the infinities of time and space—and it seemed to him that the possibility of man's conforming to the moral law within made him a participant in this kind of infinitude, thanks to intelligence. With Kierkegaard, it was just the other way. What impressed him about the stars was not their size, but their otherness, their genuine differentness from the human, and the impossibility of our participating in *that* kind of infinitude—in fact, of our coming to any real understanding with nature. And this applied not only to the stars and all large-scale phenomena but also to the small-scale and to the most intimate "communings" of man with nature. It was the indifference and self-sufficiency of nature that made it so distressing to the spirit in man. Man could not get along without nature, but it certainly seemed that nature could get along very well without him. This state of affairs produced a certain melancholy longing in man that made him a wanderer and a stranger in the midst of nature's most moving loveliness, as much as in his contemplation of her marvelous construction:

    [6] "The Critique of Pure Practical Reason," *The Philosophy of Kant,* ed. and trans. Carl J. Friedrich ("The Modern Library Edition" [New York: Random House, 1949]), pp. 261-262.

And what a puzzling arrangement the army of stars presents! Yet there seems to be an agreement between them that they shall arrange themselves in this fashion. But the stars are so far away that they cannot see the wanderer. It is only the wanderer who can see the stars, hence there may come no agreement between him and the stars. So this melancholy of poetical longing is grounded in a deep misunderstanding, because the lonely wanderer is everywhere surrounded in nature by that which does not understand him, even though it always seems as if an understanding must be arrived at.[7]

In our time this deep misunderstanding is characteristic also of some of our scientists, who think that simply because their knowledge has given them a certain undeniable control over nature, they have "come to an agreement" with nature. But nature, which allows herself to be probed and controlled and even pushed around, never responds to man. She appears to us as a reserved type of personality, like the man who may be sociable, amusing, and even entertaining, regaling the company with the most witty accounts of things that happened to him—but when you look into his eyes for a glimpse of that self revelation which is the source of human understanding, it is like looking at a stone wall, and you realize that he is not really telling you a thing about himself. So it is in astronomy, where the controlling aspect of our knowledge is not so obvious, that we become aware most clearly that nature is not telling us a thing about herself. We cannot come to an understanding with her because she does not understand our need for a response, and her silence and self-sufficiency serve only to produce in us a melancholy wonder and a half-resentful questioning.

Kierkegaard's epistemological views are nowhere explicitly stated, but one gathers from many passing references that he regarded all knowledge as either an approximation process in principle endless (empirical knowledge), or as an exhibition of relationships that are necessary and cannot be any different (logic), a process in principle tautological. So, although he was in agreement with Kant as to the fact that human knowledge is limited, his view of the nature of the limitation was a good deal more "realistic," in the sense of epistemological realism, than Kant's. For Kant it was the categories of the intellect (space, time, causation, substance, and so on) which, while they imposed a certain orderliness

[7] *Purity of Heart*, pp. 20-21.

on our knowledge of things, at the same time stood in the way, almost as a sort of veil or screen, between us and those things as they might be "in themselves," that is, as they might be for a presumably nonhuman knower or for an omniscience such as is predicated of God. But, for Kierkegaard, what stood in the way was not so much the forms of thought as the richness and complexity of reality itself as compared with the relative coarseness of human thought; therefore the mind had to fall back on an approximation process, always adding details here and there, but never quite able to exhaust the subject matter. Reality, he said, cannot be conceived, that is, exhausted in ideas. "To conceive reality is to reduce it to *possibility*—but in that case it is impossible to conceive it, because to conceive it is to reduce it to possibility, and consequently not to hold fast to it as reality."[8] Possibility consists of ideas against which no evidence can be brought at the present moment, but who knows what evidence may not show up in the future, when the approximation process is more advanced? There is always this gap between reality and possibility, because reality cannot be exhausted in ideas, only represented by the best ideas now available, and because, as epistemological realism holds, reality precedes thought, and thought must accommodate itself to reality as best it can, not the other way around.

So, I believe that Kierkegaard had a more realistic strain in him than Kant. And, having the idea of knowledge as an approximation process, Kierkegaard was not inclined to give comfort either to skeptics or agnostics. Of course, the agnostics could always hold out on the grounds of perfectionism, by pointing out that knowledge that is incomplete is not really and truly knowledge—an unanswerable argument in any case. But skepticism, the desire to doubt everything, cannot hold out against an approximation theory of knowledge, unless it is trying to evade responsibility. Kierkegaard tried to point out that in real life it is not so easy to doubt everything as the philosophers claim—those who pretend to, doubt everything except that they are doubting. He recommended that anyone who is so eager to doubt everything should try it out on some of the simpler things in life—that he is crossing the street, or that he is hungry—and see where this gets him. What interested

[8] *Journals*, No. 1054, p. 373.

Kierkegaard most, however, was that skepticism should not and must not be used as an excuse to evade the responsibility of self-knowledge.

Thanks to the rising interest in science and the scientific method, there was now the curious spectacle of people claiming to know more and more about nature and less and less about themselves. Early in the *Journals* appears a passage behind which we cannot help feeling there is some evidence that Kierkegaard had considered and rejected the possibility of becoming a scientist himself, and for these reasons:

The main objection, the whole objection to natural science may simply and formally be expressed thus, absolutely: it is incredible that a man who has thought infinitely about himself as a spirit could think of choosing natural science (with empirical material) as his life's work and aim. An observant scientist must *either* be a man of talent and instinct, for the characteristic of talent and instinct is not to be fundamentally dialectical, but only to dig up things and be brilliant—not to understand himself (and to be able to live on happily in that way, without feeling that anything is wrong because the deceptive variety of observations and discoveries continuously conceals the confusion of everything); *or* he must be a man who, from his earliest youth, half unconsciously, has become a scientist and continues out of habit to live in that way—the most frightful way of living: to fascinate and astonish the world by one's discoveries and brilliance, and not to understand oneself. It is self-evident that such a scientist is conscious, he is conscious within the limits of his talents, perhaps an astonishingly penetrating mind, the gift of combining things and an almost magical power of associating ideas, etc. But at the very most the relationship will be this: an eminent mind, unique in its gifts, explains the whole of nature—but does not understand itself. Spiritually he does not become transparent to himself in the moral appropriation of his gifts. But that relationship is scepticism, as may easily be seen (for scepticism means that an unknown, an X, explains everything. When everything is explained by an X which is not explained, then in the end nothing is explained at all). If that is not scepticism then it is superstition.[9]

It was this happy "absent-mindedness" about the self, a self-forgetfulness which even appeared to some as a virtue, that Kierkegaard had in mind when he said that in the end science would be the corruption of man. The Hegelian System at least

[9] *Journals*, No. 619, pp. 185-186.

paid theoretical tribute to the self, even if it misconstrued the self's situation in existence. But, with the growing popularization of the results of empirical science, philosophy traditionally understood as the quest for wisdom and truth began more and more to take a back seat. A new thrill of excitement ran through the literate world at the amazing success which even the most modest men of science were having in their work. Why worry about China and Persia and dialectics and world-history when from a few experiments with a handful of dust or a handful of once-living tissue you could uncover the secret workings at the very heart of nature? This, moreover, was a kind of knowledge that was power, whereas speculation always left you sitting in the armchair, everything around you outwardly unchanged. There was really nothing left for philosophy to do except to defend the scientific method against both theological and philosophical conservatism, a process that could end only in modern positivism.

Meanwhile, traditional theology sat by and watched with growing horror as bit by bit the entire structure of the world as interpreted from the Scriptures was destroyed before its eyes, and an utterly alien world-picture was put in its place. In all ages people have had difficulty in finding God in the world. Even the Jews felt that God hid himself from men. But in this new scientific world-picture taking shape before the modern man's eyes there seemed to be not even a hiding place for God, not so much as a nook or cranny where He could be found, for everywhere there was law and necessity, indifference and inhumanity. To be sure, thanks to Kant, the religious-minded could fall back on agnosticism, if they could talk themselves into it, using the moral law as the "nook and cranny" where God could possibly be hiding. But who could do this except a handful of intellectual sophisticates? As the later part of the nineteenth century unrolled, and the masses began to discuss the details of evolution and to confront the Scriptures with the current jokes about the faith of our fathers who hung from the branches of trees, agnosticism turned out to be a most ascetic and demanding creed. You had to keep from making any positive or negative statements about God, and yet you had to live as if your whole moral being, your very soul, depended on Him; and at the same time you had to listen to the learned men explaining with scientific objectivity that your moral being, categorical imperative and all, was nothing but a collection of fears and taboos left over from primitive religious customs, a bunch of socially conditioned reflexes which could probably be explained by the same neural mechanism involved in the now-famous salivation of Pavlov's dogs.

4. Equality under the Category of the Individual

Kierkegaard did not contradict the scientific picture of the world as it was taking shape in his day. He merely pointed, over and over again, to the big "X" that was in it, the observer. And he saw that not only science but also philosophy and political behavior were attacking the selfhood of man so as to dissolve it in abstractions. All three were in different ways tending toward the same end, toward the complete eradication of the Christian idea of what it means to be an individual, namely, an integral spirit capable of feeling responsibility, guilt, and repentance before God. To him the need for restoring and defending the category of the individual was an unavoidable prerequisite to his central concern, the problem of how to become a Christian in Christendom. That is why he called it "his" category, not because he had invented it, but because it became his task, providentially understood, to use that category on behalf of an understanding of what is distinctive about Christianity.

For example, he used the category of the individual to combat certain characteristically nineteenth-century political and metaphysical notions that were floating about in the intellectual atmosphere, some of them quite oblivious to their anti-Christian implications. From our vantage point a hundred years later we can see that he also used this category to fight certain ideas which had not yet appeared in full dress, so to speak, but were on their way; thus his polemic against them has in it an anticipatory, prophetic element. It is as though he had grasped these vaguely "liberal" and supposedly "democratic" ideas and notions in their germinal form and saw where they would lead, long before they became the motive power behind certain historical and cultural developments.

In the sphere of politics, the slogans of the French revolution, "liberty, equality, and fraternity!" were being translated into the medium of practical government in several countries, there developing into something resembling more the clever manipulation of the masses by demagogic leaders than the republican utopias imagined by the originators of the slogans. This was scarcely odd, considering how the parallel developments in philosophy and science had attenuated the idea of the individual. For it is obvious that the words liberty, equality, and fraternity mean something quite different when applied to a community of individuals who hold themselves responsible to God for their actions as separate human beings, than when applied to an anonymous, faceless mob, responding to the promptings of the leader according to the rules of mass psychology. Only lately, with the assistance of some obligingly horrible examples from recent history, have political theorists and cultural analysts come to recognize how easy it is to convert the theoretical democracy into an actual mobocracy,[10] and to recognize that this process is accomplished by making each man *forget his individual being* and sink himself mystically, participatingly, into the crowd, identifying his thoughts, feelings, and actions with those of the crowd.[11] Kierkegaard saw the danger long before it had become a reality to be reckoned with and some time before the ideas of popular democracy had become sufficiently widespread in Europe to penetrate finally even into little Denmark. For this reason he was conservative in politics and warned against what the practical effects of such democracy would be as long as the true equality of men before God was not understood by either the leaders or the followers of the new popular movements.

For wherein lies the true equality of man? And their true liberty, and their true fraternity? Only in the religious sphere can they be found, Kierkegaard claims, and even the politician, if he but pauses to think about it, must realize that it was in the religious sphere that all these ideas originated. "An impatient politician who hurriedly peeps into these pages will find little to edify him, that I must admit. Yet I am convinced that even he, if only he would be so kind as to bestow upon himself a little patience, will become aware, by merely the brief suggestions communicated in these

---

[10] See José Ortega y Gasset, *The Revolt of the Masses* (New York: W. A. Norton, 1932), and Nicholas Berdyaev's analysis of the dehumanization of man in *The Fate of Man in the Modern World*, trans. Donald K. Lowrie (London: S.C.M. Press, 1935).

[11] See Kierkegaard's description of the "crowd" on pp. 73-74.

pages, that the religious is the transfigured rendering of that which the politician has thought of in his happiest moment, if so be that he truly loves what it is to be a man, and loves people really, although he is inclined to regard religion as too lofty and ideal to be practical."[12]

Actually the truth is more nearly the other way around: the politician, with his impatience to get things done, is unrealistic, whereas religion, with its eye on eternity, has quite a different view. The politician gets his ideas of democracy from religion, but merely as ideas, as abstractions several removes from concrete reality. It does not occur to him to try to imagine what kind of concrete transformation of existence, the individual existence of individuals, is needed in order to get equality, liberty, and fraternity realized— he thinks all you have to do is to pass a few laws, throw the rascals out, and establish a constitution. But what about all the differences that remain after this formal equality has been legislated into existence? We know now that for a long time the democratic ideal fed itself upon the fond hope that given enough equality of educational, economic, cultural, and political opportunity, and given enough time, then, gradually, little by little, more and more as time went on, the natural differences among men would disappear or at least be reduced to a minimum. The truth, however, is only now becoming evident to us, now that a reasonable degree of educational opportunity, for example, has been achieved in some countries: that such opportunities merely remove the differences that are removable, and at the same time reveal the differences that are irremovable. Differences of native ability, of parentage, of cultural inclination, of temperament, of energy, of simplicity or complexity, of inborn qualities of the personality—doesn't the educational process expose such differences all the more clearly by removing the former excuse that the person had not been given the opportunity to develop himself?

On the other hand, it is also becoming more evident now than it was in predemocratic times that people don't really want equality as much as they claim they do. They *need* the differences, they count on the differences, in order to grade themselves in a whole

---

[12] "Two Notes About 'The Individual,' " *The Point of View, etc.*, ed. Walter Lowrie (New York: Oxford University Press, 1939), p. 109.

network of relationships to their fellow men and to their society. They want to be able to think of themselves as better than so-and-so in this respect and every bit as good as so-and-so in that respect, and they want to hope to excel so-and-so in still another respect. Such use of the differences (whether they are accidental or acquired or natural does not matter so long as they serve the purpose) to "place" oneself in relation to others is what Kierkegaard calls "worldliness," and worldliness cannot survive without the differences to feed upon. It was no accident, only a naïve stratagem, that monasticism withdrew from the world on the grounds that the Christian life could not be lived in the medium of worldliness. For worldliness is a tough medium. Conquered in one place or form, it simply springs up in another. Monasticism too discovered a difference which could be used by worldliness: "holier than thou!" There is no end to the ingenuity with which worldliness finds the means, the differences, through which to express itself. We have the comedy before us now of communism, having fanatically tried to extirpate economic differences, quickly inventing new differences by which people can grade themselves: skills, services to the state, production quotas, power in the party, and so forth.

The solution of this problem is to accept the differences that have to be accepted, but not in the spirit of worldliness. However, this cannot be done from within the medium of worldliness itself.

No politics ever has, no politics ever can, no worldliness ever has, no worldliness ever can, think through or realize to its last consequences the thought of human equality. To realize complete equality in the medium of worldliness . . . i.e. to realize it in the medium the very nature of which implies differences, and to realize it in a worldly . . . way, i.e. by positing differences—such a thing is for ever impossible, as is apparent from the categories. For if complete equality were to be attained, worldliness would be at an end. But is it not a sort of obsession on the part of worldliness that it has got into its head the notion of wanting to enforce complete equality, and to enforce it by worldly means . . . in a worldly medium? It is only religion that can, with the help of eternity, carry human equality to the utmost limit —the godly, the essential, the nonworldly, the true, the only possible human equality. And therefore (be it said to its honour and glory) religion is the true humanity.[13]

[13] "Two Notes About 'The Individual,' " *Point of View,* pp. 109-110.

With respect to differences and worldliness, the word "individual" has a double meaning to it that Kierkegaard was well aware of and that he thought should be used to advantage, "to provoke attention dialectically."

In every one of the pseudonymous works this theme of 'the individual' comes to evidence in one way or another; but there the individual is predominantly the pre-eminent individual in the aesthetic sense, the distinguished person, &c. In every one of my edifying works the theme of 'the individual' comes to evidence, and as officially as possible; but there the individual is what every man is or can be. The starting-point of the pseudonyms is the difference between man and man with respect to intellect, culture, &c.; the starting-point of the edifying works is the edifying thought of the universal human. But this double meaning is precisely the dialectic of 'the single individual.' 'The single individual' can mean the one and only, and 'the single individual' can mean every man.[14]

The advantage lies in the fact that in actuality both of the two meanings are true of every person. If you carry the thought of the differences to its conclusion, then every person is different from every other, not just the great from the humble, the famous from the unkown, and so on. Every humble, lowly, undistinguished person is different from every other humble, lowly, undistinguished person, and every great one from every other great one, while at the same time all these people, at least in so far as they can be called normal, share in something universal. The law, for example, whether it be a mere traffic law or a law against murder, assumes that there are certain ways of acting that can be expected from all normal people, regardless of the differences that characterize them. The law therefore by definition applies to everybody, it rests on the universal human, and to be outside of the law must mean either to be incapacitated in such a way (insanity, mental defectiveness) as to be regarded abnormal or to be guilty of failure to live up to the minimum requirements of the universal human. Of course, in the historical development of mankind, different cultures have set up different positive laws; nevertheless, they have all assumed that something universal is there in the human, to be approximated in the law. Laws are changed for the better not by doing away with the universal human but by raising the standard of its requirements,

<hr>

[14] "Two Notes About 'The Individual,'" *Point of View*, p. 126.

again regardless of the individual differences. Between the laws of a savage tribe and the laws of a civilized state there exists a difference in the quality of refinement with which the thought of the universal human has been conceived, but the fact of the universal human underlies both of them. The law, however, usually represents the minimum of what can be expected from all the people, so the *ideal* of the universal human may very well be higher in a given culture than the standard of what mere law-abidingness requires, and this higher ideal is usually represented by the land's religion.

In this connection Kierkegaard raised a difficult question: is there such a thing as a teleological suspension of the ethical (the universal)? Is it possible for the individual to be "outside of the law" in a higher rather than in a lower sense, by obeying a direct command from God? He raised this question (in *Fear and Trembling*) about the sacrificial murder that had been required of Abraham, and, by analogy, about the sacrificial "murder" of Regina's happiness that had been required of him, so he thought, by his religious vocation. But more generally one could ask: has anyone the right to be a saint, or a prophet, or an apostle, or a martyr, since that kind of an ideal cannot be demanded of every person by the universal human and might even bring about conflict with prior ethical obligation? What about the stern saying, "If a man will not leave father and mother . . ."?

The advantage of the category of the individual is just this richness, that it comprehends the fact that every individual is both the differentiated individual and the universal-human individual— and the difficulty of being and becoming an individual also lies in this richness and complexity. For the individual who exists before God must always consider both the differences and the universal human in the light of the divine providence, if God's will in the world is to be fulfilled. Milton, caught in the "difference" of his blindness, must have had this problem in mind when he wrote, half hopefully, half in fear that it might not be so, "They also serve who only stand and wait."

5. *Abstraction as a Threat to Edification*

Kierkegaard said that the nineteenth century was an age of dissolution. But by this word he was not referring to moral conduct directly, as when we speak about a dissolute person. Rather, he wished to call attention to a general intellectual tendency to dissolve the hard, brittle, discrete, even stubborn, single items of reality, with which every person was confronted in existence, into huge, soft, misty and watery abstractions. Two such abstractions, for example, were the ideas of *the human race* and of *the pantheistic universe*. People seemed to find comfort in these enormous, catchall ideas, for they gave every individual a chance to lose himself in something big. But whence came the desire of the individual to lose himself in something big? To this Kierkegaard had a ready answer: the reason people were so anxious to lose themselves in something big was at least in part because they had already lost the meaning of what it is to be a self in the Christian sense, and they were consequently finding out that to be a self in any other sense might well turn out to be a curse instead of a blessing.

As usual, Kierkegaard did not criticize these abstractions philosophically, except in an offhand, oblique manner, but went straight to the motive, or the incentive, behind them. After all, purely on intellectual grounds you could not stop the human mind from indulging in abstractions of all kinds, no matter how fantastic. He did not offer the kind of criticism that a much more jaded and "debunking" type of philosophy, semantic analysis, was later to bring against this kind of abstraction, the criticism that it had no "referent," that there was nothing you could point to and say: behold—the human race! "The human race" could therefore mean pretty much what anyone wanted it to mean. And the nineteenth century wanted it to mean: the two-legged species in which there was continuous, evolutionary, natural, and historical progress from something primitive toward something divine. In fact, Kierkegaard's was the age that was just on the verge of discovering *biological* evolution, and of interpreting it in these very terms. Not that there was anything new in the idea of progress toward perfection— rather, it was the method or the process by which progress toward perfection is supposed to take place that was characteristically nineteenth century, namely, the idea that progress was continuous, evolutionary, natural, and historical. The human race was a kind of railroad train steadily chugging its way up the side of a moun-

tain, carrying along with it all the passengers, who therefore had
nothing to do but sit back, relax, and enjoy the scenery.

And that, said Kierkegaard, was precisely the secret of its
appeal—the invitation to take a holiday from individual effort and
individual responsibility. After all, if we are all riding that wagon
of the human race which is hitched to the stars and so cannot go
wrong, why exert oneself overmuch, why work up a sweat? But
suppose this comfortable and relaxing abstraction (and even philosophically there was something flabby about it, though the sharpest
intellects of the day appeared to be too relaxed to notice it) turned
out to be the most fatuous of delusions? Suppose that whatever
progress has been made by "the human race" has always been the
result of individual effort—unpredictable, sporadic, and often un-
recognized at the time, usually against the grain and at a tragic
price—so that on closer inspection, if it can still be called *progress,*
it is certainly not continuous, not evolutionary, not natural (automatic), and not historical in that it is obvious in recorded events.

Much depends, of course, on what one wishes to call progress.
But whether it be defined more in material or more in spiritual
terms, progress comes up against the formidable fact that each
generation has to start from scratch. And if in every generation
there cannot be found a sufficient number of individuals willing to
make the effort to learn that which the ancestors have discovered,
it would not be long before the discoveries, even in the realm of
material goods, declined into disuse and became as if they had
never existed. But in the realm of spiritual goods this is even more
true, for in this sphere no one is allowed to ride on the backs of
the ancestors or to bask in the reflected radiance of their virtue.
Here every individual in every generation starts as if the whole
"human race" started with him. He may indeed admire and be
grateful for the examples of spiritual achievement provided by the
ancestors for his emulation, but admiration and emulation are only
steppingstones toward appropriation and inward transformation,
the only things that count in the ethico-religious sphere. And if
individuals did not appropriate them, the spiritual discoveries
would disappear even faster than the material goods.

Here we are in the sphere of reflection that Kierkegaard calls
"the edifying"—those thoughts and examples that preoccupy an

individual inwardly and actually cause him to change himself for the better, an event which may very well happen because of, but equally well in spite of, what the ancestors have done. Such abstractions as "the human race" or "mankind" produced the illusion of automatic progress, and they not only resulted in the relaxation of individual effort but also threatened to do away with the essential meaning of *edification,* the inward building of the self by itself, which is the only way spiritual progress could be made.

Every serious person who has any eye for the conditions of our time will easily perceive how important it is to make a profound effort and a rigorously consistent one, which does not draw back from the extreme consequences of the truth, to oppose boldly the immoral confusion which, philosophically and socially, tends to demoralize 'the individual' by means of 'mankind' or a fantastical notion of society; a confusion which proposes to teach ungodly contempt for that which is the prime condition of religiousness, namely, to be a single individual man. This confusion can only be opposed by making men if possible single individuals—yet after all every man is a single individual! Every serious person who knows what edification is—every one, whether he be high or low, wise or simple, man or woman, every one who has felt himself edified and God brought near to him —will unconditionally agree with me that it is impossible to edify or be edified *en masse,* even more impossible than to be 'in love *en quatre'* or *en masse.* Edification even more expressly than love, is related to the individual.[15]

The other favorite nineteenth-century abstraction, the *pantheistic universe,* spread itself out to cover even more ground than the human race. Pantheism invests every rock and twig with the same kind of inward divinity as the image of God in man. It sprinkles divinity so finely and so evenly over the whole of creation that soon it is impossible for even the most experienced eye to find God anywhere, since he is everywhere and nowhere. It is a curious thing how easily both the speculative and the romantic tendencies in philosophy were reduced to pantheism. Both began with an exaggerated emphasis on the self as the locus of the Absolute, sometimes as even the creator of the nonself, but, since both sought for a world-soul which animated the entire universe and made unity with itself possible in all relationships in the world, the individual soul continually tended to disappear in the all-pervading

---

[15] "Two Notes About 'The Individual,' " *Point of View,* pp. 128-129.

divine immanence (which amounted to pantheism as soon as it became evident that nothing could logically be excluded from it). But the ethical interest, the sphere in which the either/or of good or evil first arises, cannot survive the disappearance of the individual responsible self, and has no choice but to protest forever the dissolution of the self, along with all other distinctions, in the immense ocean of the pantheistic universe.

"The individual"—with this category the cause of Christianity stands or falls, since world-development has got so far along in reflection as it has. Without this category pantheism has triumphed absolutely. . . . But the category of "the individual" is and remains the fixed point which is able to resist the pantheistic confusion, it is and remains the weight which turns the scale.[16]

6. Quantitative and Qualitative Strength

Finally, Kierkegaard used the category of the individual to fight the "crowd"—the mass, any mass of people wielding the strength of its numbers, the idea of the "majority" that could pass judgment on the truth by putting truth to the ballot. In an age of popular movements, somehow, little by little, the idea of the divine right of kings had passed over into the idea of the divine right of the populace, which in practical politics meant the hidden assumption that majorities in some mysterious fashion possessed the truth. It was not, however, the majority of the voters as such that Kierkegaard had in mind as the "crowd," for there was no reason why such a majority could not consist of individuals each of whom had acted in his voting as a responsible individual. And also it was not the snobbish distinction between the "masses" and the leaders or the aristocrats that he had in mind. "The reader will . . . remember that here the word 'crowd' is understood in a purely formal sense, not in the sense one commonly attaches to 'the crowd' when it is meant as an invidious qualification, the distinction which human selfishness irreligiously erects between 'the crowd' and superior persons, &c. Good God! How could a religious man hit upon such an inhuman equality! No, 'crowd' stands for number, the numerical, a number of noblemen, millionaires, high dignitaries, &c.—as soon as the numerical is involved it is . . . 'the crowd.' "[17]

[16] "Two Notes About 'The Individual,' " *Point of View*, pp. 136, 137.
[17] *Ibid.*, p. 114, note.

It is in the sense of the numerical and especially the *strength* of numbers, that the "crowd" is untruth. This is because ethico-religious truth is qualitative and will not submit to the tyranny of numbers, in fact loses its truth as soon as it does submit to numbers. Whenever appeal is made to a large abstraction like the human race in the numerical sense—all those millions and millions of people—in order to browbeat the individual in a matter of ethico-religious truth, we have an illustration of the "crowd" as untruth. But of course the *strength* in numbers is exactly what the weak and cowardly individual is looking for to hide behind and to fortify himself with, and therein lies the hidden motive behind the popularity of "crowds" of various kinds. The weak individual hopes to count for more than *one* by joining a crowd of his kind in order to have numbers on his side, and yet thereby he reveals that he is less than *one, not* even as strong as *one.* And if there is a matter of carrying out some action about which perhaps each individual in the crowd has his doubts, the crowd can do it nevertheless, because the crowd appears to divide responsibility. Here Kierkegaard approaches the heart of a matter which today, again with the assistance of some horrible examples in recent history, we study under the rubrics of totalitarian ideology in connection with such phenomena as the Nuremberg trials. For a crowd need not be a number of people who are physically present, but can be simply those with whom one identifies oneself in his ideology.

A crowd—not this crowd or that, the crowd now living or the crowd long deceased, a crowd of humble people or of superior people, of rich or of poor, &c.—a crowd in its very concept is the untruth, by reason of the fact that it renders the individual completely impenitent and irresponsible, or at least weakens his sense of responsibility by reducing it to a fraction. Observe that there was not one single soldier that dared lay hands upon Caius Marius—this was an instance of truth. But given merely three or four women with the consciousness or the impression that they were a crowd, and with hope of a sort in the possibility that no one could say definitely who was doing it or who began it—then they had courage for it. What a falsehood! The falsehood first of all is the notion that the crowd does what in fact only the *individual* in the crowd does, though it be every *individual.* For 'crowd' is an abstraction and has no hands: but each individual has ordinarily two hands, and so when an individual lays his two hands upon Caius Marius they are the two hands of the individual, certainly not those of his neighbour, and still less those of the . . . crowd which has no hands. In the next place, the falsehood is that the crowd had the 'courage' for it, for no one of the individuals was ever so cowardly as the crowd always is.[18]

The crowd is untruth because by means of the numerical, an abstract power factor, it attempts to bypass both the individual and God. But the individual is not the numerical, and he is not abstract. He is this concrete *one,* and *one* in a sense that has nothing to do with the power of numbers. If his value depended on the numerical, it would literally be next to nothing—next to zero. And God also is not the numerical, and he is not abstract. He is the Concrete One, whose value would also be next to nothing if it depended on the numerical. For God is the Truth, and in ethico-religious matters he is the truth that is related to an individual, so that, if either God or the individual is bypassed by any device whatever, then untruth rather than truth is present. In this kind of truth,

. . . the communicator of the truth can only be a single individual. And again the communication of it can only be addressed to the individual; for the truth consists precisely in that conception of life which is expressed by the individual. The truth can neither be communicated nor be received except as it were under God's eyes, not without God's help, not without God's being involved as the middle term, He himself being the Truth. It can therefore only be communicated by and received by "the individual," which as a matter of fact can be every living man. The mark which distinguishes such a man is merely that of the truth, in contrast to the abstract, the fantastical, the impersonal, the crowd—the public which excludes God as the middle term (for the *personal* God cannot be a middle term in an *impersonal* relationship), and thereby excludes also the truth, for God is at once the Truth and the middle term which renders it intelligible.[19]

In view of present-day experiments with "group dynamics" and "participation" it might seem at first glance that Kierkegaard overemphasizes the individual, but on closer inspection it would rather appear that it is precisely his concept of the individual that the group experience here in question either presupposes or is trying to preserve. The interactions of the members of such a group are based on the idea that each member is a responsible individual to whom respect as such must be accorded, that he is

---

[18] "Two Notes About 'The Individual,' " *Point of View*, pp. 114-115.
[19] *Ibid.*, pp. 119-120.

neither a child to be overwhelmed by authority nor a faceless, abstract unit to be outvoted by a majority nor a thing to be manipulated by techniques. Such a phenomenon as, for example, the Quaker meeting for business, in which decisions are not arrived at by voting but by arriving at a "sense of the meeting," would be impossible if it were not assumed that each individual in the meeting had a responsible relationship to the truth as he was best able to understand it, and that, in the maintenance of this relationship to the truth he was careful neither to browbeat others nor to submit to others. Such groups are trying to avoid becoming exactly what Kierkegaard characterizes as the "crowd" by their awareness that each individual in the group is under the eye of God in that relationship to the truth in which neither God nor the individual can be bypassed.

Equality in the realm of worldliness, the human race, the pantheistic universe, and the crowd—to these abstract ideas Kierkegaard opposed the single, solitary, concrete person, from whom they had been abstracted but whose reality they did not comprehend and could not touch, unless the individual himself, under peril of being dissolved in them, permitted it. Embattled Kierkegaard! With the category of the individual he laid about him on all three fronts of the problem of becoming a Christian in his age, a cause which he had chosen to defend.

In his attack on speculative idealism he used it to confound the System. The System claimed to be the final revelation of the meaning of history both for the self and the Absolute, and yet every single individual could simply laugh the System out of existence if he chose not to take it seriously, and the System could not laugh back. While it claimed to be his savior, the System was really at the mercy of the individual. This was because every single individual, as he consciously became an individual, especially an individual before God—every such single person, even if he was nothing but a garbage collector in the eyes of the world, had more of the true eternity in himself than there was in all the grandiose perspective offered by the System, for the kind of panoramic vision it offered was the foreshortened, horizontal, false eternity of contemplation, not the true vertical eternity that intersects existence in every individual.

In attacking aesthetic romanticism Kierkegaard used the category of the individual to show that the only escape from the futility and despair of the aesthetic stage was for the individual to choose *himself* in his despair, to become conscious of his eternal significance as an individual, if necessary through his consciousness of being a despairing individual, and thus to enter into the ethical stage by means of this eternal choice on the outer fringes of existence. Romanticism was willing enough to let man be an individual—at least at the start, before it dissolved him in the pantheistic universe. But it "arrested" his development as an individual from the aesthetic to the ethical and religious stages by inviting him, in the case of the more happy temperaments, to submerge himself in an orgiastic or mystical union with nature, or, in the case of the more tragic temperaments, to glory in his despair at failing to achieve unity with nature, defiantly and heroically denouncing the whole world from his standpoint as the tragic individual. But this glorying in its own despair by the ego was the unmistakable sign of the romantic individual's basic frivolousness in regard to the self. The problem here was to get the romantic individual to despair in earnest, which meant that one really had to drive him to the edge of suicide, with all the risk that that involves. For as long as the romantically despairing person kept talking about his despair, or writing poetry or music to let the whole world know how his despair felt, he was still far from despairing in earnest and therefore still far from finding himself in seriousness, in his despair. The real despair is always the silent despair. Perhaps that was why romanticism flourished among the literary and the musical rather than among the common people or the more scientifically-minded, for these latter had no means of pouring out their despairing feelings. Ordinary people couldn't afford to flirt with despair, because for them it might turn out to be the real thing, the silent despair that waits in silent patience behind the daily round of activities, to be discovered there by each individual in silence.

And Kierkegaard also used the category of the individual in his third "front" of the problem of becoming a Christian: the restating, "if possible in a more heartfelt way," of what it might mean in the deepest and most crucial sense for any individual to become a

Christian. All the religious discourses are directed entirely toward the individual; they are concerned for the individual, concerned to make him conscious of himself as an individual before God; they are unconcerned about glittering abstractions and world-historical perspectives, and always, even where they are most severe and repelling, they are concerned with "what is edifying for *thee*."

IV

What Christianity Is, and What It Is Not

1. The Choice Among "Top Values"

Although Kierkegaard believed that every man had it in him to be—and more and more to become—an individual in the various meanings of the term explored in the last chapter, he did not imply that this process could take place in an intellectual vacuum, or in any wilful isolation from the great ideals and examples provided by individuals of the past. This meant that the various views of life, accumulated by the history of mankind and presented to the individual of the present generation as an assortment of possibilities, had to be examined, tested, and even "tasted"— especially by the youthful, reflective individual, still in the years of his education—for the purpose of discarding the worthless and ignoble ones, and selecting for attention and emulation those that inspired the energy of devotion. Kierkegaard's own youthful years at the university constituted just such a searching and sifting, and he sighed over the fact that he felt like an Alcibiades to whom the fates had failed or forgotten to grant a Socrates.

When the sifting process is carried out with sufficient thoroughness and consistency, the individual will find himself in the end faced with not one but several, indeed with a whole collection of quite distinct and different "views of life" from which to choose for emulation the one he thinks most worthwhile. The more clearly the distinctions and differences between the various views of life are made, therefore, the more the individual is helped to make his choice, with full knowledge of what he is embracing and what he is rejecting in his act of decision. But the tendency of the Hegelian habit of thinking was to do just the opposite: to slur over all distinctions and differences in the endless "annulled and yet preserved" process of mediation, so that choice became not only more and more difficult but in the long run (the process having worn out the individual's metaphysical patience) utterly confusing. The various views of life were held up to be the necessary phases of the development of the Absolute Spirit: a given view would some- how inevitably lead to its opposite, then to a synthesis; then that synthesis, as a new point of departure, would inevitable lead to *its* opposite, then to a new synthesis, and so on and on down the infinite vistas of history. Surely the individual, who by seeking the truth was attempting to occupy even momentarily the position of the Absolute Spirit with his finite spirit, could be excused if he were to exclaim with some weariness, "Do we have to go through all that?"

But, the various views of life that history presents to the individual as choices for emulation are actually not, on closer inspection, nicely paired-off logical opposites of one another, nor are they all syntheses of other "earlier" pairs. Rather they are evaluations of existence, in which now this and now that element, or aspect, of life is raised to pre-eminence or is even recommended as the highest value, while other aspects are correspondingly de- valuated. It could hardly be otherwise, for if *evaluation* is taking place, this can only mean the holding of some things dear, other things less dear, still others worthless, and still others evil. The different views of life are merely attempts at arranging in a hier- archical fashion the many elements and factors of life, such ar- rangements differing according to whatever element is placed at the top of the hierarchy; thus, in choosing among the views of life, the individual is really choosing among different "top values." In making this choice, he is not, as some modern value theory holds, making an "arbitrary value judgment." He is also not deciding whether the "top value" of a given view of life is a fact or a value, but rather whether this particular value deserves to be at the top of the hierarchical scale. He is making a judgment of comparative value among the "top values" of the different views of life, every item on each of their scales being a "value" of some degree if it is capable of being chosen or being placed in order. In Kierkegaard's view, this judgment of comparative value that is made by the individual when he chooses among the "top values" of the different views of life is anything but arbitrary. Rather it is the end of and the result of the great learning process of life wherein the individual allows himself to be "educated" by existence itself. For there *is* a criterion whereby one can decide whether a given value deserves to be the "top value" of a view of life, namely, whether that value, when the existing individual consistently places it in the position of the highest value, leads to hope or leads to despair. If it leads to despair, it may still be a relatively high value on the human scale, but it cannot be the highest value, which must issue in hope. Unfortunately, only experience, the bitter education by existence, will teach most men that a value which they had thought held hope, in reality holds only despair in the long run; and the real difference among men in this respect is that a man of thoughtfulness and imagination is able to "see through" his own mistakes concerning the highest value faster than the dullard or the scatter-brain is able to "see through" his misjudgments.

To help the individual make his choices, therefore, the best thing one could do for him, Socratically, would be to make as clear as possible the distinctions between the several alternatives. What particularly irritated Kierkegaard about Hegelian speculation was that it had practically obliterated the distinction between two honorable and venerable "views of life" which for some two thousand years had been live options for individuals coming to maturity in European civilization—Greek rationalism or humanism on the one hand, and Christianity on the other. The Hegelian System pretended to reconcile these two views of life by going beyond both of them in the process of mediation, but actually it succeeded only in so confusing and mixing them up together that an individual could no longer understand what each of them claimed to teach and what it stood for, let alone make an intelligent and responsible choice between them. Kierkegaard decided that he must once more make the distinction as clear as possible for the benefit of the nineteenth century "individual," if indeed any such creature was still to be found.

We know of course which side Kierkegaard was on, and that perhaps he had chosen decisively before he set himself this task, but at this stage he saw it as his task to act Socratically, merely to make the distinctions clear. And the task divided itself into two parts, corresponding to the fact that Kierkegaard's opposition to speculative idealism had two sides, an intellectual one and an existential one. Doctrinally, as a Christian, he found its teachings on Christianity heretical, while existentially he found them utterly inadequate to reality. He had to show the heresy inherent in speculative idealism by restating in contrast the orthodox Christian faith as he understood it to be; and he had to expose the unreality, the fantastic element, in speculative idealism by describing the inescapable conditions of existence under which the decision between Greek humanism and Christianity or between any other alternatives had to be made.

The first part of this task he carried out in *Philosophical Fragments,* in which the contrast between Christianity and Greek rationalism is developed in objective terms, as an experiment in thought. A brief, schematic statement, as abstractly put as a problem in algebra, is developed on what each of these two different views teach. Kierkegaard knew well enough how to be objective when the necessity for it arose, and he certainly believed that there must be an objective statement of what Christianity claims to be and to do—otherwise, the subjective appropriation of it which must follow would be mere shadow-boxing. Such an objective statement must be simple and brief, not necessarily owing anything to philosophy; it must approximate the naïve language of the Gospels and like them must be addressed to every man. (Kierkegaard would often refer to such an objective statement offhandedly as "what any schoolboy can learn from the catechism.") Such a statement of what Christianity teaches, contrasted with the same kind of statement for Greek rationalism, is the core of *Philosophical Fragments.*

The second part of the task was undertaken in *Concluding Unscientific Postscript,* which goes on to "clothe the problem in its historical costume." This book describes the existential thinker and the conditions of existence in which the problems of life must be faced and the choices made. It also points out the Hegelian misrepresentations of these conditions, and finally it develops the idea of the three existential stages, the aesthetic, the ethical, and the religious, a schema he had already begun to set forth poetically and dramatically in *Either/Or* and in *Stages on Life's Way.* The next five chapters will be largely concerned with the *Fragments* and the *Postscript.*

2. The Individual and "The Showdown"

Before we begin a study of the *Fragments* we may perhaps be excused if we ask for the ulterior motive behind Kierkegaard's setting himself the task of once more making clear the distinction between the Greek and the Christian views of life, between rationalistic humanism and the claims of this revealed religion. In that way we can keep more constantly in mind the subject which is the chief concern of this book, namely, Kierkegaard's idea of the individual, and the individual's development (the pilgrimage through existence).

To carry out the Socratic task he created the pseudonymous character of Johannes Climacus, a witty, brilliant, worldly-wise man, by turns ironical, poetical, humorous, analytical—and also a deeply angry man. For irony is only a roundabout verbal expression of a deep-seated and self-possessed anger, and in this respect Socrates was also an angry man, angry with all forms of stupidity, inconsistency, sophistry, and wilful ignorance. Behind all of Johannes Climacus' negativities, his sarcastic asides about professors, his jokes about the System, his continual disclaimers of having any authority to speak or any academic standing in the intellectual community, his warnings to the reader that truth is usually more painful than delusion, and his pretended attacks against that which he is really defending—behind all these gambits may be seen occasional flashes of the angry man who cannot bear to let the truth fail to get a hearing.

Johannes Climacus is no more the detached man he pretends to be than Socrates was. He does not present you with the alternatives and then "not care" which way you choose. The very manner in which he presents the alternatives shows which one he thinks you ought to choose, but he will not choose for you. So Socrates used to trap his listeners between alternatives, one of which he obviously thought right while the other, though easier and perhaps more popular, involved some damaging admission by him who chose it. Behind Johannes there stands the Kierkegaard who was convinced that Christianity was the superior way, the choice you ought to make, or, if you didn't, to take the responsibility for not making. He goes so far as to let Climacus say that if he himself does not choose Christianity, it will at least be not because he did not understand what it was and what it demanded, but because he was overawed by its difficulty.

If we leave aside for the moment the tricks and devices of the method of "indirect communication" (which is not to say that they are unimportant), we become aware that Kierkegaard is, in the *Fragments* and the *Postscript,* really calling for a showdown between Christianity and humanism. The showdown is on the question of which of these two views of life really has the right and the power to create an individual (the "single person" previously described) and to bring the individual through the vicissitudes of his existence to the goal of his completion. Which of the two, God or man, has the right and the power to do this? However, no one can understand the seriousness of this conflict, this showdown, as long as there persists the general conviction that Christianity is just another of the clever ideas of man, a purely human program invented to solve some purely human predicaments. There can be no seriousness in this conflict until it is once more made clear who the contenders are, and especially who the "owner" of Christianity really is. Listen to Kierkegaard the angry man speak on this subject directly, without a trace of irony:

"The individual"—that is the decisive Christian category, and it will be decisive also for the future of Christianity. The fundamental confusion, the original sin, of Christendom is that year after year, decade after decade, century after century, it has pursued the insidious purpose—just about half unconscious of what it would, and essentially unconscious of what it did—of tricking God out of his rights as the proprietor of Christianity, and has got it into its head that the race, the human race, was itself the inventor, or had come pretty close to inventing Christianity. Just as in civil law a fortune reverts to the state when it has lain unclaimed for a certain period of years and no heir presents himself—so has the race, perverted by observation of the trivial fact that Christianity is a thing that actually exists, thought within itself as follows: 'It is now so long a time since God has let Himself be heard from as proprietor and master that Christianity has consequently reverted to us, who can either decide to abolish it altogether, or to modify it *ad libitum,* very much as we might deal with our own possession or invention, treating Christianity, not as something which *in obedient subservience to God's majesty* MUST be believed, but as something which in order to be acceptable must try by the aid of *reasons* to satisfy "the age," "the public," "this distinguished assembly," &c. Every revolt in science . . . against moral

discipline, every revolt in social life . . . against obedience, every
revolt in political life . . . against worldly rule, is connected with and
derived from this revolt against God with respect to Christianity. This
revolt—the abuse of 'the human race' as a category—does not, however, resemble the revolt of the Titans, for it is in the sphere of
reflection, insidiously carried out from year to year, from generation
to generation. Reflection constantly takes only a tiny little bit at a
time, and about this little bit one can constantly say, 'Why, in small
matters one may well yield'—until in the end reflection will have
taken everything without anybody noticing it, because it came about
little by little, 'and in small matters one may surely yield.' Hence
men must become single individuals in order to get the proper
Christian-pathetic impression of Christianity. The individual, every
individual, will surely beware of initiating a legal process against God
in heaven to determine which of the two, absolutely and unto the
least tittle, has the right of proprietorship in Christianity. God must
again become effectually the decisive factor. But to God as the decisive
factor corresponds the individual. If the 'race' is to be the court of
last resort or even have subordinate jurisdiction, Christianity is abolished—if in no other way, at least by the *wrong and unchristian form*
one gives the *Christian* message.[1]

A showdown between Christianity and humanism always gets
around to this fundamental point of contention: whether the
"trivial fact" that Christianity exists, that it happened, that even
the most hostile historians must make a note of it in the history
books—whether this *fact* is to be interpreted as something that
God has done for man, or as something that man has attempted
to do for God (and then perhaps even mistakenly, clumsily, like
one of those misguided human inventions that never should have
been made and now must continually be amended). Of course,
Kierkegaard realized that the idea of God's ownership of Christianity could be terribly misused, by ecclesiastical authority, for
example; but that could not be used as an excuse for suppressing
it, for, after all, there was scarcely any idea about God, no matter
how true, which could not be terribly misused by man.

3. *Two Answers to One Question*

The problem which *Philosophical Fragments* poses as a thought-
experiment is stated as follows on the title page of the book: "Is
an historical point of departure possible for an eternal conscious-

[1] "Two Notes About 'The Individual,' " *Point of View,* pp. 135-136.

ness; how can such a point of departure have any other than a mere historical interest; is it possible to base an eternal happiness upon historical knowledge?" This rather complicated question turns out to be, on closer inspection, the age-old question about the possibility of salvation for man through the knowledge of an eternal truth, with the exception that it is concerned with whether it would be possible for man to learn a truth in history which is in reality eternal truth. Here Kierkegaard is really doing homage to Socrates, who was concerned with the same question when he asked, how far does the truth admit of being learned? Kierkegaard saw that in order to prove his point that Christianity cannot be reduced to any kind of mere rationalism, he must contrast it with rationalism at its best, not at its worst (as in the Hegelianism that had lost its bearings in existence). He therefore began with what he calls the Greek consciousness, for in the Greeks he considered rationalism to have made its finest attempt to provide a rational salvation for man. In the Greeks rationalism had gone as far as it could go in all essentials without pretending to know something that it didn't know on grounds of reason alone, that is, without borrowing surreptitiously and dishonestly from revealed religion.

So, although Kierkegaard intends to show that the Christian answer to the question raised in the *Fragments* is quite different from the Greek answer, this difference is something for which Socrates can scarcely be held to blame, since, from the Christian standpoint, the eternal truth had not yet appeared on the scene. It is right to honor Socrates for having attempted an answer and for having also fulfilled the highest function of philosophy by developing the question properly.

How did Socrates answer his own question, namely, how far is it possible to gain knowledge of the truth? Socrates saw that the question creates a peculiar situation: in so far as the truth is something a man seeks for, looking about him in the world and in his own mind, it is something he does not yet possess; but, on the other hand, it seems as though he must already possess it in some sense, or how would he know what to look for, and how would he recognize it when he had found it? Socrates solved this difficulty with the Doctrine of Recollection. According to this doctrine, "all learning and inquiry is interpreted as a kind of remembering; one who is ignorant needs only a reminder to help him come to himself in the consciousness of what he knows. Thus the Truth is not introduced into the individual from without, but was within him."[2]

A number of typically Greek ideas are associated with the Doctrine of Recollection—for example, the idea of a pre-existence of the soul, a kind of backward immortality referring to an aeon before the creation of the world when the human soul lived in the direct knowledge of the eternal Ideas and Forms. Another typically Greek idea stemming from the Doctrine of Recollection, one that also appears in modern rationalism, is that the knowledge of the good is inherent in man and needs only to be brought to his attention by a wise teacher; thus, a rational man never does evil out of bad intentions but only out of ignorance. The good is therefore defined as that which the rational man does when he knows what he is doing—or, as Socrates put it, virtue is insight. "In the Socratic view each individual is his own center, and the entire world centers in him, because his self-knowledge is a knowledge of God."[3]

It is through self-knowledge that a man comes to know the eternal truth, because this truth is present in each man; and the fact that this is so sets up for each man the ethical obligation of knowing himself. Now if this is true, whoever the teacher might be that helps each man to come to this knowledge in himself (which is the eternal truth) is really a matter of indifference to the one who is learning. The teacher merely acts the part of a midwife in helping to bring to birth what is already inside of the learner, and one teacher can do this as well as another. The learner does not really owe anything to the teacher, except the accidental gratitude that all learners owe to all teachers for expounding that which must sooner or later become obvious. In the same way, the particular historical circumstance which serves as an occasion for starting him off on this learning process is also of no special importance to the learner, for any historical event or item of experience is just as good as any other when it comes to pointing out the direction in which the eternal truth may be found, that is, within the man himself.

[2] *Philosophical Fragments*, trans. D. F. Swenson (American-Scandinavian Foundation; Princeton, N.J.: Princeton University Press, 1936), p. 5.
[3] *Fragments*, p. 7.

And now, how is it with Christianity? Without mentioning it by name, Johannes Climacus draws attention to the fact that there is a certain view of life which, while it begins with the same question Socrates began with, namely, how far is it possible to gain a knowledge of the truth, comes forth with an entirely different answer. In contrast with the Socratic view, where man is in possession of the truth and the teacher's function is merely to act the part of a midwife in bringing it to birth, in the Christian way of thinking man is *not* in possession of the truth. He is destitute of the truth, is not looking for it, is backing away from it, is afraid of it, and is instinctively hostile toward it whenever he happens to run into it. (This is of course the eternal truth, the saving truth, not assorted bits of truth about the world.) In this respect man may be said to be from the very beginning in a state of Error, but, since this is not an error in physics or astronomy but the far more serious error concerning the meaning of his life, and since he chooses to remain in this error even when glimpses of the Truth are shown to him (not because he cannot understand the Truth, but because he does not like the Truth), it is necessary to use a stronger word to describe the error he is in, and such a word is "sin." Now if man is in a state of Sin, he cannot be taught the Truth by his fellow men, for they are in the same condition. So if he is to learn the Truth, God himself must become his teacher. But even before He can teach him the Truth, God must give the man the condition for receiving the Truth; the condition is that he should not hate the Truth but love it, and this condition is called Faith. In other words, God must turn him around in his attitude toward the Truth, must turn him from hating it to loving it; this turning around is called Conversion. And since it is only at the moment of Conversion that the man is able to understand his previous state of Sin for what it really was, a hating of the Truth, the conversion must be accompanied by remorse for the past and hope for the future, namely, Repentance and Reconciliation based on the Forgiveness of Sins. Now if the Teacher is really God himself, giving the man the Truth, and if he is a teacher that can enable the man to turn from hating the truth to loving it, then the identity of such a teacher cannot be a matter of indifference to the man, but, on the contrary, that teacher must be the one to whom the man owes the very meaning

of his life, namely, his Savior. And, similarly, the historical circumstance which made it possible for him to receive the Truth from the
Teacher, who is God himself, cannot be a matter of indifference to
him; thus there are at least two decisive points in history as far
as the man is concerned—the moment or instant in which God
entered the world as a Teacher (the Incarnation) and the second
historical moment in which he, the learner, received the Truth.
Later on Kierkegaard shows that these two moments become one
and the same—the Moment, in which Eternity intersects time and
history, and the disciple becomes contemporaneous with the
Teacher.

This is how Climacus describes Christianity for the purpose of
his thought-experiment, the capitalized items being as it were the
algebraic terms of the nonequation. And, not to omit the ontological element, he also describes the Moment of Conversion as a
change of being:

In so far as the learner was in Error, and now receives the Truth and
with it the condition for understanding it, a change takes place within
him like the change from non-being to being. But this transition from
non-being to being is the transition we call birth. Now one who exists
cannot be born; nevertheless, the disciple is born. Let us call this
transition the *new birth,* in consequence of which the disciple enters
the world quite as at the first birth, an individual human being knowing nothing as yet about the world into which he is born, whether it
is inhabited, whether there are other human beings in it besides himself; for while it is indeed possible to be baptized *en masse,* it is not
possible to be born anew *en masse.* Just as one who has begotten
himself by the aid of the Socratic midwifery now forgets everything
else in the world, and in a deeper sense owes no man anything, so
the disciple who is born anew owes nothing to any man, but everything
to his divine Teacher. And just as the former forgets the world in his
discovery of himself, so the latter forgets himself in the discovery of
his Teacher.[4]

4. The Absolute Paradox

Here then we have a simple, objective statement ("what any
schoolboy can learn from the catechism") of the Christian answer
to the Socratic question which places it in the sharpest possible
contrast with the answer given by Socrates himself, and, by impli-

---

[4] *Fragments,* pp. 13-14.

cation, with all modern rationalistic, humanistic, and idealistic answers, which are only variations and elaborations of the Socratic answer. It tells what Christianity is, and what it is not. Christianity is not the "perennial philosophy" dressed up in Hebrew poetry and Greek metaphysics, nor can it be incorporated or taken up into the latest version of humanism without being changed so that it is no longer Christianity but something else.

In stressing the paradoxical nature of Christianity over against rationalism, Kierkegaard was not inventing any new paradoxes just to make things hard for modern minds. We must remember that this same Christianity of the Incarnation was foolishness to the Greeks in the time of St. Paul. Kierkegaard is merely calling to the attention of modern rationalists, who have a regrettable tendency to gloss over differences with peculiar phrases like "annulled and yet preserved," that at least the simple Greeks of St. Paul's day recognized instantly that here was a claim which, from the point of view of pure reason, must be called absurd.

The absurdity lies in the claim that the Eternal has a starting point in time, which is a contradiction in terms, for if it were to start in time it could not be eternal. When viewed from the standpoint of Greek rationalism, the Christian claim that Jesus is the Incarnation of God presents a double contradiction, that is, the contradiction has a human side and a divine side. First there is the contradiction that man, who is a mixture of the temporal and the eternal, can be saved by a relationship to something which is temporal, a historical event, the very historicity of which can never be more than a strong probability for succeeding generations of men no matter how many eyewitnesses have written reports on the event. To the Greeks a historical fact was always inferior to a logical or rational fact, for while each generation of men can prove to its own satisfaction that things equal to the same thing are equal to each other, not every generation is able to verify a given historical fact as well as any other, and all of them put together can build up only a high probability and never a certainty comparable with logical certainty. So the idea of basing man's salvation on a historical event, which, even if it had happened, allowed of many interpretations, was to the Greeks absurd.

The second contradiction, on the divine side, consisted in the fact that this historical event itself claimed the impossible, namely, that the Eternal should enter into time in order to save man. From the Greek standpoint, the Eternal and the temporal were two distinct spheres of which the latter was an inferior imitation of the perfection of the former, and for the Eternal to enter into time would mean for it to lose just that perfection which makes it an ideal for human striving. In other words, for the Greeks, salvation meant being lifted out of the temporal into the Eternal, and decidedly not that the Eternal should get itself mixed up in the temporal, thereby contradicting its own nature.

This double, or two-sided, contradiction is what Kierkegaard calls the Absolute Paradox. And the fact that several centuries of early Christian theology were devoted to the metaphysical problems raised by the paradox of the Incarnation shows that Kierkegaard did not invent the paradox. The early Church Fathers were for the most part well versed in Greek philosophy, and they had to tackle this problem either to find some solution for themselves, or for the sake of converting the Hellenistic world. All those christological and trinitarian controversies of the fourth and fifth centuries A.D., which we now think so unimportant, constituted nothing less than a ransacking of all possible ideas of how Christ could be fitted into the Greek scheme of thought without at the same time losing those distinctive qualities which Christian faith claimed for him. And the same problem exists today for any modern version of rationalism or idealism which would like to incorporate the Christian Savior into its system of thought, or for any Christian theology which rests its case on humanism.

But although we may honor the Greeks for recognizing immediately an instance of the absurd, the fact remains, as Kierkegaard points out, that the Greeks really did not have what it takes to plumb the depths of this particular absurdity, the Incarnation. This was because, as we have just seen from the thought-experiment, the pagan consciousness, resting as it did on the Doctrine of Recollection, could not comprehend that man is from the beginning in a state of error with respect to the Eternal. This state of error manifests itself, among other ways, in the feeling that only when one has understood an idea metaphysically, has he understood it essentially and completely, and that only then can he draw ethical

and religious implications from it. In this way metaphysical ignorance can be made a perpetual excuse for ethical and religious
inaction or misunderstanding. But if the Eternal is the living God
(in the Christian sense of the Creator and Redeemer) and not
just a device of human thought, the ethico-religious understanding
of any idea about God must be given precedence over the metaphysical understanding. Herein lies the great difference between
the Greeks and the Jews as far as a pre-Christian approach to the
saving truth is concerned.[5] The Old Testament Jews did not have
Christ either, but because for them the ethico-religious understanding of every idea and every relationship with respect to the
Eternal took precedence over the metaphysical understanding, they
began to understand what it means to be in error with respect
to the Eternal, and thus they provided the preparation for the
Truth when He appeared. And when the Truth arrived on the
scene, those who believed did not argue as to whether He
was metaphysically possible, but they *believed*, because ethico-
religiously they saw that he was meat and drink for all who
hunger and thirst, the life-saving Truth.

5. The King and the Humble Maiden

To get back to the thought-experiment, the real problem it presented, both for the Greeks and, as Kierkegaard was trying to
point out, for the metaphysically-minded nineteenth century, was
to get the learner to understand that he is in error. But how can
the learner be made to understand that he is in error when he
has not committed any logical fallacies or factual mistakes which
could be demonstrated to him? And how can the learner be made
to understand that his error does not consist of his ignorance? This,
in a Christian sense, is God's problem, not man's, since it is God
who must become the Teacher if man is to learn the Truth. However, as Kierkegaard says, by dint of speaking foolishly a little
and permitting ourselves some flights of the imagination, we can
picture to ourselves how God went about solving his pedagogical

[5] Consider, for example, the very form of the questions they asked. The
Greek question—"How can the truth be learned?"—expects as an answer
some idea or doctrine about the metaphysical foundation of the very nature
of things, such as the Doctrine of Recollection; whereas the typical Old
Testament question—"What doth the Lord require of thee?"—expects not
a doctrine but an imperative, a command.

problem, namely to show the learner that he is in error, and to give him the condition for receiving the Truth.

Socrates—and everyone who would teach Socratically—always stands in a reciprocal relation to the disciple. "As between man and man no higher relationship is possible; the disciple gives occasion for the teacher to understand himself, and the teacher gives occasion for the disciple to understand himself." [6] But God as Teacher cannot stand in a reciprocal relationship to the disciple, because God does not need the disciple to understand Himself, but the disciple needs him. What then can be God's motive in becoming a Teacher, in making his appearance in time, if it is not his need, "as if he could not endure the strain of silence, but had to break out in speech"?[7] What else could his motive be but love?

Moved by love, God is thus eternally resolved to reveal himself. But as love is the motive so love must also be the end; for it would be a contradiction for God to have a motive and an end which did not correspond. His love is a love of the learner, and his aim is to win him. For it is only in love that the unequal can be made equal, and it is only in equality or unity that an understanding can be effected, and without a perfect understanding the Teacher is not God, unless the obstacle comes wholly from the side of the learner, in his refusing to realize that which had been made possible for him.[8]

Now we are approaching the heart of Christianity, and it is characteristic of Kierkegaard that even in this "algebraic" presentation of it as an experiment in thought he does not forget to make room for that which the intellect might like to forget if left to itself. For at the heart of Christianity the real problem (or the real mystery) is neither transcendence versus immanence, nor paradox versus reason, but it is the misunderstood love of God. Without the understanding of this misunderstanding, there is no real understanding of Christianity, either by those who are for it or those who are against it. God loves the learner:

But this love is through and through unhappy, for how great is the difference between them! It may seem a small matter for God to make himself understood, but this is not so easy of accomplishment if he is to refrain from annihilating the unlikeness that exists between them.

[6] *Fragments,* p. 17.   [7] *Ibid.,* p. 18.   [8] *Ibid.,* p. 19.

. . .Much is heard in the world about unhappy love, and we all know what this means: the lovers are prevented from realizing their union, the causes being many and various. There exists another kind of unhappy love, the theme of our present discourse, for which there is no perfect earthly parallel, though by dint of speaking foolishly a little while we may make shift to conceive it through an earthly figure. The unhappiness of this love does not come from inability of the lovers to realize their union, but from their inability to understand one another. This grief is infinitely more profound than that of which men commonly speak, since it strikes at the very heart of love, and wounds for an eternity; not like that other misfortune which touches only the temporal and the external, and which for the magnanimous is as a sort of jest over the inability of the lovers to realize their union here in time. This infinitely deeper grief is essentially the prerogative of the superior, since only he likewise understands the misunderstanding; in reality it belongs to God alone, and no human relationship can afford a valid analogy.[9]

Nevertheless, he suggests such an analogy in his parable of the king who loved a humble maiden. The problem for the king was to bring about the union between them in such a way so as not to deny or destroy the unlikeness between them, for to do that would be to base the whole relationship upon a deceit and would be an unworthy expression of the king's love; and yet the union must be brought about in such a way that the difference between them would not overwhelm her and make her more unhappy than if she had never known the king's love. It is possible of course that in this story the humble maiden might understand the difficulty and possess the courage to live it down by the side of the king, so in order to make the analogy better we must assume that she does not understand it, that the understanding of the possible misunderstanding resides entirely on his side, and that only the king understands how his love for the humble maiden could easily make her the most unhappy of women. And such is the situation between God and the learner. For God loves the learner and desires to teach him and to bring him to equality with himself.

If this equality cannot be established, God's love becomes unhappy and his teaching meaningless, since they cannot understand one another. Men sometimes think that this might be a matter of indifference to God, since he does not stand in need of the learner. But in this we forget—or rather alas! we prove how far we are from under-

[9] *Fragments*, p. 19.

standing him; we forget that God loves the learner. And just as that kingly grief of which we have spoken can be found only in a kingly soul, and is not even named in the language of the multitude of men, so the entire human language is so selfish that it refuses even to suspect the existence of such a grief. But for that reason God has reserved it to himself, this unfathomable grief: to know that he may repel the learner, that he does not need him, that the learner has brought destruction upon himself by his own guilt, that he can leave the learner to his fate; to know also how well-nigh impossible it is to keep the learner's courage and confidence alive, without which the purposed understanding and equality will fail, and the love become unhappy. The man who cannot feel at least some faint intimation of this grief is a paltry soul of base coinage, bearing neither the image of Caesar nor the image of God.[10]

Kierkegaard then goes on to show that the union cannot be brought about by the elevation of the learner, much as the learner might like this, for this elevation would rest on a deception, namely, the learner's ignorance of the fact that he was in error. Nor can God simply reveal himself directly, thereby overwhelming the learner by his power and glory, for this would not bring about the equality of love either, only the prostration of a slave before the mightiest master. The Old Testament Jews had at any rate some intimation of the problem confronting God, even if they could not fathom the grief in it because they had not yet seen all the love. Kierkegaard says, "There once lived a people who had a profound understanding of the divine; this people thought that no man could see God and live.—Who grasps this contradiction of sorrow: not to reveal oneself is the death of love, to reveal oneself is the death of the beloved!" [11] Thus God is always in the position of having to deny the learner what the learner wants, because God loves him with a love that will not rest on a deception.

Let us recall again the contrast with the Socratic conception, that between man and man the Socratic midwifery is the highest relationship—one man can only assist another man to come to the realization of that which he already bears in himself. Therefore, for Socrates the deception (one of the most insidious of deceptions) would be if one man, in becoming the teacher of another, tried to make the learner feel that he owes his teacher something.

[10] *Fragments*, pp. 21-22.
[11] *Fragments*, p. 23.

But when God becomes a Teacher, his love cannot be merely second-ing and assisting, but is creative, giving a new being to the learner, or as we have called him, the man born anew; by which designation we signify the transition from non-being to being. The truth then is that the learner owes the Teacher everything. But this is what makes it so difficult to effect an understanding: that the learner becomes as nothing and yet is not destroyed; that he comes to owe everything to the Teacher and yet retains his confidence; that he understands the Truth and yet that the Truth makes him free; that he apprehends the guilt of his Error and yet that his confidence rises victorious in the Truth.[12]

And so, finally, by a kind of process of elimination and by speaking foolishly a little, we come to the solution of God's peda-gogical problem, a problem created by the fact that God loves the learner but the learner is in Error. Since the union cannot be brought about by the false elevation of the learner, it must be attempted by the true descent of the Teacher. "Let the learner be *x*. In this *x* we must include the lowliest; for if even Socrates refused to establish a false fellowship with the clever, how can we suppose that God would make a distinction! In order that the union may be brought about, God must therefore become the equal of such a one, and so he will appear in the likeness of the humblest. But the humblest is one who must serve others, and God will therefore appear in the form of a *servant*." [13]

Here are some excerpts from the long passage in which Johannes Climacus, our Socratic pseudonym, describes with the assistance of a little poetry the "solution" God has decided upon, in the Christian way of answering the Socratic question:

But the servant-form was no mere outer garment, and therefore God must suffer all things, endure all things, make experience of all things. He must suffer hunger in the desert, he must thirst in the time of his agony, he must be forsaken in death, absolutely like the humblest —behold the man.
. . . He is God; and yet he has not a resting-place for his head, and he dares not lean on any man lest he cause him to be offended. He is God; and yet he picks his steps more carefully than if angels guided them, not to prevent his foot from stumbling against a stone, but lest he trample human beings in the dust, in that they are offended in him. He is God; and yet his eye surveys mankind with anxious care,

[12] *Fragments*, pp. 23-24.
[13] *Fragments*, p. 24.

for the tender shoots of an individual life may be crushed as easily as a blade of grass. How wonderful a life, all sorrow and all love: to yearn to express the equality of love and yet to be misunderstood; to apprehend the danger that all men may be destroyed, and yet only so to be able really to save a single soul; his own life filled with sorrow, while each hour of the day is taken up with the troubles of the learner who confides in him! This is God as he stands upon the earth, like unto the humblest—by the power of his omnipotent love. He knows that the learner is in Error—what if he should misunderstand, and droop, and lose his confidence! To sustain the heavens and the earth by the fiat of his omnipotent word, so that if this word were withdrawn for the fraction of a second the universe would be plunged into chaos—how light a task compared with bearing the burden that mankind may take offense, when one has been constrained by love to become its saviour! . . .

Every other form of revelation would be a deception in the eyes of love; for either the learner would first have to be changed, and the fact concealed from him that this was necessary (but love does not alter the beloved, it alters itself); or there would be permitted to prevail a frivolous ignorance of the fact that the entire relationship was a delusion. (This was the error of paganism.) Every other form of revelation would be a deception from the standpoint of the divine love. . . .

And now the learner, has he no lot or part in this story of suffering, even though his lot cannot be that of the Teacher? . . . When the seed of the oak is planted in earthen vessels they break asunder; when new wine is poured in old leathern bottles they burst; what must happen when God implants himself in human weakness, unless man becomes a new vessel and a new creature! But this becoming, what labors will attend the change, how convulsed with birth-pangs! . . . And how wrapt in fear; for it is indeed less terrible to fall to the ground when the mountains tremble at the voice of God, than to sit at table with him as an equal; and yet it is God's concern precisely to have it so.[14]

6. Faith or Offense

In this way, with the assistance of a little algebra and a little poetry, by appealing both to logic and to the imagination, and, as he says, by speaking foolishly a little about the divine in earthly figures, Kierkegaard sets forth what he believes to be the objective truth of the Christian claim, in contrast to the claims for objective truth by rationalism or at least humanism. From the standpoint of logic, Christianity is the paradoxical; from the standpoint of the poetic imagination, it is the miraculous. The Incarnation is

[14] *Fragments*, pp. 25-27, *passim*.

an invention of the poetic imagination which, by all the laws of reason, should not have happened; but since it did happen (or perhaps I should say, for those who claim that it did happen), it ceases to be mere poetry and becomes The Miracle.

The next part of the *Fragments* is concerned with what sort of relationship a human being might sustain toward this Miracle, the Absolute Paradox. The relationship of rational understanding is ruled out by definition: you don't *understand* a paradox. You may recognize a paradox when you see one, but it is precisely because your reason is offended that you recognize it as a paradox. Similarly, you don't *understand* a miracle. Your reason may recognize when something that claims to be miraculous is placed before you, but this recognition is based on the fact that your reason rises up in protest against it and tries in every way to destroy the evidence on the basis of which the supposedly miraculous event claims to be true.

But in the preceding section on God as Teacher and Savior we have just finished trying to "understand" the paradox of the Incarnation with the assistance of the poetic imagination—and then it didn't seem so unreasonable that God should have to take on the likeness of a man, and the humblest at that, in order to become man's Teacher and give him the Truth. In fact, we were drawn to the "conclusion" that that was the only way it could be done if the revelation was to be consistent with the divine love, and if it was to express the fact that God loves the learner and wishes to be equal to him in love. The poetic imagination deals not with the possible nor even with the probable, but with the ideal clothed in the concreteness of the real. If you want to know what God has to do in order to save man, you imagine Him with the qualities of love, understanding, power, patience, and willingness to suffer, all raised to an ideality that is altogether divine and yet human enough for a human being—even one who is in Error—to understand with his own altogether human equipment of the same qualities. But to jump from this ideal representation to the realm of history, and to claim that this is what actually happened in the life of one particular man, is to run into a collision with the possible and the probable, and it is Reason that is concerned with the possible and the probable. So the problem is, what is Reason to do in the face of this claim that the paradoxical, the miraculous, has actually happened in history, seeing that rational understanding is ruled out by definition?

We say that when Reason is presented with something that cannot be understood, then Reason is *offended*. But why should Reason be *offended,* under any circumstances? Offense is after all not an act of judgment; it is the emotional response of a whole person to some kind of insult or attack. Offense is a passive form of anger, for the offended one believes he is suffering an unprovoked attack. And not only is it passive, but it is also likely to be introverted, especially if the source of the attack or insult is a beloved object. Offense then takes on a sad or melancholy aspect; it is something that, in spite of the absence of any outward signs of anger, smoulders deep inside the offended one simply because he cannot actively express it. Reason is angered by something that contradicts Reason, and when this contradiction comes from something with which Reason is secretly in love, namely, the divine itself, Reason is offended, both passively and introvertedly. One might say, Reason's feelings are hurt, thereby admitting that Reason *does* have feelings after all. Reason is not just a machine, like a cream-separator, for separating true judgments from false judgments, itself remaining indifferent to the results. On the contrary, Reason feels its own fate to be somehow involved in the results.

But this involvement, Kierkegaard claims, is the true characteristic of all existential thinking, thinking that comes to grips with existence, in contrast to the supposed objectivity of Reason claimed by the speculative philosophers—as if Reason were an absolute monarch who legislates for the whole country but himself remains above the law. Reason in existence is always supported by a feeling or passion, usually suppressed or kept on the fringes of consciousness, and this passion is somehow connected with the individual's deepest hold on existence, either threatening it or supporting it at any given moment. The problem of what Reason can do in the face of the paradox or miracle of the Incarnation must therefore be examined on this level—the affective relation of the individual to existence, or what Tillich calls the individual's "unconditional concern"—rather than on the level of Reason itself, which in this case has already been transcended by the very fact that the question of its basis in existence has been raised. Now Kierkegaard claims that Reason does not run into a paradox merely by accident, and thereby get itself hurt, or offended. Deep down in Reason there is a restlessness, a passion which drives Reason to seek out the paradoxical, in spite of the fact that the paradoxical may make it angry. For it is only by seeking out a collision with the paradoxical that Reason is able to transcend itself, or rather, become aware of its self-transcendence, which is there in any case, waiting to be discovered. It is only by seeking its limit that Reason can become aware that it has a limit and that therefore it must rest on something beyond that limit. Thus,

. . . one should not think slightingly of the paradoxical; for the paradox is the source of the thinker's passion, and the thinker without a paradox is like a lover without feeling; a paltry mediocrity. But the highest pitch of every passion is always to will its own downfall [that is, to find its limit]; and so it is also the supreme passion of the Reason to seek a collision, though this collision must in one way or another prove its undoing. The supreme paradox of all thought is the attempt to discover something that thought cannot think. This passion is at bottom present in all thinking, even in the thinking of the individual, in so far as in thinking he participates in something transcending himself.[15]

So then Reason is driven to seek its own limit, but whenever it arrives at the limit it is confronted with the problem of trying to conceptualize this limit, which is by definition unthinkable, or it would not be the limit of Reason. But Reason has to call it something, so it calls it the Unknown, or the Unknowable, or God (in so far as God must be thought of at least in part as the Unknown). "The paradoxical passion of the Reason thus comes repeatedly into collision with the Unknown, which does indeed exist, but is unknown, and in so far does not exist. The Reason cannot advance beyond this point, and yet it cannot refrain in its paradoxicalness from arriving at this limit and occupying itself therewith." [16]

[15] *Fragments*, p. 29.
[16] *Fragments*, p. 35.

Reason tries to conceive of its limit as the Unknown, and yet the minute it tries to put some content into what is unknown, for example by filling the idea of the Unknown with the content "God," it finds itself back in the known, and therefore not yet at the limits of Reason but only approaching the limit again from another side. The trouble is that in relation to Reason the unknown must be the absolutely different, and it is just this absolute difference that Reason cannot think or express. As Kierkegaard here puts it:

What then is the Unknown? It is the limit to which the Reason repeatedly comes, and in so far, substituting a static form of conception for the dynamic, it is the different, the absolutely different. But because it is absolutely different, there is no mark by which it could be distinguished. When qualified as absolutely different it seems on the verge of disclosure, but this is not the case; for the Reason cannot even conceive an absolute unlikeness. The Reason cannot negate itself absolutely, but uses itself for the purpose, and thus conceives only such an unlikeness within itself as it can conceive by means of itself; it cannot absolutely transcend itself, and hence conceives only such a superiority over itself as it can conceive by means of itself. Unless the Unknown (God) remains a mere limiting conception, the single idea of difference will be thrown into a state of confusion, and become many ideas of many differences. The Unknown is then in a condition of dispersion (diaspora), and the Reason may choose at pleasure from what is at hand and the imagination may suggest (the monstrous, the ludicrous, etc.).[17]

The dilemma of Reason is, therefore, that even if Reason is willing to admit that there *is* a limit to Reason and that this limit is somehow to be thought of as God under the aspect of the Unknown, Reason still cannot express or understand the Unknown because it cannot express or understand the absolutely different from itself; and yet this is just what it needs to understand in order to get a true conception of the Unknown.

From this there would seem to follow the further consequence, that if man is to receive any true knowledge about the Unknown (God) he must be made to know that it is unlike him, absolutely unlike him. This knowledge the Reason cannot possibly obtain of itself; we have already seen that this would be a self-contradiction. It will therefore have to obtain this knowledge from God. . . . Merely to obtain the knowledge that God is unlike him, man needs the help of God; and

[17] *Fragments*, p. 35.

now he learns that God is absolutely different from himself. But if God and man are absolutely different, this cannot be accounted for on the basis of what man derives from God, for in so far they are akin. Their unlikeness must therefore be explained by what man derives from himself, or by what he has brought upon his own head. But what can this unlikeness be? Aye, what can it be but sin; since the unlikeness, the absolute unlikeness, is something that man has brought upon himself. We have expressed this in the preceding by saying that man was in Error, and had brought this upon his head by his own guilt; and we came to the conclusion, partly in jest and yet also in earnest, that it was too much to expect of man that he should find this out for himself. Now we have again arrived at the same conclusion. . . . [What he lacked was] the consciousness of sin, which he indeed could no more teach to another than another could teach it to him, but only God—if God consents to become a Teacher.[18]

To get back to the problem of what Reason can do when confronted by the paradox of the Incarnation, there are really only two things that can happen. The situation is already on the limits of Reason, so it won't be decided by Reason, but rather by the passion that drives Reason to its limits, the individual's concern for the ultimate ground of his being. The encounter between this concern and the paradox will be like a love affair, that is to say, it will be a happy encounter, or an unhappy encounter, between a passion and its object.

In case it is an unhappy encounter, however, the only analogy with love that can be allowed here is with that particular form of unhappy love which has its roots in misguided self-love. No temporal accidents or external circumstances (as when romantic love encounters its traditional obstacles in family feuds and misfortunes) can be allowed to make this love unhappy, for here we are dealing entirely with an inward relationhip, with each individual's own relationship to God. The obstacles that could make this love unhappy must come entirely from within the man himself, and the valid analogy here is provided by the relationship between an individual's self-love and his love for another.

Self-love underlies love; but the paradoxical passion of self-love when at its highest pitch wills precisely its own downfall. This is also what love [for another] desires, so that these two are linked in mutual understanding in the passion of the moment, and this passion is love.

[18] *Fragments*, pp. 36-37.

Why should not the lover find this conceivable? But he who in self-love shrinks from the touch of love can neither understand it nor summon the courage to venture it, since it means his downfall. Such then is the passion of love; self-love is indeed submerged but not annihilated; it is taken captive and becomes love's *spolia opima,* but may again come to life, and this is love's temptation. So also with the Paradox in its relation to the Reason, only that the passion in this case has another name; or rather, we must seek to find a name for it.[19]

Here then are the two alternatives: "If the Paradox and the Reason come together in a mutual understanding of their unlikeness their encounter will be happy, like love's understanding, happy in the passion to which we have not yet assigned a name. . . . If the encounter is not in understanding the relationship becomes unhappy, and this unhappy love of Reason if I may so call it . . . , may be characterized more specifically as *Offense.*" [20]

Let us drop for the moment the terminology of Kierkegaard's thought-experiment (for all this is still part of the comparison and contrast between a certain view of the world called X and the Socratic view) and see what the above might mean in the usual terminology of Christianity. The "happy passion" referred to is of course *faith;* and we see that the two alternatives for a man who is confronted by Christ are *faith* or *offense.* Christ said, "Blessed is he who is not offended in me." But the man who is offended, what exactly is the content of this offense? According to the above, when Christ and man come together in a mutual understanding of their unlikeness, their encounter will be happy; if not, it will be unhappy. But what is this mutual understanding of their unlikeness but the admission on the part of man that he is a sinner, since Christ already knows this? The understanding of the unlikeness therefore involves the need for *repentance* on the part of man, and this obstacle forms the real content of the offense. So the analogy with self-love is not so bad. Reason is offended at the touch of Christ, just as the wrong kind of self-love is offended at the touch of love and shrinks away from it in mistaken self-defense. But it is not the laws of Reason that are offended; they merely take note of the fact that here is a paradox. It is the man behind the Reason who is offended, because repent-

---

[19] *Fragments,* p. 38.
[20] *Fragments,* p. 39.

ance is required of him, and he shrinks back from repentance in mistaken self-defense, using Reason as his shield as he backs away from this encounter.

But it is otherwise in case the encounter is a happy one. The man understands that repentance is required of him and that Reason cannot teach him to repent. He stops fighting in mistaken self-defense, and simply puts Reason aside momentarily in the tremendous realization of what is about to happen to him—in that instant he has faith, he succumbs to the demands of love and repents gladly. His Reason is not annihilated—it is transcended by being put in its place. The man no longer cares to use it as a weapon in this encounter, since he is no longer on the defensive.

The happy encounter is the turning point, the conversion, the turning around of the man himself, and with that the turning upside down and inside out of his whole world. As soon as he realizes what he has done, the converted man asks himself where he got the strength to do it, and whence he received the courage to stop fighting in mistaken self-defense. Certainly not from Reason, which was both shielding him and egging him on to resist. He must have got it from that by which he has been taken captive, so that now he owes everything to his Teacher and Savior, including the fact that he was able to believe in him.

It is testimony of this kind by the believer himself which is the source of the doctrine of the Holy Spirit, and is the truth behind every theory of predestination, no matter how fantastic such theories may become as a result of too much human speculation. In all relationships between man and God, God is there first. But man cannot realize this priority until after the relationship is there for himself, that is, until after he has faith. Kierkegaard goes to the greatest pains to protect the divine initiative in the Holy Spirit, remembering the words, "Flesh and blood hath not revealed this to thee." But if the divine always takes the initiative, and if even faith can understand the divine only in so far as the divine takes the initiative, then from the human or rational standpoint faith must also be regarded as a miracle. Faith is the miraculous organ of apprehension that is required to appropriate the miraculous event of the Incarnation, and both Faith and the Incarnation are the temporal or historical expression of the divine initiative motivated by the divine love. Faith is therefore the "condition" that the Teacher must give to the learner if the latter is to know that he was in Error, and if he is to learn that the Teacher and the Truth are one.

7. Discipleship Then and Now

The remaining parts of the *Philosophical Fragments* are devoted to the question whether a would-be disciple who is contemporary with Christ has any advantage in the matter of attaining faith over the would-be disciple who comes along hundreds or even thousands of years later. It is easy to predict from the foregoing what his answer to this question will be, but Kierkegaard is in no hurry to rush up with the answers. He explores the situation of the contemporary disciple, who, to be sure, is in a position to go where he can see the Teacher, listen to his voice, touch his garments, ask questions about his teachings, and so on. Nevertheless, it does not follow from this that he will become a disciple, and of course we know from the testimony that not everyone who followed the Teacher around in the throng surrounding him became a believer on that account.

And this not because he lacked time and opportunity (in the immediate sense), but because of something else, which could be lacking even if he himself had been present, and favored with opportunities for seeing and hearing to the fullest extent, and had not permitted these opportunities (in the immediate sense) to go unused. But what does it mean thus to say that one can be a contemporary without being contemporary . . . what does this mean except that it is quite impossible to be an immediate contemporary of such a Teacher and of such an event; so that the real contemporary is not the real contemporary by virtue of an immediate contemporaneity, but by virtue of something else? . . . *ergo*, it must also be possible for a non-contemporary (in the immediate sense) to be a contemporary, by virtue of that something which makes the contemporary a real contemporary. But the non-contemporary (in the immediate sense) is of course the member of a later generation, whence it must be possible for an individual so situated to be a real contemporary. Or what do we mean by being contemporary? Is it perhaps this kind of a contemporary that we praise, one who can speak as follows: 'I ate and drank in his presence, and he taught in our streets. I saw him often, and knew him for a common man of humble origin. Only a very few thought to find something extraordinary in him; as far as I am concerned, I could see nothing remarkable about him, and I was certainly as much of a contemporary as anybody.' Or is this what we mean by calling anyone a contemporary, and is he a contemporary to whom God must say if they meet in another life, and he seeks to urge his contemporaneity: 'I do not know you?' . . . Only the believer, i.e., the non-immediate contemporary, knows the Teacher, since he receives the condition from him, and therefore knows him even as he is known.[21]

But such a real contemporary every believer becomes, regardless of the generation into which he is born, regardless of whether a few years or thousands of years have elapsed since the event.

The first generation, then, has no advantage in an absolute sense over the latest generation, for only faith can make one really contemporaneous with the Eternal in time. But the first generation does have a relative advantage over the last generation, and this is compensated for by an equally relative advantage which the latest generation has over the first. The first generation

has the relative advantage of being nearer to the shock produced by the impact of our fact. This shock and its reverberations will help to arouse the attention. . . . The being somewhat nearer to it in comparison with later generations, well, suppose we call it an advantage; . . . The advantage is entirely dialectical, like the aroused attention itself. It consists in having one's attention aroused, whether the result is that one believes or is offended. The aroused attention is by no means partial to faith, as if faith followed from the attention by a simple consequence. The advantage is that a state of mind is induced in which the crucial nature of the decision confronting the individual becomes more clearly evident. This is an advantage, and the only one of any account; aye, so significant is it that it is fearful, by no means an easy and comfortable convenience.[22]

The latest generation, to compensate for the absence of the shock advantage, ambiguous though it is in the matter of producing faith, can point to the "results," the eighteen or nineteen hundred years of Christian history. And this advantage is just as ambiguous as the shock advantage which the first generation holds. The latest generation

is far removed from the initial shock, but it has on the other hand the consequences to lean upon, the proof of probability afforded by the results. It has before it, as immediate datum, the consequences with

[21] *Fragments*, pp. 54-55.
[22] *Fragments*, p. 78.

which this fact must doubtless have invested everything; it has an obvious recourse to a demonstration of probability, from which however no immediate transition to faith is possible, since as we have shown faith is by no means partial to probability; to make such an assertion about faith is to slander it. If this fact came into the world as the Absolute Paradox, nothing that happens subsequently can avail to change this. The consequences will in all eternity remain the consequences of a paradox, and hence in an ultimate view will be precisely as improbable as the Paradox itself.[23]

And suppose the whole thing were a mistake, a misunderstanding—"may not a misunderstanding also have consequences, may not a lie also be powerful? . . . But consequences founded on a paradox are humanly speaking built over a yawning chasm, and their total content, which can be transmitted to the individual only with the express understanding that they rest upon a paradox, are not to be appropriated as a settled estate, for their entire value trembles in the balance." [24]

The advantage of the consequences would seem to lie in a gradual *naturalization* of this fact [the Paradox]. . . . Under the assumption of naturalization, it will be possible for a later generation to appropriate the fact without the slightest embarrassment, without sensing anything of the ambiguity of the aroused attention, from which offense may issue as well as faith. However, this fact [the Paradox] is no respecter of the drill-master's discipine; it is too proud to desire a disciple whose willingness to attach himself to the cause is based upon the favorable turn that events have taken; it disdains naturalization, whether under the protection of a king or a professor. It is and remains the Paradox, and cannot be assimilated by any speculation.[25]

"Naturalization" is precisely the danger of this advantage of the later generation, when the most wonderful thing that ever happened in history becomes the most commonplace of all institutions; everybody becomes included in this naturalized institution, and everywhere the sense of fear and wonder and the need for decision is smothered. As soon as this later generation sees that the relative ease provided by the "results" easily becomes the greatest danger to true faith, it sees that it has no real advantage over the first generation, and then it will be "gripped as primitively by awe and fear as the first generation." [26]

[23] *Fragments*, pp. 78-79.   [24] *Ibid.*, p. 82.
[25] *Ibid.*, p. 80.   [26] *Ibid.*, p. 83.

But the later generation of disciples has nothing to go on except the testimony of the contemporary disciples—isn't that a one-sided relationship? Not in the democracy of faith that prevails among all the generations of disciples, for "just as the historical gives occasion for the contemporary to become a disciple, but only it must be noted through receiving the condition from God himself, since otherwise we speak Socratically, so the testimony of contemporaries gives occasion for each successor to become a disciple, but only it must be noted through receiving the condition from God himself." [27]

The only thing the contemporary can do for the successor is to testify to his own faith, and precisely in such a form as to give occasion to the same ambiguity of the aroused attention, with its possibility of offense, that the witness himself has experienced. The quantity and accuracy of historical detail in the testimony of the witness here sinks into insignificance, in comparison to the astounding claim that in faith is made for this historical fact. For this is the one historical fact that one human being cannot communicate to another directly, and which

if communicated in the form of faith is so communicated as to prevent the other, so far as possible, from accepting it immediately. If the fact spoken of were a simple historical fact, the accuracy of the historical sources would be of great importance. Here this is not the case, for faith cannot be distilled from even the nicest accuracy of detail. The historical fact that God has existed in human form in the essence of the matter; the rest of the historical detail is not even as important as if we had to do with a human being instead of with God. Jurists say that a capital crime submerges all lesser crimes, and so it is with faith. Its absurdity makes all petty difficulties vanish. Inconsistencies which would otherwise be disconcerting do not count for anything here; they make no difference whatsoever. . . . If the contemporary generation had left nothing behind them but these words: "We have believed that in such and such a year God appeared among us in the humble figure of a servant, that he lived and taught in our community, and finally died," it would be more than enough. The contemporary generation would have done all that was necessary; for this little advertisement, this *nota bene* on a page of universal history, would be sufficient to afford an occasion for a successor, and the most voluminous account can in all eternity do nothing more.[28]

[27] *Fragments*, p. 84.
[28] *Fragments*, p. 87.

The above statement has brought Kierkegaard considerable criticism from *our* contemporaries, some of whom have accused him of Gnosticism, and others of fideism, on its account. The statement is so flat and exaggerated that it seems to reduce the whole content of Christianity to the simple challenge: either you believe or you do not believe that God has existed in human form, and thereby you are saved or damned. In fact such exaggerations, such verbal punches, are to be found quite thickly sprinkled all through Kierkegaard's writings, and they show him up for the polemicist that he was. I believe the only way to deal with them is to see them in the total setting of the entire authorship, counterbalanced by emphases in other directions, and perhaps understandable in terms of the polemical purpose at hand—rather than to throw back in his face certain isolated quotations that supposedly contain the gist of his whole thought. So, I think that in this case Kierkegaard's extensive and profound preoccupation with the biblical accounts, both in the discourses and throughout all his writings, as well as in the *Journals,* counterbalances the impression given by this statement that he actually thought the historical details had little value. The polemical purpose here seems to be to warn those who were looking for the essence of Christianity in the ever increasing historical research that they were on the wrong track; that the accumulation of historical details tends instead to obscure the distinctive, essential, and paradoxical claims made by Christian faith for these historical details; and that only by peeling the proposition down to the bare bones—God has existed in human form—does one become aware of the essence of Christianity in contrast to other ways of salvation.

V

The Question of Kierkegaard's Orthodoxy

1. Essential Truths in the "Colossus"

Philosophical Fragments is at the very least a curious little book. Though its content is severely theological and obliquely philosophical, it reads now like a fairy tale, now like a piece of propaganda on behalf of the Greeks, now like a textbook of grammar or logic, and now like a quiet joke between the writer and the reader. Theodor Haecker says about the *Fragments,* "Poetically and philosophically the work is a Platonic myth. Furthermore the God who appears as teacher in *Crumbs of Philosophy* is not the historical Jesus Christ of the seed of David, who was foretold and came amid signs and wonders testifying to his office; he is a poetic creation, the aim of which is to stress the paradox that a man is God by exaggerating it." [1]

I should like to call this book a philosophical parable rather than a philosophical myth, for we now regard the word "myth" as containing more than a purely illustrative or pedagogical meaning. But a parable has a teaching purpose, and this philosophical parable certainly has one: to teach the nineteenth century speculative idealists the difference between Christianity and rationalism. Just as Jesus used the processes of nature and the relationships between men as material for parables pointing up comparisons and contrasts between this world and the world of the Father, so Kierkegaard uses the concepts of idealistic philosophy (the temporal, the eternal, the absolute, the truth, etc.) to point up the contrast he wishes to make, driving it of course to the extreme for the sake of logical clarity. Yet he can suddenly turn these abstractions into a drama between the Teacher and the learner or into a fairy tale about a king who loved a humble maiden. Kierkegaard does not claim that by reading this book a person

[1] Theodor Haecker, *Søren Kierkegaard,* trans. Alexander Dru (New York: Oxford University Press, 1937), p. 16.

will become a Christian—on the contrary, he may be repelled from becoming one by reading it. Nevertheless, the role of God as Teacher and Savior is portrayed in the most appealing terms. The motive behind the role is love and love's desire to make equal that which can never be equal in any other way: God and man. So the book arouses attention in the same ambiguous fashion that Kierkegaard says must be true of all communications about faith —they must attract and repel at the same time, thus making each man feel the weight of the decision.

In regard to the category of the individual, the importance of *Philosophical Fragments* lies in the fact that it contains the most objective statement of what Kierkegaard believed Christianity to be that can be found anywhere in his writings. That is to say, it answers the question about the degree of Kierkegaard's orthodoxy or unorthodoxy. And this is a very important question to have answered, in view of the tremendous claim Kierkegaard made for Christianity regarding the individual and his development through the stages of life. To put it briefly and mildly, Kierkegaard claimed that Christianity is the goal and the crown of the individual's development, that it is the only power in life capable of bringing that development to completion and fulfilment, by establishing the right God-relationship. But what sort of Christianity was able to do this? Surely not the denatured and decontaminated version of Christianity that had been incorporated into idealistic philosophy. *Philosophical Fragments* deals with and supports, on a small scale, all the chief doctrines of the Protestant orthodoxy, doctrines which idealistic philosophy had found to be so objectionable that they had to be explained away somehow. And yet it deals with them in such a way that it also cuts the nerve of the scholasticism of Protestant orthodoxy, by showing the true character of Christian faith and obedience to be something quite different from intellectual assent to a set of revealed doctrines, as the Protestant scholastics had presumed.

This philosophical parable, then, is a two-edged sword. With respect to the theological situation which Kierkegaard was trying to change, it cuts both ways. Although Kierkegaard may with some justice be called the father of the neo-orthodox movement, the prefix "neo" must in his case be understood as a new and revitalized vision of the major doctrines of the orthodoxy, not as a relapse into Medieval or Reformation modes of theological speculation. Indeed, we have Kierkegaard's own words on his relationship to the Protestant orthodoxy: "As you know, I grew up, so to speak, in orthodoxy; but as soon as I began to think for myself the tremendous colossus began to totter. I call it a colossus with purpose, for taken as a whole it is very consistent and in the course of centuries the different parts have fused so tightly together that it is difficult to quarrel with it. I could of course agree with it on certain points, but these would have to be treated like shoots, found in the cracks of a rock." [2]

We have only to remind ourselves of the aims and methods of the Protestant scholastics to see how far removed they were from the spirit and temper of Kierkegaard. As soon as the Reformation churches had become established churches (supported by the state), matters of religion became the concerns of law and political jurisprudence, a question of the legal standing of citizens. Therefore it was necessary to have a source of authority and guidance as objective and unchangeable as that which the Catholic Church had in the tradition on its side, and this unchangeable authority the Protestant theologians decided must be the Bible, taken both as the source and the proof text of systematic theology. As one church historian says, "Like the schoolmen of the Middle Ages, the Lutheran theologians had, in the *Formula of Concord,* a closed system. Its acceptance was regarded as necessary to salvation, because it set forth the true interpretation of the Bible. To depart from it or correct it in any way was out of the question. Theological speculation must take it for granted, and the duty of the theologian was to move always within set bounds, systematising, elucidating, and defending truth already fully given and unalterably fixed. As in all scholasticism the importance of a particular doctrine came to depend upon its place in the system rather than upon its practical relation to life. Truth was gained, not from the religious and moral experience of individual or church, but by logical deduction from the accepted system, and it was tested by its consistency with the larger whole." [3]

[2] *Journals,* No. 16, p. 8.
[3] Arthur C. M'Giffert, *Protestant Thought Before Kant* (New York: Scribner's, 1911), pp. 144-145.

There were five cardinal doctrines of the Reformation which had been attacked directly by the Enlightenment and which remained as the chief stumbling blocks to be overcome by the more conciliatory and reconstructive liberal theologians of the nineteenth century: (1) the authority of the Bible; (2) original sin; (3) justification by faith; (4) the double predestination; and (5) the nature of the eucharist. In the Protestant scholasticism, these doctrines had been chosen for especially hard and fast definition in opposition to the Catholic Counter-Reformation, which in turn had hardened *its* formulations at the Council of Trent in order to stress opposition to the Reformation ideas. Now while Kierkegaard was as much opposed to the abstract definitions of the Protestant scholasticism as he was to the abstract speculations of the German idealists, he did not on that account turn his back on what he thought were the existential, the experienced truths contained within these now-despised dogmas, as did most of the liberal theologians, who tended to leave them out of the picture altogether. In the *Philosophical Fragments,* four of the five doctrines are dealt with, the argument over the eucharist being, obviously, much too metaphysical a piece of speculation to be of any concern to Kierkegaard. The other four he apparently thought contained truths which must be defended against the "dissolving" tendency of the philosophers if Christianity was to be itself and not changed into something else. Let us now examine these doctrines in the form in which they appear in this philosophical parable.

2. The Real Authority of the Bible

The entire discussion about the difference between the contemporary disciple and the disciple of a later generation[4] is an attempt to show wherein lies the true authority of the Bible, or at least of the New Testament. The nineteenth century was after all the time of the flowering of biblical criticism. The same kind of logic that was applied elsewhere to historical material in an effort to develop a scientific historiography was now applied to the Bible in an effort to discover at least probable authorship and the order of appearance of its various books. A great effort was made to extract from this brief but fantastic collection of writings a picture

---

[4] See chap. IV, sec. 7.

of something called the historical Jesus. Biographies of Jesus were attempted, in which Paul's writings were devaluated in an effort to get at "the religion *of* Jesus" as against "the religion *about* Jesus." There were two motives behind such biographies and such historical and critical research. For the skeptical and the emancipated there was the intention of showing how scanty indeed were the verifiable historical evidences on which the entire Christian religion rested; *ergo,* the inference ran, one did not have to believe it. On the other hand, for those who *wanted* to believe the Christian religion but could not square the Gospel accounts with what their reason told them, the intention was to distil from these accounts a kind of minimal, de-theologized, believable picture of the real Jesus as he must have appeared to his contemporaries.

Now Kierkegaard was mildly in favor of biblical criticism and historical research, and certainly any sort of biblical literalism or proof-text quoting or what we now call fundamentalism was utterly alien to his spirit. One has only to look at the way he handles the New Testament passages in the religious discourses. But he could not allow to pass unchallenged the implications behind this research, that historical details decide the question of faith and that "the picture of the historical Jesus," assuming it could be achieved, would make belief in him as the Christ easier. Kierkegaard strikes at the heart of this argument by showing that the real object of faith is not the historical Jesus at all, but the Eternal Christ. The believer does not *believe* that the historical Jesus existed; this he *assumes* on the basis of probabilities which are as risky here as anywhere else in history. But the believer *believes* that the historical Jesus, whose existence is thus assumed, is at the same time the Eternal Christ; the unbeliever does not believe this, even though he may allow that the historical person named Jesus probably existed. It is the confession "Thou art the Christ, the son of the living God" that makes a man a Christian, and this confession can be neither forced nor prevented by historical evidences piled up pro or contra. Jesus' contemporaries, as Kierkegaard points out, were in a position to know the historical Jesus as well as they wished, but this did not necessarily lead them to confess that he was the Christ. We are deluding ourselves if we think that had we been in their position, we would have believed or at least would have found it easier to believe than we do now, in our present position.

No, the stumbling block is the same for all generations, and the possibility of offense is the same for all generations, and herein lies the true contemporaneity of all believers, for to be contemporary with the Eternal Christ is the only way you can be contemporary with this particular historical event. If you do not see the Eternal Christ in the historical Jesus in so far as he is portrayed in the New Testament, historical evidence will not help you to do so, just as the evidence of their own eyes did not help the actual contemporaries. The true authority of the New Testament lies in the fact that it is a believing interpretation of the event. It is the testimony not just of witnesses to a historical event (as, for example, witnesses to an automobile accident might give testimony to what they saw); it is at the same time the testimony of believers to what they have believed. And just as "flesh and blood" did not reveal to the contemporary disciples that Jesus was the Christ, so "flesh and blood," that is, the ordinary understanding of the past as the historically probable, will not reveal to the present generation that this man Jesus is also the Christ.

Kierkegaard is here defending the Christian doctrine of the Holy Spirit. He is not defining it, but simply making room for its activity, since if the activity of the Holy Spirit is left out of the account or is swallowed up in something else, there can be no really Christian understanding of either history or the authority of the Bible. At the same time he is putting his finger on one of the sore spots in the relationship between Christian theology and philosophy, namely, the effort of philosophy to understand history as determined according to some universal law. For if the Holy Spirit is a reality and not a fiction, every effort to subsume the particularities of history under a law of history is an effort to subjugate the Holy Spirit under a higher authority. Kierkegaard places a little interlude (to give the illusion that eighteen hundred years are passing) between his discussions about the disciple at first hand and the disciple who comes along eighteen hundred years later, in which he considers what it really means to apply the category of necessity to history. For this is what much of nineteenth century interest in history was hoping to do, whether to show, rationalistically, that history had to happen the way it did, or to demonstrate, more empirically, that since it did happen the way it did we are given some grounds on which to predict what it will do next. He examines the nature of the change involved in *becoming,* and asks,

Can the necessary come into existence? Becoming is a change; but the necessary cannot undergo any change, since it is always related to itself, and related to itself in the same manner. All coming into being is a kind of *suffering,* and the necessary cannot suffer; it cannot suffer the suffering of the actual, which is that the possible (not only the excluded possibility, but also the accepted possibility) reveals itself as nothing the moment it becomes actual; for the possible is annihilated in the actual. Everything that comes into being proves precisely by coming into being that it is not necessary; for the necessary is the only thing that cannot come into being, because the necessary is.[5]

And how is it with history?

What has happened has happened as it happened; in this sense it does not admit of change. But is this immutability identical with the immutability of the necessary? The immutability of the past consists in the fact that its actual "thus" cannot become different; but does it follow from this that its possible "how" could not have been realized in a different manner? The immutability of the necessary, on the contrary, consists in its constant relation to self, and in its being related to itself always in the same manner, excluding every change. . . . The future has not yet happened. But it is not *on that account* less necessary than the past, since the past did not become necessary by coming into being, but on the contrary proved by coming into being that it was not necessary.[6]

Elsewhere he says, "Distance in time tends to promote an intellectual illusion, just as distance in space provokes a sensory illusion. A contemporary does not perceive the necessity of what comes into being, but when centuries intervene between the event and the beholder he perceives the necessity, just as distance makes the square tower seem round." [7] Thus history may be seen as the graveyard of possibilities. In the present we are more aware of the many possibilities that are rejected for every one that is realized, so we do not see the necessity in what happens. But imagination

[5] *Philosophical Fragments*, p. 60.
[6] *Fragments*, p. 63.
[7] *Fragments*, p. 65.

fails us when we try to visualize the rejected possibilities that accompanied every event in the past, and this failure of the imagination promotes the illusion of necessity.

This interlude is written against Hegel's philosophy of history, according to which history is the unfolding of an immanent logic —that is to say, history happens as it happens because of an inner necessity, and it simply could not have happened otherwise. Kierkegaard objects that the necessary cannot determine history because history changes and the necessary cannot change. Hegel thought he could import *movement* into logic by making necessary relations between ideas serve as causes of change. Such a feat could happen in the medium of thought (depending on how one *defined* the terms of one's logic) but not in reality. Again we run into the priority of reality over thought. There is certainly a determinate element in history, because man is not a disembodied spirit and his historical being is everywhere imbedded in nature, in biological, psychological, geographical, economic, and cultural conditions. But what he does or does not do within these conditions is such an inextricable mixture of necessity and freedom that the only way to approach history objectively is with the category of probability. Kierkegaard claimed, however, that calculations of probability are incommensurable with the decision by which a man decides his relationship to God. Logically such calculations are inconclusive, since history, the meaning of which is being decided on, is still unfinished and may yet reverse the best hypothesis. And, from a motivational standpoint, to use them to decide this issue is ignoble—a far greater objection, since it is the eternal that is at stake and not some finite venture. The use of probability calculations here betrays the mean-spirited person, one who will not take a chance on a high cause until the probable success of it appears plainly evident. It betrays the shrewd success-calculator, a disciple who is in reality only a bandwagon-climber.

The probable and the eternal are ill-matched companions. There is something eternal in man which wants to know what the eternal is but which realizes that the concrete, historical realm presents it only with probabilities. That is why the Greeks deserted history for the realm of essences, and that is why modern rationalism does essentially the same thing when trying to explain history, for every logic of history always turns out to be a certain possible structure of human thought rather than an explanation of history, thus driving the eternal in man again to desert history for an understanding of the eternal. Then along comes Christianity, and utterly confounds the rational in man by placing the eternal just where his reason tells him only probabilities can be found, in the very heart of the historical. At the end of the *Fragments*, Kierkegaard says,

It is well known that Christianity is the only historical phenomenon which in spite of the historical, nay precisely by means of the historical, has offered itself to the individual as a point of departure for his eternal consciousness, has assumed to interest him in another sense than the merely historical, has proposed to base his eternal happiness on his relationship to something historical. No system of philosophy, addressing itself only to thought, no mythology, addressing itself solely to the imagination, no historical knowledge, addressing itself to the memory, has ever had this idea: of which it may be said with all possible ambiguity in this connection, that it did not arise in the heart of any man.[8]

Reason tells you, you shall become conscious of the eternal by abstracting from all the natural and historical particulars their abiding and unchanging aspects, whether you do this a priori as in idealism or a posteriori as in empiricism, and certainly this avenue to the eternal is open to all men who possess a normal endowment of reason. Christianity tells you, you shall become conscious of the eternal not by abstracting from all particulars but by seeing the eternal in this one particular man, by seeing God in Jesus of Nazareth, by which act of apprehension or vision he is known to you as the Christ. Small wonder that this avenue to the eternal is not necessarily open to all men who possess a normal endowment of reason, but requires instead a new organ of apprehension, faith, and a new source of authority, the Holy Spirit. Not in the definitions of theologians, nor in the creedal pronouncements of the Church, nor in the legal power of the state, but in the witness of the Holy Spirit lies the true authority of the Bible.

3. Original Sin and God's Transcendence

The second doctrine of the Protestant orthodoxy that is supported and yet reinterpreted in this philosophical parable is per-

[8] *Fragments*, p. 92.

haps the one that was pragmatically the most unbelievable to the
nineteenth century frame of mind—the idea of original sin. For
this was the century in which the idea of progress became enthroned
as a metaphysical principle at the core of even the most skeptical
and materialistic philosophies, not as a logical consequence of basic
tenets, but simply as a mood or temperament or atmosphere. The
human race was, to be sure, not pictured as perfect—there were
plenty of "realists" and muckrakers at work—but its *perfectibility,*
especially through the application of reason, was questioned no
more by the conservatives who liked to bask in tradition and take
improvement in small doses than by the radicals who wanted to
change everything overnight. In this atmosphere the doctrine of
original sin was mostly ignored or misunderstood. People could not
understand that "original sin" did not mean improvements should
not be made, but that it meant man is quite capable of corrupting
the improvements too, when they are made, and yet this does not
excuse him from making the improvements in the first place.

Kierkegaard, on the contrary, places the doctrine of human sinfulness at the very heart of the Christian understanding of man,
not as an appendage or a regrettable detail to be added later. Man
is from the beginning in a state of Error (sin), and he cannot learn
the truth from his fellow men because they are in the same condition. Nor can the Doctrine of Recollection help him, even if he
were so fortunate as to have a Socrates with him in every generation
to be his midwife. For this doctrine may bring him to some knowledge of himself, but not to the knowledge that he is in Error. If
man is to learn the truth, God must become his Teacher, and the
first thing God must teach him is that he is in a state of Error,
since this Error, this sin, is precisely an error in his God-relationship and not necessarily an error about the world of things and of
men considered apart from their God-relationship.

Here is a whole theory about the relationship between reason
and revelation. Reason will indeed tell us many true and interesting
things about the world and about ourselves and our fellow men.
But reason will not tell us that in relation to God we are sinners,
because reason is itself a human faculty susceptible to sin, and it
has neither the authority, nor the holiness, nor the righteousness,
nor the criterion of divine love, with which to condemn us. Only

a God who transcends both man and the world (including what reason tells man about himself and the world) and who transcends them precisely in the sense of holiness and love rather than in the merely metaphysical sense of space and time—only such a God has the authority to condemn man as a sinner, to reveal his condition to him, and to make him actually feel the need for redemption. And yet the nineteenth century was busily bending all its intellectual and poetic and moral efforts to the task of doing away with the transcendence of God.

It would seem that the ideas of divine transcendence and human sinfulness go hand in hand, while the ideas of divine immanence and human goodness also go hand in hand. However, the two pairs of ideas are not logical opposites, nor are they mutually exclusive. It might be that only through divine transcendence can human goodness be achieved. All depends on how one thinks about transcendence and immanence. The nineteenth century thinkers were determined that God, both as transcendent and immanent, must be conceived in terms of what is rationally definable; hence the difference between his transcendence and his immanence must be a relative difference, a matter of degree. This determination is betrayed by the very fact that instead of giving him any special attributes, they called him the Absolute. Absolute what? The Absolute in this connection could only mean the infinitization and eternalization of some quality or essence that was assumed to be *relatively* present in every man. Thus, whether man was defined as essentially reason, essentially self, or essentially moral purpose, God, in his transcendent aspect straightway became Absolutized (human) Reason, Absolutized (human) Self, or Absolutized (human) Moral Purpose. There could be no qualitative, *essential* difference between God and man, only the relative difference between a finite being, embodying the essence in a particular body limited in space and time, and an infinite being, embodying the same essence in the whole universe and to all eternity. And that is what it means for reason to absolutize anything—to take a concept and attribute it in an ultimate and infinite way to the whole universe as its basic purpose or principle.

This is just what Kierkegaard pointed out when he said that reason cannot conceive of an absolute difference in relation to the unknown—only a relative difference. "The Reason cannot negate itself absolutely, but uses itself for the purpose, and thus conceives only such an unlikeness within itself as it can conceive by means of itself; it cannot absolutely transcend itself, and hence conceives only such a superiority over itself as it can conceive by means of itself." [9] Such is the predicament of reason in relation to the problem of conceiving the transcendence of God, the unlikeness of the unknown. If reason is to be self-sufficient, if reason is to be the revealer of the ultimate truth to man, it cannot afford to allow— in fact, it must not permit there to exist—anything that is ultimately beyond reason's own capacity. Thus, when this kind of reason, which we might call self-sufficient reason, arrives at its limits and confronts the unknown, it cannot just stand there with folded hands and say: behold, a mystery. It must insist that the unknown can be nothing but an extrapolation into the infinite out of that which is known in the region where reason naturally operates, the visible, historical world of space and time, things and people. Self-sufficient reason will thus never be able to instruct man concerning his unlikeness to God or concerning the real transcendence of God.

But reason need not be self-sufficient unless it wills to be self-sufficient. As Kierkegaard himself points out, there is something in man, a passion or a restlessness he calls it, that makes him drive reason to its limits precisely because thereby he becomes aware that he is something more than reason. If man were not something more than reason, he would never be able to question the ground of reason nor to seek the limits of reason. At this point Kierkegaard would probably disagree with the evaluation of reason made by the Protestant orthodoxy, which simply declared reason to be weak and depraved by sin and by its involvement in material things and desires. But that is not the proper way to put reason in its place. Reason is an insufficient instrument for finding the eternal, not because man is a poor logician, but because he is something more than the best logician. And reason is not *necessarily* depraved by weakness and sin; rather it would be more correct to say that reason is limited and confused by its own inability to conceive the unlikeness between man and God in such terms or dimensions as would do justice both to the transcendence of God and to that something

[9] *Fragments*, p. 35.

more in man himself which transcends reason. Reason may *also* be corrupted by sin (be used for selfish ends), but that is something quite different from its inability to understand the real dimension of sin and the real transcendence of God, making it necessary for man to learn these from God, if he is to learn them at all.

We should recall here that when the reaction eventually set in (at the end of the First World War) against the liberal theology which was based largely on some form of rationalistic idealism, it was heralded by a prophet who proclaimed first and foremost the "otherness" of God. Karl Barth, admittedly influenced by Kierkegaard, declared to the world the bankruptcy of reason's efforts to capture and domesticate the Almighty, Just, and Merciful God of the Bible, whose thoughts are not our thoughts, nor his ways our ways. The "otherness" of God became practically the rallying slogan of the neo-orthodox movement, and it has since also received its peculiar metaphysical distortions among the professional Barthians; but in Kierkegaard's parable, the "otherness" in all its majesty and mystery still appears side by side with God's determination in love to make this unlikeness into likeness, as illustrated by the tale of the noble king who loved a humble maiden.

4. God's Omnipotence and Man's Freedom

The other two doctrines of the Protestant orthodoxy that are supported and yet reinterpreted in *Philosophical Fragments* can be discussed together. They are the doctrine of justification by faith, the principal contribution of Luther to Protestant thought, and the doctrine of predestination, the principal contribution of Calvin. Together they express the idea of the divine initiative with respect to man. It is God who makes the gesture of love toward man and who takes the first step that is necessary for the redemption of man. He consents to become the Teacher and Savior of man, in order to show man that he is in Error and to give him the condition for understanding the Truth. This God does out of love for man. All that man can do is to understand that this is so and to understand that if this is not so, his situation is desperate indeed. For of what avail are all his own attempts at salvation if God still does not love him and chooses to remain withdrawn? This very thought, when pondered together with the coming of the Christ, has in it such revealing power that when it occurs to a man he attributes it to the source of the revelation.

It is not impossible that it might occur to a man to imagine himself the equal of God, or to imagine God the equal of man, but not to imagine that God would make himself into the likeness of man; for if God gave no sign, how could it enter into the mind of man that the blessed God should need him? This would be a most stupid thought, or rather, so stupid a thought could never have entered into his mind; though when God has seen fit to entrust him with it he exclaims in worship: This thought did not arise in my own heart! and finds it a most miraculously beautiful thought.[10]

Unfortunately, the idea of the divine initiative as a miraculous element in the religious man's experience with the deeper implications of his God-relationship was quickly obscured, both by Luther and by Calvin, in their attempts to explain this experience on the theological level in terms of the still-prevalent Aristotelian logic of substance and attributes. According to this logic a substance could not have contradictory attributes; it had to be one thing or another, but could not be both at the same time, and could not even imply both attributes in a dialectical fashion. Thus Luther argued, if we are saved by faith, we cannot be saved by works. Such a dichotomy ignores the possible relationship between faith and works whereby only the wholehearted devotion to works, along with the experience of always falling short of the glory of God, can lead one to the personal conviction that he must be saved by faith if he is to be saved at all. Such indeed had been the experience of Luther himself in the monastery, as we all know, but when he came to theologizing about it, and especially when his followers came to systematizing his theology into a set of hard and fast and supposedly consistent doctrines, faith and works were so far separated as to take on the meaning of logical opposites. Faith became the unconditional intellectual acceptance of a set of doctrines supposedly representing the dogmatic substance of Christian teaching, and this acceptance assured the believer's justification in the eyes of God. Works, on the other hand, became an increasingly suspect activity, the meritorious interpretation of which might at any moment endanger the believer's justification in the eyes of God. However, as an expression of love and gratitude in return for the mercies received

[10] *Fragments*, p. 28.

in the justification, works could be allowed. By the time the nineteenth century rolled around, a veritable faith-righteousness had supplanted work-righteousness in the lives of those who still subscribed to the Protestant orthodoxy. As for the works, these became reduced almost entirely to the official charitable activities of the Church. Individuals found the line between the right and wrong interpretation of works very had to draw; it was so much easier to forget about works altogether, and thereby also absolutely assure one's salvation by faith alone.

Calvin applied the same sort of mechanical, legalistic logic to his experience of the absolute sovereignty of God. He said: if some are predestined to be saved, the others must be predestined to be damned; *ergo,* we have the double predestination. His related concept of grace as irresistible completed the purely mechanical picture of the relationship between God and man: man became a puppet, God the Great Puppeteer who moved some to salvation and others to hell, according to his inscrutable, proprietary will. Compare this with the picture Kierkegaard draws of God as Teacher and Savior who in love for the disciple determines to become the equal of the humblest.

He is God; and yet he picks his steps more carefully than if angels guided them, not to prevent his feet from stumbling against a stone, but lest he trample human beings in the dust, in that they are offended in him. He is God; and yet his eye surveys mankind with anxious care, for the tender shoots of an individual life may be crushed as easily as a blade of grass. How wonderful a life, all sorrow and all love: to yearn to express the equality of love and yet to be misunderstood; to apprehend the danger that all men may be destroyed, and yet only so to be able really to save a single soul. . . .[11]

Elsewhere Kierkegaard comments directly on the question of God's omnipotence, pointing out that only true omnipotence can make anything free, although it would seem that it should make everything dependent.

But if we rightly consider omnipotence, then clearly it must have the quality of so taking itself back in the very manifestation of its all-powerfulness that the results of this act of the omnipotent can be independent. That is why one man cannot make another man quite free, because the one who has the power is imprisoned in it and con-

[11] *Fragments,* p. 25.

sequently always has a false relation to him whom he wishes to free. That is why there is a finite self-love in all finite power (talent and so forth). Omnipotence alone can take itself back while giving, and this relationship is nothing else but the independence of the recipient. God's omnipotence is therefore his goodness. For goodness means to give absolutely, yet in such a way that by taking oneself back one makes the recipient independent.[12]

In this respect God is the greatest respecter of persons—indeed, this is how he makes persons out of men. All mechanical or "substance" analogies fail here, and even personal relationships must be probed to their deepest to afford an analogy to the power and love of God. Just as in the human case a strong and noble love seeks to make the beloved person free rather than to enslave him, but never quite succeeds, so God's love makes men free just at the point where they would seem to be most dependent. God does not browbeat anyone, and to speak of his grace as irresistible is to have an ignoble conception of his power—the very power which in the form of love allows itself to be misunderstood in the world every day in order that men might become persons. Predestination in these terms becomes a most mysterious relationship. It is the feeling on the part of one who has responded freely to the divine love that even this freedom he owes in some way to the divine love itself.

What Kierkegaard has done in this philosophical parable about the difference between Christianity and rationalism is to set forth some of the most difficult and distinguishing doctrines of Christian theology in such a way that they cannot possibly be mistaken for the natural products of human reason. But neither are they merely intellectual beliefs to be blindly accepted on the authority of the Church, tradition, or the Bible. They are in fact not mentioned as *doctrines* at all. They are described as the marks, the characteristic features, of a certain kind of God-relationship that is possible for man. That this kind of God-relationship is now possible for man is something over which man has no control, since it depended upon a divine act in the first place, upon the appearance of God in history. Human reason may rationalize this fact after it has happened, but in so doing it often obscures the primary, antecedent response of faith, which alone apprehends *what* has happened, for

[12] *Journals*, No. 616, p. 180.

man's benefit, in this event. As Kierkegaard often says, once the primacy of faith and the related distinctive features of this kind of God-relationship are understood and granted, everything returns to the Socratic order of things. There is nothing "irrational" about this kind of God-relationship, and the premise on which it rests, that the historical can be a point of departure for the eternal, should be described rather as *beyond* reason than as *against* reason, for the discovery of the paradoxical is merely the signal that reason has reached its limits. Of course, to self-sufficient reason the paradoxical appears as the absurd, the enemy of reason, because self-sufficient reason is offended by the idea that it has limits.

This kind of God-relationship therefore has its own inner dialectic, its own inner rationale, one might say, once the premises are granted. It offers itself to the individual as something he can think about and think through, in so far as it implies certain attitudes, actions, and feelings which are consistent with it, as well as others which are inconsistent. It offers no prizes to dolts and dullards, but is indeed as great a challenge as existence is capable of presenting. It is an invitation, the greatest ever given—Ho, everyone that thirsteth!—to the individual to discover the truth of this God-relationship by exploring it from the interior, by trying to express in his life the attitudes, actions, and feelings which are consistent with it. Taking up this invitation is what Kierkegaard meant by the "subjective appropriation" of the truth, and it is the appropriation by the individual of the Christian truth that he undertakes to explore in *Concluding Unscientific Postscript.*

VI

Christianity Appropriated by the Individual

1. The Larger, More Difficult Question

According to Kierkegaard's own estimation, *Concluding Unscientific Postscript* represents "the turning point" of his entire authorship. It was originally intended to be the conclusion of his authorship, following which he planned to retire to the countryside as a rural pastor. His collision with the *Corsair*[1] prevented this, and the volume of his subsequent writings reached such proportions that even from the standpoint of quantity, the *Postscript* became more or less the central point in his production.

Its sheer size, in comparison with the slender volume to which it is supposed to be a postscript, seems designed to draw attention to the difference between what happens when one asks, "What is Christianity?"—something which any schoolboy can answer out of the catechism—and what happens when one asks, "But how can *I* become a Christian?" For the answer to the latter question is by no means simple, or easy, or of equal proportions with the answer to the first question.

Johannes Climacus asks the second question on his own behalf at the beginning of the book, his attitude being that of the man in the Bible who wisely counts the cost before he sets out to build a tower, lest he find himself unable to finish what he had begun. As we would probably put it now, Johannes wants to know "what he is getting in for" in the matter of becoming a Christian. We know already that the "author" is a humorist and a dialectitian, and he is by no means undeveloped religiously, but here he uses all his powers for one purpose only—to show how difficult the answer to the question of becoming a Christian can be as soon as one really takes it seriously. And of course he assumes that Christianity intends itself to be taken seriously.

---

[1] *Korsar*, a satirical and humorous periodical published in Copenhagen, with which Kiergekaard engaged in a bitter literary duel starting in 1845.

His attitude of lightness toward himself and his purpose ("So there I sat and smoked my cigar . . .") gives him a vantage point from which to attack, with pathos and ridicule, what was being put forward as the serious intellectual's Christianity in his day— that high-flown aesthetic-philosophical-scientific mishmash which claimed to have incorporated and superseded "simple," "primitive" Christianity, thereby automatically making everybody into a Christian of some sort, and the professor into something even better. He himself does not claim to be a Christian, or even that he will become one in due course. But he makes it clear that if he does not become one, it will not be because he could not understand what it was and what it demanded; it will be because he understood it so well, seeing so clearly what it implied in the way of existing and becoming, that he decided it was too high, too difficult for him. In this way he would at least honor Christianity by taking it seriously, even if he did not become a Christian.

Although at the time he wrote this book Kierkegaard himself was already living in the religious categories, it is evident that Johannes Climacus represents an earlier stage in his own development— that of a highly reflective, dialectically and passionately endowed personality who felt it necessary, before he could accept Christianity, to state its case in the severest terms possible in order to know the worst it could mean, the most it could demand of him. Generally, when people deliberate about Christianity in this way, they quickly decide that of course the worst it could mean would be death, that surely the most it could demand of any man would be his physical life. A man then pictures himself in the role of a martyr, and while this gives him a thrill of horror it is not an altogether unpleasant picture. However, the probabilities being against such a melodramatic occurrence, he decides to accept Christianity on the grounds that the worst it could do to him is to make him a martyr, a fate which, if it had to happen, would not be such a bad thing, but which at the moment is comfortably improbable.

The trouble, Climacus complained, was that people had forgotten what it means to live. They had been hypnotized by the spirit of the times into a dreamy, speculative trance, in which one grandly surveys the pageant of world history; compared with this the living

out of a single life seemed hardly worth thinking about. In case it
was suggested that something might demand their life, they thought
of physical death. But Christianity demands of every man his life,
not always in order to burn it away at the stake, but always in
order to burn it in the crucible of the Holy Spirit so that what remains might become the life that is called everlasting. What it
means to live out a life in the context of those possibilities that are
actually live options when one is such a creature as man is (and is
destined to become) is described in the *Postscript* under the
categories of existence, the existential thinker, truth as subjectivity,
becoming subjective, and so on, in order to contrast this kind of
life as sharply as possible with the metaphysical daydreaming
(while playing the truant from life) that the spirit of speculation
encouraged. Men had forgotten what it means to live as the
individual *has* to live, and Kierkegaard was determined to remind
them of it in no uncertain terms.

2. The Objective Approach: Historical

First of all, however, it was necessary to remove the objective
"props" which supported the world-historical speculators in their
supposedly superior position above the plane of existence. In
Kant's day, the religious and philosophical problems had revolved
around the actual doctrinal conflict between science and religion,
between, that is, the dogmas of the Protestant orthodoxy and the
defiant pronouncements of an overconfident, dogmatically inclined,
youthful science. Kant hoped that he had cut the nerve of this
controversy by pointing out the limitations of the theoretical
reason and by reducing the knowable content of religion to the
moral law of practical reason, the categorical imperative. But then
a curious thing happened. Science, having been given a "dressing
down" by this critical philosophy, became perhaps a little less rau-
cous and boorish in its claims; nevertheless, it calmly set to work
and produced triumph after triumph in the so-called "merely"
phenomenal knowledge that had been assigned to it as its realm.
The faith that had been "made room for," however, somehow had
lost its specific Christian content during the controversy and had
become a mere empty possibility of faith, looking toward philosophy
for a new content. And philosophy, faced by this wistful demand

from faith, and unable to stand the tension of suspended judgment logically demanded by the Kantian agnosticism, let go of its grip on life and abandoned itself to an orgy of speculation. Kierkegaard's problem was therefore not to destroy knowledge in order to make room for faith, but to destroy the illusory support of "objective" speculation in order to get people back into the realm of existence, where, as he says, "God could educate them."

There are, Kierkegaard says, two ways of going at the problem of Christianity, the objective way and the subjective way. The first part of the *Postscript* sets forth and disposes of the objective way in some thirty-odd pages, while the rest of the book is concerned with the subjective way and runs to some five hundred pages, because as soon as the question of the subjective way is raised one runs into the whole concept of existence, and existence is not easily disposed of.

When anyone goes at the problem of the truth of Christianity objectively, he asks first of all: what is Christianity? and then: is Christianity true? In the first case he wants to know what Christianity claims to be about, what special doctrines it teaches, and in the second case he wants to be shown evidences for the truth of the doctrines in question. By dividing the objective question into two parts one avoids the confusion that would be caused by first of all stating what one believes to be true about Christianity, then saying that this is what Christianity teaches. Kierkegaard assumes that the *what* of Christianity can be stated without any reference to the truth of its claims, it being in the last analysis the *what* of the New Testament. This kind of objective analysis is nowadays sometimes called "kerygmatic" theology, which simply sets forth some paraphrase of the New Testament message, in contrast to "apologetic" theology, which raises the question of how the truth of this message is to be understood and defended against competing doctrines. In *Philosophical Fragments,* Kierkegaard had already done a little piece of kerygmatic theology, in as much as he had simply stated the *what* of Christianity in contrast to the *what* of Greek humanism in order to show how they differ, without raising the question of the truth of either. He could now refer the objective questioner to the *Fragments* for the *what* of Christianity and go at once to the second question, evidences for the truth of Christianity.

The truth in this objective sense may mean, first, the historical truth; second, the philosophical truth. Viewed as historical, the truth of Christianity must be determined through a critical examination of the various sources, and so forth; in short, in the same manner that historical truth generally is determined. When the question of the philosophical truth is raised, the object is to determine the relationship of the doctrine thus historically given and verified, to the eternal truth.[2]

The historical part of the objective evidence for the truth of Christianity concentrates itself on three subjects: (1) the holy Scriptures; (2) the authority of the Church; and (3) the proof of the centuries for the truth of Christianity.

(1) As far as historical and critical research touching upon the Scriptures is concerned, Kierkegaard makes it clear that he has not the slightest intention to disparage these intellectual labors or even to hint that they might be irreverent. All honor to scholarship and the painstaking work of rendering the Scriptures in what is probably the most correct form! If we show our respect for the ancient classics by taking care that we have left no stone unturned, no scroll undeciphered, to arrive at the most probably correct form, the least we can do is to show the same respect for the Holy Scriptures. Kierkegaard enters his protest as a dialectician only at the point where it is claimed that the results of this scholarly research are supposed to make a difference to the believer *as believer*. A believer is one who has made a decision involving his eternity, in response to that which the Holy Scriptures proclaim as historically true. And yet the historical evidence for this event, like the historical evidence for any event at any time in history, can never be more than a high probability, and a high probability is incommensurable with a decision about eternity. There is nothing wrong with historical research unless it should claim that by its method of approximation you can reach a decision on eternity, but this is at least in part what the nineteenth-century "higher criticism" of the Holy Scriptures was trying to do, at the same time hiding this motive behind a screen of objectivity. In comparing the biblical criticism with researches on any other ancient writing, Kierkegaard points out:

It constantly seems as if this labor of criticism were suddenly about to yield a result for faith, issue in something relevant to faith. Here lies

[2] *Concluding Unscientific Postscript,* p. 23.

the difficulty. When a philologist prepares an edition of one of Cicero's writings, for example, and performs his task with great acumen, the scholarly apparatus held in beautiful subservience to the control of the spirit; when his ingenuity and his familiarity with the period, gained through formidable industry, combine with his instinct for discovery to overcome obstacles, preparing a clear way for the meaning through the obscure maze of the readings, and so forth—then it is quite safe to yield oneself in whole-hearted admiration. For when he has finished, nothing follows except the wholly admirable result that an ancient writing has now through his skill and competence received its most accurate possible form. But by no means that I should now base my eternal happiness on this work; for in relation to my eternal happiness, his astonishing acumen seems, I must admit, inadequate. Aye, I confess that my admiration for him would be not glad but despondent, if I thought he had any such thing in mind. But this is precisely how the learned theologian goes to work; when he has completed his task (and until then he keeps us in suspense, but holds this prospect before us) he draws the conclusion: *ergo*, now you can base your eternal happiness on these writings.[3]

In order to show the dialectical difficulty due to the incommensurability of historical knowledge with a decision on eternity, Kierkegaard shows what happens when either the historical defenders or the historical attackers of the Bible prove their opposing cases as best as they can ever hope to do.

I assume, accordingly, that the critics have succeeded in proving about the Bible everything that any learned theologian in his happiest moment has ever wished to prove about the Bible. These books and no others belong to the canon; they are authentic; they are integral; their authors are trustworthy—one may well say, that it is as if every letter were inspired. More than this it is impossible to say, for inspiration is an object of faith and subject to a qualitative dialectic; it is incapable of being reached by a quantitative approximation. Furthermore, there is not a trace of contradiction in the sacred writings. . . .

Well then, everything being assumed in order with respect to the Scriptures—what follows? Has anyone who previously did not have faith been brought a single step nearer to its acquisition? No, not a single step. Faith does not result simply from a scientific inquiry; it does not come directly at all. On the contrary, in this objectivity one tends to lose that infinite personal interestedness in passion which is the condition of faith, the *ubique et nusquam* in which faith can come into being. Has anyone who previously had faith gained anything with respect to its strength and power? No, not in the least. Rather is

[3] *Postscript*, p. 27.

it the case that in this voluminous knowledge, this certainty that lurks at the door of faith and threatens to devour it, he is in so dangerous a situation that he will need to put forth much effort in great fear and trembling, lest he fall a victim to the temptation to confuse knowledge with faith. . . .

I assume now the opposite, that the opponents have succeeded in proving what they desire about the Scriptures, with a certainty transcending the most ardent wish of the most passionate hostility—what then? Have the opponents thereby abolished Christianity? By no means. Has the believer been harmed? By no means, not in the least. Has the opponent made good a right to be relieved of responsibility for not being a believer? By no means. Because these books are not written by these authors, are not authentic, are not in an integral condition, are not inspired (though this cannot be disproved, since it is an object of faith), it does not follow that these authors have not existed; and above all, it does not follow that Christ has not existed.[4]

As soon as we put the question in terms of these extremes it is easy to see that while the form of the Scriptures may be changed somewhat by historical research, nothing can be proved conclusively either one way or the other concerning the challenge to faith that they present. Both sides leave the situation in a residue of uncertainty, since both sides base their views on an approximation knowledge-process which is in principle endless. That there is this residue of uncertainty has, according to Kierkegaard, either the salutary effect of arousing the passion of the infinitely interested subject whose eternal blessedness is at stake, or the unsalutary effect of postponing the decision on the grounds that future research will reduce the amount of the uncertainty and thus force a conclusion.

The more an objective attitude dominates the questioner, the more he tends to postpone the decision on the grounds that the evidence is not yet conclusive, refusing to face the fact that the evidence never can be conclusive. The more the subjective attitude dominates the questioner, that is, the more he realizes that something infinitely precious is at stake here, on which a decision must be made, the more helpful is the residue of uncertainty in getting the questioner to make the decision of faith or unbelief, and to make it wholeheartedly, that is, with passion. The insidiousness of the objective attitude lies in the fact that it gives the questioner an

[4] *Postscript*, pp. 29, 30, 31, *passim*.

excuse for not facing the decision, for evading the issue by hiding behind historical probability, which will never be anything other than historical probability even though thousands of years should pass. The objective evidence for the truth of Christianity from the Scriptures is therefore simply inconclusive, and it appears to become more and more inconclusive as the objective attitude of the questioner prevents him from coming to a decision and as he uses the residue of uncertainty as an excuse for postponement, instead of seizing upon the residue of uncertainty as an aid toward clarifying what is here at stake and what is demanded of him.

(2) The second source of the historical evidence for the truth of Christianity is supposed to be the Church itself, that is, the very fact that there is now a Christian Church in existence where there was none before Christ and that this existing Church's living word and sacraments testify to the truth of Christianity. "Just as [above] it was the Bible which was to decide objectively what is Christianity and what is not, so now it is the Church that is to serve as the certain objective recourse. More specifically, it is the living word in the Church, the confession of faith, and the word in connection with the sacraments." [5] This, Kierkegaard points out, is even a Danish idea, attributable to his illustrious contemporary, Pastor Grundtvig.[6] "Grundtvig had rightly perceived that the Bible could not hold out against the encroaching doubt; but he had not perceived that the reason was that both attack and defense were involved in an approximation-process which in its everlastingly continued striving is dialectically incommensurable with an infinite decision, such as that on which an eternal happiness is based." [7] In the case of the Church it seems as though the historical difficulty (probability) has been obviated at least in so far as existence is concerned, for here is the church right in front of our eyes, and we surely do not have to prove that it exists. "So then the Church exists; and from the Church as something present, as contemporaneous with the inquirer . . . , one may learn what is essential to Christianity; for this is what the Church professes." [8]

[5] *Postscript*, p. 37.
[6] N. F. S. Grundtvig (1783-1872), Denmark's well-known religious patriot, poet, and founder of the Folk High-Schools.
[7] *Postscript*, p. 37.
[8] *Postscript*, p. 39.

Unfortunately, it turns out to be not quite so easy as that.

After it has been asserted of the Church that it exists, and that one may learn from the Church what Christianity is, it is further asserted of this Church, the present Church, that it is the Apostolic Church, the same Church which has persisted for eighteen centuries. The predicate: Christian, is thus more than a present predicate. When predicated of the present it implies a past, and thus involves a historicity in quite the same sense as the Bible. The only historical factuality which is superior to proof is contemporaneous existence; every determination of pastness requires proof. . . .

The moment we make use of the living word to urge the continued existence of the Church through past centuries, the issue is brought back to precisely the same point where it was in the Bible theory. . . . But let the Church theory endure attack as the Bible theory has had to endure it; let the whole swarm of possible objections arise to seek its life: what then? Then we shall here again consistently find that an introductory discipline becomes necessary; for every other procedure would nullify the Church theory itself, and transfer the problem to the realm of the subjective where it properly belongs, though the objective Grundtvig does not think so. This discipline would have the task of proving the primitive character of the confession of faith, its identity of meaning everywhere and in every moment through eighteen centuries (where criticism will stumble on difficulties that the Bible theory never knew); and so again there will be a nosing about in ancient documents.[9]

Thus the Church theory, in spite of the fact that the Church exists before our very eyes, is no more conclusive than the Bible theory, for in this way "the approximation-process again begins; the parenthesis is launched, and no one can say when it will end; for it is and always remains only an approximation, and this has the remarkable property of being able to continue indefinitely." [10]

(3) Finally, there must be considered from the historical-objective standpoint the proof of the centuries, both the fact that Christianity has lasted so long and the results that it has wrought in history. This argument, Kierkegaard says, "cannot really be treated in a strictly dialectical manner at all, for at the very outset it transforms itself into an hypothesis. And an hypothesis may become more probable by maintaining itself against objections for three thousand years, but it does not on that account become an

[9] *Postscript,* pp. 39-40, *passim.*
[10] *Postscript,* p. 41.

So much, then, for the objective evidences from history for the truth of Christianity. As arguments for Christianity they constitute just so much approximation-knowledge, plus a rhetorical expounding of the "results" after the manner of a sales talk which dwells on the testimony of the many satisfied users of the product. As arguments against Christianity, they still constitute just so much approximation-knowledge, plus a rhetorical attack on the results which succeeds only in proving that the results might have been different had certain men been better Christians, not in disproving the truth of Christianity objectively. This inability of the objective historical evidence to help a man decide on the truth of Christianity is, however, quite salutary, for it helps the man see that the decision must be based on something entirely different.

3. The Objective Approach: Philosophical

There remains the question of whether or not Christianity can be shown speculatively to be the eternal truth. Here Kierkegaard introduces the supposition that is to become the presupposition of all the rest of the *Postscript*. The problem is to contemplate Christianity philosophically in order to discover whether it can be shown to be the eternal truth, and to do this the speculating philosopher must get himself into such an objective frame of mind that Christianity itself must be a matter of indifference to him. Only the truth of its speculative content must interest him—whether or not anyone is a Christian and whether or not he himself is a Christian must not matter to him, because such subjectivity is not supposed to enter into the argument, in order to ensure that the argument is an argument and not an exhortation. But now suppose, says Kierkegaard, just suppose for the moment that Christianity is such an affair, such a phenomenon, that anyone who is really indifferent to it cannot understand it and that his very indifference to it assures his misunderstanding of it.

The philosopher contemplates Christianity for the sake of interpenetrating it with his speculative thought. . . . But suppose this whole proceeding were a chimera, a sheer impossibility; suppose that Christianity is subjectivity, an inner transformation, an actualization of inwardness, and that only two kinds of people can know anything about it: those who with an infinite passionate interest in an eternal happiness base this their happiness upon their believing relationship to

Christianity, and those who with an opposite passion, but in passion, reject it—the happy and the unhappy lovers. Suppose that an objective indifference can therefore learn nothing at all.[13]

This supposition is not an excuse which would beg to exempt Christianity from any objective treatment at all, in so far as such treatment is possible and necessary. Rather it points to certain conditions in the very nature of the situation which even the most objective observer ought to take into account. There happens to be an analogy to this situation in the natural sciences. Suppose a physiologist wishes to examine the characteristics of living tissues. He arranges his experiment as carefully as possible to preserve these characteristics, and yet he cannot help but observe that there are certain instances where the very instruments which he must use to probe the tissues disturb the characteristics he is trying to study, and to such an extent that they are no longer the characteristics of living tissues but only those of tissues under the artificial conditions of his experiment. If he is a good scientist, he will recognize that here is a situation in which the conditions of experiment impose a limitation upon the knowledge, and he will simply suspend judgment on the results, not attributing them to tissues in their normal state. In the case of Christianity, even an objective person ought to recognize that the way to get "inside" Christianity to the truth of it is to become a Christian, even if he should reject it after giving it a try. But to presume to find out what it is on the inside by prodding and testing it from the outside will merely result in a deception. The philosophical approach comes to grief therefore over the objectivity of the speculator, who cannot be inside and outside at the same time, since he cannot be infinitely, passionately interested and completely disinterested at the same time.

In this manner, Kierkegaard disposes of both the historical-evidence approach and the speculative-philosophical approach to Christianity, quickly and lightly, as if the whole matter were so obvious that it is hardly worth spending another moment's thought on. But perhaps he is too fast for us. Let us take time to notice a few points before we pass on to Book Two of the *Postscript,* the part devoted to the subjective approach to Christianity.

First it should be noted that his rejection of historical evidence

<hr>

[13] *Postscript*, p. 51.

does not appeal to despair of knowledge beyond phenomena, that is, to the Kantian agnosticism. Historical knowledge is unsatisfactory not because it is not real, but because it is not complete. In fact, the hope of its increase is the motive that logically puts off decision. The increase is an increase in real knowledge, but this knowledge, by the very fact that it is never finished, shows that it is incapable of forcing a decision upon the ultimate. At what point in history would it be possible to say, *"Now* the evidence is conclusive, but yesterday it was not"? Nevertheless, historical knowledge is real knowledge, and the ambiguities and uncertainties in it are due to such factors as the inaccessibility of data, the multiplicity of variables, and the element of human freedom, rather than to some inherent defect of reason. Kierkegaard is not at all trying to destroy knowledge to make room for faith, but rather he is trying to clear the way for the subjective approach to the truth of Christianity by removing the objective "props" which the believer misuses by imagining that they give his faith some sort of unshakable, external support, and the unbeliever misuses by imagining that they give him an excuse for putting off the decision of faith.

We know that Kierkegaard was not interested in epistemology in the way Kant for example was, making it the cornerstone of his entire philosophical system. Kierkegaard was interested in the individual and in getting the individual to go through his development toward personhood without missing anything—and, above all, without being sidetracked by the dazzle and fascination of the many-faceted objective world, including the whole history of the human race, that was held shimmering before his eyes in the form of the many new kinds of knowledge. He talks about the individual getting "lost in the huge parenthesis," that is, never getting to the end of the sentence to find out what it had started out to say, never getting to the meaning of the whole thing. So the very manner in which he situates the individual in existence has epistemological overtones. It is a question here of the relation of parts to a whole. One would think that a summation of the parts, of the millions of details supplied by the approximation process, would yield a resounding conclusion about the whole—but no, such a summation, even in so far as it is possible for the limited human mind to make it, yields a huge question mark. What is missing is a knowledge of the individual relation of each of the parts to the whole, yet surely only Omniscience could claim to have that.

But what about the individual human being, considered as a part in relation to the whole, can't he, without claiming omniscience, attain to some knowledge of how he himself, this particular individual, is and ought to be related to the whole? Suppose this kind of knowledge were possible for the individual, how could he afford to neglect it? And indeed what good would all his objective knowledge be, if he were to miss this entirely, if he were to fail entirely to perceive his own individual connection with the whole? But let us listen to the more personal terms in which the youthful Kierkegaard raised this question for himself:

The thing is to understand myself, to see what God really wishes *me* to do; the thing is to find a truth which is true *for me*, to find *the idea for which I can live and die*. What would be the use of discovering so-called objective truth, of working through all the systems of philosophy and of being able, if required, to review them all and show up the inconsistencies within each system;— what good would it do me to be able to develop a theory of the state and combine all the details into a single whole, and so construct a world in which I did not live, but only held up to the view of others;—what good would it do me to be able to explain the meaning of Christianity if it had *no* deeper significance *for me and for my life*;—what good would it do me if truth stood before me, cold and naked, not caring whether I recognised her or not, and producing in me a shudder of fear rather than a trusting devotion? I certainly do not deny that I still recognise an *imperative of understanding* and that through it one can work upon men, *but it must be taken up into my life*, and *that is* what I now recognise as the most important thing. That is what my soul longs after, as the African desert thirsts for water.[14]

He also speaks of the connection with the whole as "the precious stone," the "anchorage," the "something which grows together with the deepest roots of my life, through which I am, so to speak, grafted upon the divine . . .,"[15] and it is just this that the individual might miss entirely if he continued to lean on the crutches of the objective evidences. That is why Kierkegaard demonstrates in the first book of the *Postscript* that the objective supports are indeed makeshift and unreliable, and that the individual who leans on

[14] *Journals*, No. 22, p. 15.
[15] *Journals*, No. 22, pp. 16, 17, *passim*.

them just puts himself at the mercy of the shifting winds of doctrine
or at the mercy of any skeptic who is determined to kick them out
from under him. Whereas if the individual will only turn away from
the objective to the subjective approach and strive to lay hold of
that precious stone, that anchorage, that something by which he
is grafted upon the divine, then he will need no crutches, and he
will have something to hold fast to, "even though the whole world
fell apart."[16]

4. Subjectivity as Opposed to Subjectivism

Having disposed of, as misleading, the objective approach to the
truth of Christianity, Kierkegaard turns next to his exposition of
the doctrine that in ethico-religious matters subjectivity is the
truth. It is in this exposition that his Hegelian terminology is likely
to be most grating on modern ears, which have come to prefer a
more psychological, or at least a more concrete, everyday terminology in discussing these matters. But I must simply beg the reader's
patience here. The doctrine can be stated in many different ways,
and it must first be defined negatively against an idea too close to
it to be ignored, *subjectivism*. All kinds of apparently endless misunderstanding of Kierkegaard would be avoided if the phrase
"subjectivity is the truth" were never allowed to appear without its
guardian and modifier, "in ethico-religious matters." Kierkegaard
never claimed anything so stupid as, for instance, that in physical,
astronomical, or mathematical matters, subjectivity is the truth.
Subjectivity does not mean, as the term *subjectivism* usually does,
arbitrariness of judgment about matters that can properly be decided objectively, such as if someone should maintain against all
evidence that the world is flat. And subjectivity, as Kierkegaard
uses it, also does not mean the special preference for one's own
likes and dislikes which seeks to remove them from all possible
criticism by others, as in the defense of the arbitrariness of
"taste" in manners and morals. This is where Kierkegaard's treatment differs so signally from much of modern discussion of "theory
of value," which so often mires down in—or simply goes in circles
around—the problem of *subjectivism,* or the arbitrariness of values.
The whole effect of Kierkegaard's development of the idea of sub-

[16] *Journals*, No. 22, p. 16.

jectivity is to remove more and more of the element of arbitrariness from it.

The subjectivity that is the "truth" can perhaps be described in modern terms as the quality or condition of being in the process of becoming a person, or as the selfhood of man in its concrete and real, not its abstracted or idealized, aspect. Subjectivity is thus the being-a-subject, that is, being the originator and receiver, the actor and sufferer, of happenings—being, as he calls it, an existing individual. Kierkegaard broke through the pretensions of academic philosophy in both its idealistic and its empiricist forms, not by playing these two off against each other, but by demanding that attention be focused once more upon the person for whose benefit it was claimed that both of these kinds of knowledge were being sought. He assumed that there was no great disparity or irreconcilable conflict between the two schools. Both were concerned with truth as the conformity of thought with being, although they approached it from opposite sides. From the empirical side, truth was defined as the conformity of thought to being, whereby truth became a *desideratum,* an endless approximation process that logically could not become conclusive, since it had the peculiar property of being in principle unfinished. From the idealistic side, the conformity of *being to thought* was asserted a priori, thereby reducing truth to a tautology, since the "being" thus envisaged was not concrete existence at all, but it was "being" already abstracted by thought; thus the assertion was reduced to the statement that abstract thought (being) is abstract thought.

What both of these approaches to the conformity of thought and being failed to ask, what they most blissfully and irresponsibly ignored, was the question: what kind of a person, what kind of subject or knower, would it have to be, for whom this admittedly desirable conformity of thought and being could become an actuality, that is, real knowledge? Well, in the case of idealism it would have to be the abstract subject-object identity, the fantastic "I-am-I" which was the presupposition of the whole idealistic enterprise, while in the case of the empirical approach it would have to be some imaginary eternal being who could afford to wait until the end of time for the approximation process to be finished —for the last, clinching argument or conclusive bit of evidence to be turned in at the end of history—before he could be said to have the truth; in other words, he would have to be a quite godlike being. No doubt the conformity of thought and being, no matter how achieved, *would* be the eternal truth if and when achieved, but Kierkegaard questioned the responsibility of the whole undertaking if it simply ignored the fact that man was not that kind of a "critter"—he was not a god, and he was not the I-am-I.

How can it help to explain to a man how the eternal truth is to be understood eternally, when the supposed user of the explanation is prevented from so understanding it through being an existing individual, and merely becomes fantastic when he imagines himself to be *sub specie aeterni*? What such a man needs instead is precisely an explanation of how the eternal truth is to be understood in determinations of time by one who as existing is himself in time. . . .[17]

The next question to ask, if we really wish to take the poor existing individual seriously, and if we do not wish to poke fun at him by dangling before him an unattainable goal as the carrot is dangled before the donkey, is this: how then is it possible for such a creature as man really is to be related to the truth? Is it possible at all? On the other hand, who can say that it is impossible? Or, what is the best that man can hope for here, what is the highest possibility?

Kierkegaard saw that these questions and the predicament they delineate could never be answered by logic or dialectics alone, but only with the aid of an insight into the *pathos,* the emotional dimension, of the situation. Once the subject saw the nature of his predicament, everything depended on the attitude he was inclined to take toward the fact of finding himself in such a predicament, whether it be the attitude of protest, of denial, of outrage, of rebellion, of defiance, of desperation, of struggle, of acceptance, of defeat, resignation, or of anything else. The attitude that Kierkegaard seems to recommend in this book is *acceptance* of the predicament in full knowledge of its difficulties, but with the passion of the infinite, to keep the individual rightly oriented in his predicament. Acceptance of the predicament is the same as "remembering what it means to be a man," but the passion of the infinite is needed to supply the driving force for the struggle, under such forbidding conditions.

[17] *Postscript,* p. 172.

For the difficulty lies precisely in the fact that the individual cannot free himself from the concern for the truth so long as there is even a suspicion that some kind of truth is available to him. If he could convince himself that *no truth,* absolutely none, is available to him, if he could become wholeheartedly agnostic, he could also become lightheartedly irresponsible about the whole matter and dismiss the question as one of no concern to him.

Kierkegaard's recommended attitude, combining acceptance of the predicament with the passion for the infinite, sets him apart from the aesthetic romanticism we have already discussed, as well as from some of the existentialisms of the twentieth century. Romanticism stood for defiance, and recommended arbitrary, emotional, antirational self-assertion as the only possible *noble* response for the glorious human spirit trapped in such a predicament. And as we know, some modern existentialisms, such as that of Sartre, stand for despair, or the desperate assertion of despair. They recommend the arbitrary invention of purposes by man's freedom for man's freedom, the act of *invention* constituting simultaneously the assertion of the freedom and the denial of the validity of approximation knowledge. Both the romantic and the existential attitudes constitute a regression to agnosticism, and therefore they remove the *pathos* of the individual's situation in existence, a pathos generated just by the fact that as long as there is the possibility of *some* knowledge there is also the possibility of some way of being related to the truth that the individual might miss. In order to avoid deliberately both of these attitudes, or rather, to avoid all attitudes secretly based on radical agnosticism (and also all shoulder-shrugging, "I give up" attitudes), the individual must have in him the passion for the infinite, an infinite concern to be somehow related to the truth.

5. *"Essential" Knowledge and "Accidental" Knowledge*

Accordingly, it must be emphasized over and over again that Kierkegaard's doctrine that subjectivity is the truth is not based on agnosticism with respect to objective knowledge. It is based on affirmation of the approximation knowledge as far as this goes, but also on recognition of the dialectical-pathetic difficulty that the approximation process creates for man, who is himself in a process of becoming and needs a norm to guide him, but who cannot pretend that he occupies the position of eternity. For such a creature as man is, subjectivity, personhood, is the truth, because subjectivity is the *locus,* the interior arena, where he can realize ethico-religious truth by performing it.

At this point it is necessary to call attention to the distinction Kierkegaard makes between ethico-religious truth (all positive values, norms, philosophical and cultural ideals, moral codes, the teachings and requirements of various religions, etc.) and all other kinds of truth (science, logic, technology, etc.). Both of these kinds of knowledge are incomplete and are approximations or attempts to approach an ideal, but only the former are concerned with the subjectivity of man, with what kind of a person he shall become. This distinction corresponds roughly with the distinction drawn in college curricula between "the humanities" and "the sciences." Kierkegaard calls the former "essential knowledge" and the latter "accidental knowledge," but be it noted that he calls both of them knowledge. The former is "essential" because "only ethical and ethico-religious knowledge has an essential relationship to the existence of the knower."[18] The latter is "accidental" because the amount and scope of it is essentially indifferent to the existence of the knower, to what he as a person shall become. For example, a simple, unlettered man may become a saint, although a saint need by no means be a simple, unlettered man; the relationship of the amount and scope of "accidental" knowledge to the sainthood is in both cases accidental. But all "essential" knowledge is essentially concerned with what a person ought to be or ought not to be; if not, then the person has essentially misunderstood it.

Now in the face of the approximation-process of "accidental" knowledge the subjectivity of man is helpless, unable to wait for its completion or to anticipate it by some godlike contemplation from outside of existence. But in the face of "essential" knowledge, even though it too be partial or fragmentary, his subjectivity is challenged to a realization. Here is a kind of knowledge the very essence of which is that it demands to be done, and so it is a truth to which one can be related by doing it. The individual can

---

[18] *Postscript*, p. 177.

be "in" the truth by incorporating the truth "in" himself, by himself becoming that which the truth asserts. This too is a kind of approximation-process, but an inward approximation-, or rather, an appropriation-process. It is a value-learning, value-testing process in which the individual goes through "stages," learning the higher possibilities by working through and then transcending the lower ones. And if the individual has in him the passion of the infinite, this process, this "pilgrimage through existence," can end, or find its goal, only with the attainment of the Christian God-relationship, according to Kierkegaard.

A reflective person cannot help but notice that a very curious relationship obtains between the appropriation-process, the selfhood of the one who is appropriating, and the conditions of existence. To exist at all is to be forced to act, and to act is always, upon reflection, to act, or to *have* acted, "as if" a certain value were true. Thus a murderer, whatever his motive for the act, has acted "as if" life were not a very precious thing. And he has also, in the act, irrevocably become what he has done, namely, a murderer. All this is equally true for all of the individual's acts, the thousands of less spectacular acts of everyday life that constitute his existing. And furthermore, it is even true of inward acts, such as decisions and resolutions and feelings and attitudes, even where no outward actions are immediately recognizable. These inward acts are also "done" inescapably "as if" such and such values were the highest, and they also irrevocably make the person what he has inwardly "done." So, since the very fact of existing involves this acting and deciding, both of which determine not only what the individual does but whom he thereby becomes, the real crux of the matter lies in his becoming *conscious and deliberate* about the inescapably ethico-religious quality or coloration of his existential becoming. In this way, by becoming conscious and deliberate about his becoming, he not only begins to determine the self that he becomes, but he consciously becomes more and more a *person*, a self-related subject. The dimension or intensity of selfhood increases with the degree of deliberateness and resolution with which one becomes. Whoever refuses to face the fact of his becoming becomes something anyway, but he forfeits something in that kind of becoming, for he loses what he might

have gained along with the becoming, namely, the increased stature
of selfhood.

Kierkegaard assumes that as soon as anyone realizes these characteristics of selfhood in existence, he will, out of *self-respect,*
choose the highest he knows in the ethico-religious realm to be
the goal of his appropriation. This of course is the ideal case, and
many will not choose the highest for reasons of weakness and
indolence and absence of that passion for the infinite which supplies the driving force. But, even in the ideal case, his choosing
the highest-he-knows by no means removes the element of risk
which is part of the pathos of existence and which is the price of
having any relationship to the truth at all. For suppose . . . and here
we could imagine no end of ways in which an individual might
easily choose something far less than the highest, both by accidents
of birth and history and by accidents of temperament and capacity.
All granted. But the important thing for the existing individual
to realize is that for him there can be no such thing as objective
certainty about *any* of the ideas that present themselves to him
as ethico-religious possibilities, and that there is a limit to the
time he can spend examining and comparing them objectively
(for example, in a critical study of systems of philosophy, ethics,
and religion) because all the time he is doing this, the time for
appropriating them subjectively, which is here of the essence, is
running out. Sooner or later he must venture himself in appropriating one of them, and better sooner, "for," as Kierkegaard
says, "if I have ventured amiss—very well, then life helps me by
its punishment. But if I have not ventured at all—who then helps
me?"[19] It is life itself through which God "educates" the appropriating individual, for life by its "punishment" helps him to get
from the treacherous to the trustworthy, from the fleeting to the
abiding, from the "lower" to the "higher" values.

6. Appropriation of the "Paradoxical"

Kierkegaard now joins the issue with Christianity by restating
the doctrine that subjectivity is the truth in such a way that it is
at the same time a definition of faith. *"An objective uncertainty*

---

[19] *The Sickness unto Death,* tran. W. Lowrie (Princeton, N. J.: Princeton
University Press, 1941), p. 52.

held fast in an appropriation-process of the most passionate inward-ness is the truth, the highest truth attainable for an *existing* individual."[20] This definition expresses the antithesis to the objective approach, so as to be a constant reminder of the fork in the road "where the way swings off," where the individual has realized that the objective approach is not getting him anywhere and that it is time to start in on appropriation. Corresponding to the certainty which is the goal of the objective knowledge, on this new way there is only what has to be acknowledged as an objective uncertainty, no more. Corresponding to the approximation-process that can end only with the end of history, there is the appropriation-process that can end only with the individual's life. And, corresponding to the objective indifference of the contemplative attitude, there is the "holding fast" in the "most passionate inwardness." As for the fork in the road:

At the point where the way swings off (and where this is cannot be specified objectively, since it is a matter of subjectivity), there objective knowledge is placed in abeyance. Thus the subject merely has, objectively, the uncertainty; but it is this which precisely increases the tension of that infinite passion which constitutes his inwardness. The truth is precisely the venture which chooses an objective uncertainty with the passion of the infinite. I contemplate the order of nature in the hope of finding God, and I see omnipotence and wisdom; but I also see much else that disturbs my mind and excites anxiety. The sum of all this is an objective uncertainty. But it is for this very reason that the inwardness becomes as intense as it is, for it embraces this objective uncertainty with the entire passion of the infinite. In the case of a mathematical proposition the objectivity is given, but for this reason the truth of such a proposition is also an indifferent truth.

But the above definition of truth is an equivalent expression for faith. Without risk there is no faith. Faith is precisely the contradiction between the infinite passion of the individual's inwardness and the objective uncertainty. If I am capable of grasping God objectively, I do not believe, but precisely because I cannot do this I must believe.[21]

This definition of faith marks as yet only the general religious relationship to the eternal, rather than the specifically Christian. "In the principle that subjectivity, inwardness, is the truth, there is comprehended the Socratic wisdom, whose everlasting merit

[20] *Postscript*, p. 182.
[21] *Postscript*, p. 182.

it was to have become aware of the essential significance of existence, of the fact that the knower is an existing individual. For this
reason Socrates was in the truth by virtue of his ignorance, in the
highest sense in which this was possible within paganism."[22] The
fact that existence forces the existing concrete person to embrace,
with a wholeheartedness befitting only eternal, unchanging truth,
something which nevertheless remains for him objectively uncertain
—this is a characteristic of all religious conversion, not just the
Christian, and it renders this eternal and essential truth paradoxical
for man. But not for God. "But the eternal essential truth is by
no means in itself a paradox; but it becomes paradoxical by virtue
of its relationship to an existing individual."[23]

Since the term "paradoxical" arouses the accusations of irration-
alism from time to time hurled at Kierkegaard, we must try to see
exactly how he is using the term in this connection. He is describing
the general religious situation of man everywhere, even in paganism,
even in the Oriental and other non-Christian religious traditions.
And surely one has only to cast a not too jaded eye upon the historical manifestation of man's religious situation in all ages to
observe that "paradoxical" is hardly too strong a word to apply to
it. All religions demand some act of conversion or devotion, a
fact that is appropriately expressed when we say, for example, that
so-and-so "embraced" Islam. Impartiality to the gods, or, in
modern times, impartiality to the several religious traditions, even
on the reasonable grounds that all of them probably reflect some
aspect of the divine truth, simply means that the impartial individual
has not yet become religious in the strict sense of the term, that he
has not yet begun to appropriate. Existence itself is so stubborn
and intractable on this point that it does not allow man the privilege
of religious impartiality, for, as we have seen, whenever he acts, he
acts "as if" one or another of the several basic religious orientations
were true, even if he has never heard of it as a religion, or even if he
refuses to admit the ethico-religious implications of his acts. It is
just this stubbornness of existence, combined with man's increasing
rationality and self-consciousness about his acts and their implications, and his desire to bring about an increasing consistency

[22] *Postscript*, p. 183.
[23] *Postscript*, p. 183.

between his acts and his beliefs that actually makes him aware of the paradoxical character of his religious situation, and of the paradoxical character of his existence as an individual.

Then, as if this realization or awareness weren't trouble enough for the poor existing individual, along comes Christianity and *intensifies* the paradoxical character of existence by proclaiming a revelation of the eternal truth which increases the tension on both sides of the paradox. On the objective side it increases the tension by proclaiming something that is not merely an objective *uncertainty* (such as, let us say, the Hindu doctrine of the Wheel of Kharma) but an objective *unlikelihood*, namely, that the eternal Godhead appeared in history in the likeness of a man. And on the subjective side, it increases the tension by proclaiming that the "appropriation-process" is doomed, that it is headed toward frustration because the subject is a sinner and cannot save himself by his own hand. He needs the help of Christ even to "appropriate" in the right way.

Thus the tenor of the polemic which the *Postscript* directs against speculative philosophy seems to be as follows: if it is ridiculous, in view of the existing individual's paradoxical situation with regard to the religious truth, to try to reduce the content of the general religiousness of mankind to a few moments or steps in the march of Absolute Reason through history, then it is piling misunderstanding upon misunderstanding to apply this explanation to Christianity, claiming subsequently to have "gone farther" (on this march), since all that Christianity does is to accentuate to the highest possible degree the already paradoxical character of the would-be knower's predicament. Christianity did not come into the world in order to receive an explanation from the obliging philosopher, but in order to transform men. And, as if to warn men away from the idleness and futility of speculation, it straightway tells them that in this matter of having a relationship to the truth their situation is much more paradoxical than they had ever imagined or suspected, before they had heard of Christianity.

Now it must of course be admitted that Kierkegaard's polemic against speculative philosophy has lost some of its force today, for not many, today, are engaged in reducing Christianity to a paragraph in an all-embracing system of thought. To be sure, there are still "dons" and "professors," but these have rather tended to become pathetic figures in our time—as pretentious figures worthy of Kierkegaard's attacks, they have been more or less replaced by the "engineers," the "technical experts," and the "executives." We have to look back with some wonder and nostalgia at the nineteenth century, especially at the fact that it could still afford to be condescending toward Christianity, in its broad-minded attempts to save religion for the intellectual. To the present century Christianity recommends itself, if at all, by the fact that it is the least idealistic of all religions, and by the fact that the hope it offers is promised only on the basis of man's facing and accepting a most unflattering appraisal of himself and his situation, proclaimed since Old Testament times. But by the same token, and to the degree that the present century has given up the attempt to transcribe Christianity into the terms of rationalistic idealism, the word "paradox" has lost some of its offensive sting. Modern man has become so puzzled about himself and fearful for the future that he tends to accept this word as merely one of several negative descriptive terms equally applicable to his disasterous condition, rather than as the insult to reason it was intended to be. His reason has been far too humbled and confounded by historical events to be in a position to take affront. He is not surprised to find both his condition and the Christian cure described in paradoxical terms—he rather revels (sometimes almost gleefully) in this fact. It is almost as if he were looking for exoneration in the piling of paradox upon paradox—after all, if existence has played such a dirty trick on him, how is he to blame?

By this attitude the modern man simply betrays the fact that he is still in what Kierkegaard calls the "aesthetic stage," still unwilling to be responsible, still trying to put the blame for his condition on "something out there," still unaware of what it means to be an individual, a single person, still playing around with theories and possibilities, without himself *becoming* anything. For it is one thing to understand in theory both the disease and the cure, and quite another matter actually to undergo the cure. For example, it is one thing to acknowledge that in ethico-religious matters subjectivity is the highest truth available to man, and another thing to live out one's life on this basis.

"The same thing happens to Christianity, or to becoming a Christian, as to all radical cures, one puts it off as long as possible."[24] No, Christianity is "put off" not because it is paradoxical but because it is difficult, because of the deep change it has to work in the very nature of the person. Kierkegaard loved the medical analogy so much because among other things it allowed for the fact that the cure takes *time,* takes, in fact, the lifetime of the person. For it is the very life of the whole man, in the sickness of his fallen human nature and in the particularity of his individual nature, that is the subject matter of the cure. With such notoriously recalcitrant material to start with, Kierkegaard never tired of warning against haste and impatience in this department, against the "quick cures" whose illusory efficacy succeeded only in bringing Christianity into disrepute. He was, in the words of the modern Christian martyr, Dietrich Bonhoeffer, in favor of "costly grace" as against "cheap grace," constantly berating the Danish Church for selling Christianity at too low a price. What is usually called his doctrine of the "three stages," to which we turn in the next chapter, may from one standpoint be understood as his attempt to show how deep the cure had to go before it was effective, how radical were the changes in character-structure of the whole man that it required, and how futile it was for anyone to want the final results without being willing to go through the preliminary stages.

[24] *Journals,* No. 27, p. 21.

VII

The Pilgrimage Through Existence

Part One: The Setting Out

1. Stages, Spheres, or Patterns of Life

If reality cannot be conceived, cannot be exhausted in ideas, if its richness and variability, its many-sidedness and hiddenness, constantly put even our best ideas about it to shame, how could the case be otherwise with the individual? How can the individual be conceived? The individual—that living, thinking, changing, acting entity, who is part of reality himself and yet stands over against it as one facing a challenge, who is a part in relation to the whole and yet in some sense always has the whole within him, if only as an urge toward wholeness. All attempts to conceive the individual must fall short of the reality—and yet the attempt must be made, because man must find some way of talking about himself if he is to gain self-understanding (even in the most partial sense) as opposed to complete self-bafflement, inarticulateness, opaqueness.

Kierkegaard's theory of the three stages should be thought of as his attempt to conceive the individual—admittedly in a schematic and therefore nonexhaustive way—in the individual's aspect of *becoming*, as an entity that actually changes qualitatively in time, while in another sense remaining itself, remaining that particular individual whose name and parentage we know. It should not be thought of as a philosophy of religion. For one thing, it does not necessarily lead to religion, and in fact, it provides as good an explanation of why some people never get to religion as of why they do. Then Kierkegaard never allowed it the pretensions of a philosophy of anything; he did not intend it to be objective, logically self-consistent, comprehensive, or exhaustive of the subject. His theory is no more than a scheme for describing what one would be tempted to call (if it were not for the deterministic biological connotations the word now has) the *evolution* of selfhood in the individual. In fact, I do not see why we should not appropriate this word, keeping in mind, however, that nothing biological, like inevitable growth or physically determined change, is at all meant by it.

There are many different ways of describing Kierkegaard's doctrine of the three stages. This is partly because he himself used two metaphors in talking about them—both "stages" and "spheres" or "spheres of existence"—and the several meanings of these metaphors play upon or interpenetrate one another. Thus the metaphor of "stages" tends to emphasize temporal development, as periods of life with certain characteristics that the individual goes through. Every mother nowadays is familiar with this idea, being informed by the child physchologists about the "stage" her child is in currently, or may soon be expected to enter. On the other hand, the metaphor of "spheres" or "levels" of existence pictures a kind of quasi-solid medium arranged horizontally in layers, so that one can speak about superficial levels or deep levels, with all sorts of ontological overtones such as are implied in phrases like "the mere surface of life" as opposed to "the depths of being." And in still another way, in the terminology of values, both the stages and spheres can be thought of as constituting a pyramid or hierarchy, with the individual climbing his way upward from the "lower" to the "upper" levels in a kind of spiritual ascent. It is no accident that the pseudonym Kierkegaard created for the *Postscript* to discuss the more abstract formulation of these ideas was called Johannes Climacus. At this point I suggest the reader take a look at the schema of the stages (the frontispiece of this book), which I offer with all diffidence as at least one way of picturing Kierkegaard's theory. In this diagram I try to represent some of the metaphorical connotations of both "stages" and "spheres of existence."

But before he ever got around to discussing the stages as such, Kierkegaard had first of all created, poetically and dramatically, concrete individuals actually existing in the different stages, so that the reader might know, by means of that vicarious participation which is the goal as well as the triumph of the literary art, what it really feels like to be an existing individual in each particular stage. Those persons are not labeled—just as in the theater the actors do not come out labeled "hero" or "villain," but we are to learn in the course of the drama, by means of the feelings, motivations, and acts they play out, who they really are. Nor are they stock figures whom we can spot at once from long experience in theater-going. They are concrete individuals all bearing a slight, if sometimes poeticized and sometimes farfetched, resemblance to Kierkegaard himself, for he wrote best about the man he knew best. It is as if he had asked himself: what sort of a person might I become if I persisted or remained in this or that stage? and then had answered his question with: someone like "A," or someone like the seducer in *Either/or,* or like Judge William, or like any one of the participants in the symposium in *Stages on Life's Way,* or like the diarist of "Guilty/Not Guilty?" or perhaps like Frater Taciturnus, or like the "young man" in *Repetition,* or perhaps rather like the psychologist-author Constantine Constantius. So one could go on. The reader, of course, cannot be seriously interested in these imaginative explorations of what Kierkegaard might have become —seriously, he can be interested only in what he himself might have been and still may become. Nevertheless, these imaginary persons help him to see, to feel, to concretize the characteristic predicament of each stage. I would not care to obviate Kierkegaard's purpose by attempting any summary of these writings—for to get the intended effect one must read them for himself. Here it will be possible only to attempt a generalized description of the stages, as they pertain to the idea of the individual struggling through existence.

Each of the stages can also be described, more empirically, as a style or pattern of life organized around some one highest value or principle which thereby becomes the ordering principle. In fact, without some ordering principle there can be no pattern, and there is something in the very nature of the unitary individual that resists the chaos of patternlessness, a sort of economy of energy that demands an ordering principle, if for no other reason than that it makes efficient, directed action easier. Even the animals have their ordering principle, namely the fulfilment of their various hungers, which lends to their subrational, apparently aimless lives distinctive adaptive patterns of remarkable efficiency. In fact, the very presence of these patterns in instinctual rather than intentional form is proof of their survival value. But man, alas, has outwitted instinct and thereby has lost his "habitat," the natural, need-determined pattern. He tends more and more, from childhood on, to determine his own pattern on the basis of memory of the past and anticipation of the future—a process that involves selection and rejection, which in turn involve, as experience accumulates in quantity and variety, an appeal to a principle or criterion which would make the selection or rejection easier and more consistent, more part of an orderly pattern. The ideal pattern of life in any stage, if it could be achieved, might be pictured somewhat after the analogy of an orchestra, in which the conductor acts the part of the highest value or ordering principle and gives to each of the instruments, the other values and needs, its proper role and function in relation to the whole.

But of course in reality there are no ideal cases, only approximations, and sometimes only hints and longings in the direction of the ideal. There is something in reality itself that resists the ideal and frustrates the longing for it; otherwise there would never be anything more than a first stage, since the desired harmony of life could be achieved within it. Kierkegaard's stages are an elaboration of the doctrine that in ethico-religious matters subjectivity is the truth; the truth is something that the individual must strive for, because it is not a part of every individual's equipment at birth, it is not an inherent psychosomatic perfection. The appropriating individual, the person-in-the-process-of-becoming-existential-truth, is commited to an exploration, a pilgrimage through existence. Existence resists the pilgrim, puts obstacles in his path, leads him from one predicament to the next—and yet the very secret of the pilgrim's progress is that only in this manner can he *become the truth*. For if life itself offered no resistance, no collisions and contradictions, every individual would get stuck fast in the first pattern he managed to hit upon; he could not transcend himself, move on, he could not be a pilgrim in relation to the truth.

2. *The Scope of the Aesthetic Sphere*

The Kierkegaardian stages do not lend themselves easily to a logical subdivision, since the nature of the transitions between them is just as important as the characteristics of each pattern of life. But for practical reasons we will concentrate on the first two stages in this chapter and leave the third, dealing with the two kinds of religiousness, for the next. The aesthetic and the ethical stages are in fact the subject of *Either/Or,* wherein only hints are given that another stage awaits. The reader who is familiar with *Either/ Or* will agree that some note must be taken of the manner in which Kierkegaard uses the term "aesthetic" with regard to the first stage. In academic philosophy, aesthetics is the discipline which concerns itself with the theory of beauty and the nature of the experience elicited by beauty. What makes a thing beautiful, why some things elicit the aesthetic experience more readily or more permanently than others, how to educate one's taste and sensibility in the detection and appreciation of beauty—these are the proper concerns of aesthetics, and it is obvious that these are not Kierkegaard's concerns in his delineation of the first stage of life's way. Of course, there is no question that the pursuit of beauty as one of the many pleasures that life has to offer constitutes an important part of the aesthetic sphere, especially if the particular individual is lucky enough to have talents in that direction. But Kierkegaard uses the term aesthetic much more broadly, to indicate any manner of living in which the principle that one should seek pleasure and avoid pain is operative as the dominant, or decisive, principle. Thus the meaning of the term as he uses it is much more closely approached, I think, by the terms "hedonic" and "hedonistic." It would take another book, I suspect, to go into the matter of whether his use of the word "aesthetic" with this meaning was justified; in other words, it is a question whether the broader pleasure/ pain principle can be shown to be not only operative but also dominant and decisive in whatever has been technically defined and distinguished as the experience of beauty, or the appreciation of art. However, here we are concerned with understanding the Kierkegaardian stages, and I would suggest to the reader that he might find it clarifying throughout the following discussion to substitute in his mind now and then the words "hedonic" and "hedonistic" for Kierkegaard's "aesthetic" and "aesthetical."

The three stages are related to each other, at least in their "natural" order, roughly somewhat as youth, middle years, and old age are related to each other, but their succession is neither automatic nor inevitable—nor are they a parallel development, a sort of concomitant variable of the biological time-scale. It is quite possible for the individual to become "old" before his time, by reaching the religious stage while comparatively young in years. Kierkegaard himself, for example, felt that he was "a thousand years too old" for the young girl he was to marry. This exaggeration expresses not the extreme degree of his piety but the qualitative difference between the stages. Regina Olsen was not an irreligious girl, but the quality of her religiousness was determined by her still childlike and innocent immersion in the aesthetic stage. It is also possible to remain in the aesthetic stage all through a long life, never really growing up existentially, though in other respects becoming the most experienced of connoisseurs, the most worldly-wise of "elders." And finally, it is also possible to "regress" from a later stage back to an earlier one. It is no unusual occurrence to see an individual "lose" both his religion and his ethics, and then to console himself for his disappointment in them by immersing himself in frankly cynical pleasure hunting. Such an outcome is all the more likely if the individual has learned religion and ethics as abstract doctrines, perhaps even tyrannically imposed, without any inward appropriation.

But everyone begins, naïvely and innocently, at the aesthetic stage, for that is the stage into which we are born. No one is born dutiful or religious and then discovers the pleasure/pain principle afterward. The child is given no choice; the pleasure/pain principle is his first education in the world, his introduction to the qualities both of the environment and of his own receiving and reacting bodily and mental equipment. And, undeniably, as long as the pleasures and pains are of the simple, immediate type, with no appreciable time lag between the impulse and the resulting "lesson" (such as the goodness of food for hunger, or the hurtfulness of hot stoves for fingers), the principle that one should seek pleasure and avoid pain certainly seems to operate educatively and pre-servatively on the young human specimen.

Now it is just the *time element,* insinuating itself between the impulse or desire and its immediate result in pain or pleasure, that brings about the first crack in immediacy, the first sour note in this marvelous harmony between the young child and his apparently benign or at least undeceptive environment. Pleasure is to be sought, and pain avoided—but what about the pleasure that turns out *in the long run* to be pain or to have painful results, and what about the pain that turns out *in the long run* to be pleasure or to have desirable results? The older child, with the assistance of the teachings, warnings, and exhortations of the parents, begins to include in his experience the fact that at least some pleasures are snares to be avoided and some pains are trials to be undergone for the sake of future gains. He learns that immediacy cannot be trusted, that the pleasure/pain principle turns out to be equivocal, and he begins to see the purpose of some of the rules and traditions of conduct that his parents have been trying to teach him. There must have developed, in the course of the history of the human race, some practical ways and means of distinguishing the long-term from the short-term pleasures, the rewarding from the deceit-ful, and the worthwhile pains from the useless pains—an empirical wisdom presumably embodied in moral codes. And so the young person is gently ushered into the ethical stage, almost without his noticing it. If, however, he happens to be a reflective individual, he will have noticed, at least in retrospect, that in this transition the pleasure/pain principle has been superseded by the good/evil principle, which also brings with it the *principle of obligation* to tide him over the "long term."

But no matter how gradually, by what almost imperceptible degrees, the family or the society has managed to transpose the individual from the aesthetic to the ethical stage, if the transition is real, if it has actually occurred, it constitutes, Kierkegaard insists, a *leap,* a qualitative change from one pattern of existence to another.[1]

---

[1] The leap was Kiergekaard's answer to the Hegelian mediation, a mys-terious mental process by which the mind passed from any given quality to its opposite, pushed along by the "power of negation," and then passed on to the synthesis of the opposites, pushed along by the "power of recon-ciliation." Kierkegaard did not deny that such a mental process was pos-sible, but he thought it a mistake to imply that this is what the individual did every time he changed the quality of his life and his selfhood by a resolution of the will, a decision, or a choice. In the medium of life, if a real discontinuity between one quality and another did not occur, the change would have to be regarded as illusory. That is why he used the acrobatic term "leap," something that gets you from here to there, and does not leave you in the same place as before. Of course the famous "leap into the arms of God" was the most dramatic instance of a leap, but actually all qualitative changes in the life of the individual were accom-plished by a succession of little leaps.

So it used to be, in simple societies with traditional moralities, and the transition seemed on the whole rather painless, or natural. Even the pains involved seemed natural growing pains, which in some societies were celebrated by appropriately painful rites for entering adulthood. But now, in much more complex and dislocated societies with far more intellectualized forms of thought, something else is likely to happen. Abstract thought and worldly calculation come to the rescue of the pleasure/pain principle, to see if it cannot be saved from being superseded, and the result is "a fictitious transition, like the transition from eudaemonism to the ethical within eudaemonism."[2] In the eyes of abstract thought, which abstracts precisely *from* time in order to achieve a timeless object of contemplation, a long-term pleasure is nonetheless a pleasure, the obligations of ethics are counsels of prudence for arriving at maximum pleasure with minimum pain, and pleasure is getting what you want. And so we must conclude that the Christian martyr, for example, is just one type of the heroic hedonist, since martyrdom is what he obviously wants, more than life itself!

At this point Kierkegaard would call attention to the ease with which the quantitative determinant, here the length of time involved, can be used quantitatively, "little by little," to hide a qualitative transition, here the change from the aesthetic to the ethical principle. Our youthful individual prudently decides to aim at the long-term pleasure, but prudence also tells him that the pleasure had better not be too long delayed or require too much arduous labor for its realization, or else the bargain must surely be considered a poor one, especially if in the interval the individual himself should change, should lose his taste or capacity for the pleasure in question. Well, then, how long is not too long, how much time or work is the pleasure worth? And aren't there other pleasures clamoring for his time? The *time element,* which is just what the intellectual abstraction leaves out as being of no importance, is for the existing individual the most important, persistent, and all-penetrating element in the whole problem. What the abstract reflection hides or fails to mention is that the *kind of self* that can strive for the long-term pleasure is required to be different from the *kind of self* that simply desires immediate pleasures. What

---

[2] *Concluding Unscientific Postscript,* p. 379.

is required is a kind of self that has sufficient will power and resolution to conceive and carry out a long-term plan, sufficient discernment to choose a goal worth working for, and sufficient energy and
discipline to maintain itself through changing circumstances, always
directed toward the goal and undeviated by the clamor of lesser
goals. That which the pleasure principle itself is unable to supply
in the case of the long-term pleasures, that which can sustain and
maintain the self in the proper orientation during the interval that
stretches out between the desire and the goal—just that the ethical
principle supplies by quite simply requiring itself of every individual as a matter of obligation. So the secret of the difference
between the kinds of self lies in the fact that by the time we have
the kind of self that is able to keep itself in this relationship, we
have both an ethical self and an ethical goal, that is, we have the
self that is single-mindedly striving for the highest good. And yet
it looked at the start as though the decision was simply a matter of
short-term versus long-term pleasures, and as though you could
get from the one to the other "little by little," increasing the time
interval ever so slightly.

From the standpoint of only what is involved in the *transition*
from the aesthetic to the ethical principle, it is not necessary to
specify the objective content of the highest good. The ethical individual's ideas about the highest good may change. In fact it is
devoutly to be hoped that his idea of the highest good will grow
and enlarge with his years. But his orientation toward it remains
the same. In every changing circumstance of life, and with increasing moral insight, the ethical individual wills the highest good he
knows, and this factor of *constancy, steadfastness,* and *continuity*
becomes the medium in which he "acquires his soul" and becomes
more and more a self. We shall return to the further adventures in
existence of the ethical individual, but now we must follow what
happens to him who refuses to take this path and remains in the
aesthetic stage, still determined basically by the pleasure/pain principle, even though he may grow in the richness and diversity of
experience.

3. The Aesthetic Individual's Quest

The aesthetic individual who is at all intelligent learns soon enough how to avoid the major avoidable pains and troubles, how, for example, to restrain himself so as not to fall afoul of the law. The highest meaning of ethics for him is that of the prudential reduction of ethics—whatever the moral code that operates in his vicinity, he interprets it as a kind of minimum of necessary rules of the game to prevent the many pleasure-seekers from trespassing too much on one another's pleasures, like the laws for regulating traffic. His chief problem, however, as he grows in experience, is to maintain the quality and quantity of his enjoyments at a sufficiently rewarding level. He encounters sooner or later the two brute facts of satiation and boredom. The earlier pleasures fail, no matter how ingeniously he tries to recapture them, and so there begins for him the endless and restless search for novelty and variety, for diversification, a quest which he undertakes at first with zest and enthusiasm. At the drop of a hat he is ready for something new, and he can hardly finish with one enjoyment soon enough, for fear of missing some other enjoyment. All of Kierkegaard's representatives of the aesthetic stage are highly talented and intelligent individuals, for he wanted to show that it requires fine sensibilities and unusual gifts of the intellect to maintain oneself in this stage for very long. A simpleton, not clever at avoiding the pitfalls, or a mediocre person, whose enjoyments were limited to, say, drink and sex, would soon ruin himself or call down upon himself the wrath of society and thus be assisted into the ethical stage. But the intelligent hedonist disdains all crudities and deliberately avoids just those collisions with society which might shock him into awareness of the ethical in its true meaning as the rule of the good/evil principle.

The aesthetic individual cannot believe that the zest and enthusiasm with which he pursues enjoyments are not his own contribution to the pleasures he is able to achieve, but are simply by-products of youth and health and a responsive nervous system, and he cannot believe that they will some day leave him or at least diminish in intensity. When he finally can't help but notice that they are diminishing, he steps up his ingenuity proportionately. "The Rotation Method," an essay in the aesthetic section of *Either/Or,* bases itself on the premise that boredom is the root of all evil. To avoid boredom most intelligently the writer recommends intensive, as against extensive, cultivation of the field of enjoyments. The latter is for the vulgar and inartistic: "One tires of living in the country, and moves to the city; one tires of one's native land, and travels abroad; one is *europamüde,* and goes to America, and so on."[3] No, the sophisticated method for avoiding boredom resembles the true rotation of crops—changing the method of cultivation of the same field, and also letting it lie fallow. One becomes inventive in seeing the smallest trifles observantly, in seeing the same thing in a new light or in a different mood. One learns the art of remembering and forgetting selectively at will, in order to change the quality of both past and present, and in order to "insure against sticking fast in some relationship of life"[4]—above all one learns to avoid friendship, marriage, and business, the three traps of boredom. One learns to cultivate the accidental and the arbitrary, the fantastic or the grotesque, anything, anything that promises the revival of interest.

Thus the aesthetic individual is seen to be well advanced in the hopelessness of the aesthetic stage when he passes from the dominance of the pleasure/pain principle to that of the interest/boredom principle. After all, pain may be more *interesting* than pleasure when pleasure has gone stale. He begins to explore the dark side of life, not from any desire to comprehend it or to change it, but simply to widen the scope of the interesting and to keep away the devil of boredom. One of the analytical-lyrical essays in *Either/Or,* Part I, is called "The Unhappiest Man" and another is concerned with the inner ratiocinations of three tragic heroines of love, Marie Beaumarchais, Donna Elvira, and Faust's Margaret. The plan of existence that started out by seeking pleasure and avoiding pain thus finds itself driven to seek out the unhappy, the tragic, the sorrowful, simply because these are less boring than their opposites. Of course it would not do for the aesthetic individual to get *himself* too much involved in tragedy or sorrow, for then he would lose just that "aesthetic distance," that evaluating detachment which permits him to taste and enjoy the experience as a spectator in order to find if it is interesting or not. Metaphysically, the aesthetic indi-

---

[3] *Either/Or,* trans. David F. Swenson and Lillian Marvin Swenson (vol. 1), Walter Lowrie (vol. 2) (2 vols.; Princeton, N. J.: Princeton University Press, 1944), I, 239.

[4] *Either/Or,* I, 242.

vidual understands good and evil under the category of "fortune and misfortune." The Greek mythological view that the fortunes and misfortunes of mortal men constitute the spice and variety of life necessary to keep the gods from getting bored, suits him quite well, and when misfortune strikes him personally, he can only believe blindly that it will pass, it must pass. In other words, he secretly believes that he is a darling of the gods.

His refusal to become involved with the ethical or the religious does not mean that the aesthetic individual is ignorant of them, or even disdainful. He simply views them aesthetically, as he does everything else. This means that, as we have seen, in so far as he observes ethical rules of conduct, he regards them as counsels of prudence or even as amiable social conventions, but also that he is quite ready to admit that for some people, perhaps even for most people, ethics must be the highest, the dominant principle, in order to keep society conveniently orderly. As for reformers and such, they are manifestations of a type, the puritanical temperament, which may be interesting to observe if it does not become tedious.

Far more interesting to him in its variety of expression is the religious temperament, and it is not difficult for us to spot the aesthetic individual who happens to take an "aesthetic interest" in matters religious. He tends naturally to become the religious thrill-secker or the connoisseur of the varieties of religious experience, tasting and comparing liturgies, theologies, architectures, mythologies, music, psychological attitudes, and so on. He is the sensitive critic in the pew, attending divine worship in the same spirit as he attends exhibitions of art, the ballet, or the opera. That man is a religious animal is, he believes, not only a perfectly obvious fact, but a great stroke of luck, since it gives imagination positive tasks, and cultures a delightful variety of definite forms. As for the people who want to convert you to their form, they are interesting too, as *afficionados,* who after all have every right to defend their taste—or else they are a type of the monomaniacal mind. People who oppose religion on scientific grounds are simply bores.

4. Approaching the Boundary of the Ethical

In all his searches and researches into the possibilities of enjoyment, the aesthetic individual tries to throw himself wholeheartedly into the enthusiasm of the moment but also to leave some part of himself outside, in order with this part to stand off and observe, taste, study, and enjoy reflectively. This outside part, however, becomes just the thing he would like to get rid of when the situation is for the moment devoid of enjoyment, when he is feeling "low," melancholy, bored, restless, undecided what to do next, exhausted. This reflective part of himself informs him no less on the futility and chaos of his existence than on the enjoyments, but it does not have enough power over him to engage his will, to make him want to do anything about it. Kierkegaard calls the aesthetic stage a continuous *possibility* of existence, because the aesthetic individual lacks as yet the kind of self that would make him an existing individual. A self is continually trying to be born in him, but it is just as continually being aborted or arrested because of his debility of will in the face of alternatives he meets and his scattering out at the call of multiple diversions. This lack of a self constitutes the real, that is, the deep, underlying *despair* of the aesthetic individual, but he himself does not understand it that way, because of that very lack. He understands well enough, if he is at all thoughtful, that his situation contains despair, or that it may at any moment become desperate, and he understands that his pursuit of enjoyment is in part goaded on from behind by the need to flee the always threatening despair—but he persistently and consistently attributes this fact to something in the environment, to the world's not being amusing enough, to his not having found the right people or his proper milieu, or to his not having enough good fortune in the way of natural endowments, such as health, talents, charms, riches, and opportunities. "If only things were different," he keeps thinking to himself, so as not to face this unwelcome thought: "If only *I* were, basically, different."

The question now arises, how can the aesthetic individual be assisted out of the beguiling and debilitating medium in which he is mired and into which he sinks more and more hopelessly the longer he remains in it? There are two major possibilities here, corresponding to the two aspects of the bankruptcy of the aesthetic stage, the spiritual aspect and the intellectual aspect. Spiritually, the transition to the ethical is a matter of his acquiring a real self. Intellectually, it is a matter of his coming to a comprehension of misfortune. But the two aspects are hardly to be separated in existence, though they may be in thought. The aesthetic individual lives in immediacy, that is, in direct, even though discriminating, action-reaction with the environment, and thus he is always at the mercy of external circumstances. In Kierkegaard's terminology, he "has his dialectic outside of him, never inside." The pattern of his actions, or the rationale for them, even when he thinks he is freely responding, is determined by circumstances beyond his control. He is the slave, or the dupe, of the momentary situation, in regard to both stimulus and response. In so far as this slavery happens to be agreeable, the immediate (aesthetic) individual must consider his life as simply lucky. But when misfortune strikes he can hardly bring himself to believe that he is one of those chosen by the fates to be permanently unlucky (which would be a consistent view), and so he is brought to a halt, puzzled. Intellectually he draws a blank.

If one were to ask the immediate individual whence he has this view of life [that he is fortunate] he would have to answer with virginal naïveté, "I do not myself understand it." The contradiction comes from without, and takes the form of misfortune. The immediate individual never comes to any understanding with misfortune, for he never becomes dialectical in himself; and if he does not manage to get rid of it, he finally reveals himself as lacking the poise to bear it. That is, he despairs, because he cannot grasp misfortune. Misfortune is like a narrow pass on the way; now the immediate individual is in it, but his view of life must essentially always tell him that the difficulty will soon cease to hinder, because it is a foreign element. If it does not cease, he despairs, by which his immediacy ceases to function, and the transition to another understanding of misfortune is rendered possible, that is, his despair may lead him to a comprehension of the suffering, and an understanding of it that grasps not only this or that misfortune, but essentially arrives at an understanding of the rôle of suffering in life.[5]

A good solid misfortune that does not pass away would seem to be one way of dragging the aesthetic individual out of the bath of immediacy in which he is immersed. And surely both personal life and history bear witness to the fact that nothing short of a near-fatal catastrophe is needed sometimes to "wake up" an individual and arrest his tendency toward complete disintegration and ruin.

[5] *Postscript*, p. 388.

However, it ought not be necessary to call upon such dramatic extremes. There is at least one "misfortune" that strikes everyone and does not pass away, namely, old age, which might be called upon to perform the needed service. The trouble with age is that it comes so gradually, so insidiously, and the individual can so easily delude himself to believe that he is holding it off. The aesthetic individual has no criterion of struggle and achievement by which to calibrate time (whether it be the passing years or the passing moments) and by which to give time continuity. Time is his most pernicious problem, always going too fast in the moments of enjoyment, or not fast enough in the intervening moments. Aesthetic time is a series of disconnected moments, the moments that count separated from one another by flexible vacuums that don't count, presumably, but are nevertheless there and are always threatening to stretch, collapse, or swallow up the helpless individual who is in their grasp. An acute melancholia is hidden in these time-intervals between the moments that count, and this melancholia becomes more and more manifest as the inescapable effects of bodily aging (fatigue, satiation, the lowering of the zest-level, the loss of physical attractiveness) begin to defeat the ingenious devices formerly used to drive away the "evil spirits." Such aging can in fact happen quite soon in life, the sooner the more diligently the aesthetic individual has exhausted the possibilities open to him. So the young man in *Either/Or* complains:

Wine can no longer make my heart glad; a little of it makes me sad, much makes melancholy. My soul is faint and impotent; in vain I prick the spur of pleasure into its flank, its strength is gone, it rises no more to the royal leap. . . . My soul has lost its potentiality. If I were to wish for anything, I should not wish for wealth and power, but for the passionate sense of the potential, for the eye, which ever young and ardent, sees the possible. Pleasure disappoints, possibility never. And what wine is so foaming, what so fragrant, what so intoxicating, as possibility![6]

The aesthetic individual needs to have his attention turned from the possibilities in the external world to those in the inner world of himself, but just this turning he resists, because he cannot bear to face himself, or, rather, the lack of self, the emptiness that is

⁶ *Either/Or*, I, 33.

his equivalent of a self. If a providential misfortune (a misfortune which afterward can be providentially understood) does not force him to face himself, perhaps a friend can talk him into it with a discourse on choosing. This is what Judge William tries to do in *Either/Or* for the young man, appealing to his intellect to help him to grasp the spirit. He tells him that the aesthetic sphere is despair, either hidden, open, or intermittent despair, and that the way out of it consists of despairing in earnest, despairing whole-heartedly, so that he might find himself in his despair, find his despairing self, which is, in his condition, finding his real self; then he must choose this despairing self, choose himself in his despair, in an absolute choice. As soon as he chooses himself absolutely just as he is in his despair, he chooses himself out of despair, for by that choice he gains an absolute self, he discovers the self in its absolute validity, and, having this absolutely valid or eternal self, he is no longer strictly speaking in despair, even though he as yet scarcely knows what to do with the self he has gained by his choice.

In keeping with his doctrine that in ethico-religious matters subjectivity (personhood)is the truth, Kierkegaard will not allow a beginning in ethics to be made by an intellectual consideration of objective concepts or definitions of what is good or what is right. He insists that there must first be what amounts to a *spiritual crisis,* a dividing line or decision point, in which the individual acquires, by means of the spiritual struggle of choice, the kind of self that makes ethics possible. In other words, the individual must first know himself and choose himself in that aspect of himself in which alone it makes any sense to talk subsequently about the choosing between good and evil. Thus the first choice he has to make is not between good and evil, but between the eternal validity implied in choosing and the despair implied in not choosing. This first choice, then, is the limiting boundary between the aesthetical and the ethical. On one side is the neutrality of the aesthetic confusion of passing moods, enthusiasms, ups and downs of enjoyment, which render choice meaningless and thus prevent personality from coming to birth in its aspect as continuity. On the other side is the directedness of the ethical, with its possibility of repeated choices between good and evil and thus also the possibility of the birth, growth, and development of personality in its eternal (continuous in time) aspect. This first choice, however, is not an intellectual deliberation (although intellect may assist by making the alternatives clear) but is an act; it is not a judgment but a commitment, not a learning but a sort of being born. *After* this choosing and chosen self is born in this first choice, then it makes sense to talk about choosing between good and evil, for then what is at stake in this second choice is evident—on the one hand the growth and integration, on the other hand, the injury and disintegration of the personality in its eternal, essential, nonaccidental aspect. "What is it, then, that I distinguish in my either/or? Is it good and evil? No, I would only bring you up to the point where the choice between the evil and the good acquires significance for you."[7]

5. *How to Choose the Ethical Correctly*

Time, which for the aesthetic individual was some kind of horrible gremlin—now appearing and now disappearing, now luring him on with possibility, now exasperating him with its boring, taunting too-muchness—is, for the ethical individual, the precious medium in which the "becoming" of his ethical self can take place. The ethical plan of life *needs* time, since it *is* a plan, a striving toward a goal, a struggle with recalcitrant materials both "inside" and "outside" the person, and therefore not to be accomplished in the medium of thought, quick as a wink. Kierkegaard makes us feel the emergent ethical personality as a living, palpable, almost a biological entity, becoming one thing or another, never static, refusing to "stay put," for when it is not growing, nourishing itself, integrating, then it is dissolving, disintegrating, losing itself, dying. This fact is what makes the time element so crucial and urgent in the moments of choice, those decisive times when, as it were, the intellect is begging for more and more time in which to deliberate on the alternatives, while the spirit, the personal self, is begging to be delivered soon from the disintegrating effects of indecision. Moreover, it is part of the very nature and pathos of temporal existence that the alternatives themselves refuse to "stay put" but change even while the person concerned is intellectually weighing and appraising them. Kierkegaard describes the way choice and time accentuate each other thus:

[7] *Either/Or*, II, 142.

That which has to be chosen stands in the deepest relationship to the chooser, and when it is a question of a choice involving a life problem the individual must naturally be living in the meantime, and hence, it comes about that the longer he postpones the choice the easier it is for him to alter its character, notwithstanding that he is constantly deliberating and deliberating and believes that thereby he is holding the alternatives distinctly apart. When life's either/or is regarded in this way one is not easily tempted to jest with it. One sees, then, that the inner drift of the personality leaves no time for thought experiments, that it constantly hastens onward and in one way or another posits this alternative or that, making the choice more difficult the next instant because what has thus been posited must be revoked. Think of the captain on his ship at the instant when it has to come about. He will perhaps be able to say, "I can either do this or that"; but in case he is not a pretty poor navigator, he will be aware at the same time that the ship is all the while making its usual headway, and that therefore it is only an instant when it is indifferent whether he does this or that. So it is with a man. If he forgets to take account of the headway, there comes at last an instant when there no longer is any question of an either/or, not because he has chosen but because he has neglected to choose, which is equivalent to saying, because others have chosen for him, because he has lost his self.[8]

The ethical life is a striving toward a goal, the goal being the highest good, and the striving consisting of trying to embody somehow the highest good in all the essential acts of the person. Objective or so-called "scientific" ethics places the emphasis on the goal and tends to ignore the striving. If only the goal can be defined or prescribed, whether more empirically or more idealistically, the striving (objective ethics assumes) will take care of itself. And this would indeed be true if man himself were an abstract idea instead of being an existing individual, for then there would really not be any "striving" worthy of the name—or rather, the striving would consist of exchanging one idea for another, just like that. But man is not an idea, and, for such a creature as man is, to abstract from the time element and ignore the process of appropriation is almost to guarantee a false outcome, namely, the misappropriation of the ethical goal in such ethical "mistakes" as legalism, phariseeism, mysticism, or puritanism. In the medium of existence, to strive for the good in the wrong way is the same as to strive not for the good but for something else. Placing Kierkegaard's

[8] *Either/Or*, II, 138-139.

existential dialectic in the most extreme contrast to the objective approach, one might say that, for Kierkegaard, if only the striving is correct, the goal will take care of itself. In other words, it is impossible in the long run to strive unethically for an ethical goal, or to strive ethically for an unethical goal. If goal and striving do not correspond, there will be a breakdown of the person, even though this inward discrepancy may take a long time to achieve outward expression in telltale symptoms. Of course, Kierkegaard admits that for each particular choice it is necessary to deliberate, that is, it is necessary to weigh the alternatives to decide which one most probably contains the highest good—and in this respect it is proper to consult the informative sciences. But, since the information they give is always incomplete and inconclusive, it is just as necessary to be constantly aware that the information of itself will not *decide* anything, and that decision and its risks and responsibilities always rest with the choosing self.

Kierkegaard would be the last person to deny that the transition from the aesthetic to the ethical plan of life is fraught with dangers and difficulties. Thus, it is of the utmost importance that the would-be ethical individual, launching out into the struggle to realize the good, should come to an understanding of what an ethical self is. Right at the beginning of the ethical stage it is possible for the would-be ethical person to make a mistake by choosing himself in the wrong way, or by misunderstanding the kind of self he gets if the choice is correct. According to the delineation of the stages, whereby Kierkegaard explores and reveals the possibilities that existence holds for the individual, the criterion by which one decides if the ethical self was correctly chosen is the question of whether this new self actually does transcend or go beyond the limitations of the aesthetic self, or whether it collapses back into the aesthetic stage, thereby disclosing that it was a crypto-aesthetic choice, an ethical self understood and chosen on aesthetic grounds.

Such is the danger if, for example, the individual does not understand the relationship of the concrete to the abstract in the new self which he receives in choosing the ethical way. The difficulty here is that in choosing himself in his eternal validity, the individual has to make an *absolute* choice (since only an absolute choice can correspond to an eternal value), and yet it seems as if he must choose a concrete, *finite* thing (namely, the particular self that he happens to be) in order to maintain continuity with the self that he was in the aesthetic stage, with the empirical self that to the outward eye he still is. For if he does not maintain his continuity, he does not choose himself but repudiates himself, in favor of a pure abstraction (the sheer empty possibility of a self) containing no concrete determinants. This is a mistake, for by choosing this abstract "I-am-I" he will not only have failed to rescue anything out of the aesthetic stage, but he will have provided himself ethically with nothing to do, no concrete determinants to mold into the pattern of the good. The correct ethical choice demands that he choose himself absolutely in his full concreteness as *this* particular person who has had *this* history so far, which means that in accordance with the good there must be some elements of his concreteness of which he must repent and others for which he can only be thankful. But he must not repudiate anything, for repudiation is not repentance but a disowning of one's past that makes it impossible to achieve the self-possession which is the true mark of the ethical personality.

It may seem at the moment of choice that the self one chooses is an abstract self because one has to abstract the eternal aspect, for example, from the despairing self, in order to see that the former is there as a possibility, in the possibility of freedom—even the very freedom to choose the despairing self. And yet,

it is an illusion to suppose that the self is entirely abstract and empty, for it is not conscious simply of freedom in general, as thought might conceive it, but it was produced by a choice and is conscious of this definite free being who is himself and no other. This self contains a rich concretion, a manifold variety of determinants and characteristics, being the whole aesthetical self which is chosen ethically. . . . Hence, in the first instant of choice the personality issues forth apparently as naked as does a child from the body of its mother, the next instant it is concrete in itself and only by an arbitrary abstraction can it come to pass that a man is able to remain at this point. He becomes himself, quite the same self he was before, and yet he becomes another, for the choice permeates everything and transforms it. Thus his finite personality is infinitized by the choice whereby he infinitely chooses himself.[9]

[9] *Either/Or*, II, 187.

eternal truth, adequately decisive for one's eternal happiness. Has not Mohammedanism persisted for twelve hundred years? The guaranty of the eighteen centuries, the circumstance that Christianity has interpenetrated all the relations of life, has transformed the world, and so forth—all this assurance is nothing but a deceptive snare in which the resolving and choosing subject is held captive, lost in the wilderness of the parenthesis. Eighteen centuries have no greater demonstrative force than a single day, in relation to an eternal truth which is to decide my eternal happiness." [11]

Kierkegaard maintains that this argument from the eighteen centuries of the existence of the Church can be presented only in rhetorical form, since actually it is a browbeating administered upon the prospective believer.

The speaker isolates the deliberating or doubting subject from all connection with others. He confronts the poor sinner with innumerable hosts of past generations, with millions upon millions, and then says to him: "Now dare you be so insolent as to deny the truth? Dare you really imagine that you are in possession of the truth, and that the eighteen centuries, the innumerable generations of men, millions upon millions, have lived their lives in error? O wretched solitary man, do you dare thus to plunge all these many millions, all mankind indeed, into destruction? Behold, they arise from their graves, they pass as if in review before my thought, these generations upon generations of believers, whose minds found rest in the truth of Christianity. Their glances condemn you, O insolent rebel, until the separation of the judgment day snatches you from their sight, because you were weighed and found wanting, were thrown into the outer darkness, far from eternal bliss, etc., etc." Behind the tremendous barrage of the many millions the cowardly speaker sometimes trembles in his boots when he uses the argument, because he dimly feels that there is a contradiction in his whole procedure.

But he cannot do the sinner any harm. Such a rhetorical shower-bath from the height of eighteen centuries is very stimulating. The speaker performs a service, if not precisely in the way intended, by separating the subject out for himself over against other men—ah, and this is a great service, for only a very few are able to do this for themselves. And yet it is experience in this situation which constitutes an absolute condition for entering Christianity. The eighteen centuries ought precisely to inspire fear. As proof *pro* they are in the moment of decision worth precisely nothing to the individual subject; but as fear-inspiring *contra* they are excellent.[12]

[11] *Postscript*, pp. 45-46.
[12] *Postscript*, pp. 46-47.

Judge William observes that one reason people resist the choice of the ethical is that they are afraid they will lose the asthetical entirely, that life will become one long grim round of monotonous, unrelieved duty-performance in which all the joyful and playful aspects of life are suppressed. This fear is in part the result of a falsely rigoristic conception of ethical obligation, which makes the ethical ridiculous by dragging it into the most trivial acts and situations. Judge William is apparently thinking here of certain puritanical and perfectionistic interpretations of the ethical goal, whose adherents think they are honoring God by crediting him with an obsessive interest in the way one dresses, eats, drinks, takes his ease, etc. Such an attitude also implies that ethical obligation, for example, to love one's neighbor, is directly translatable into such terms. And fear of the ethical is due also to an unwillingness to part with the romantic overemphasis on the strange, the novel, the exotic, or the sensational, as if these, in view of their exceptional character, could be made the basis of a view of life that claims universal validity for all men, as the ethical must do.

But, correctly chosen, the ethical does not destroy the aesthetical. It rescues as much of it as it can, and preserves it precisely by subordinating it to a ministering role. There are plenty of pleasures, for example, which, instead of being the objects of a desperate chase, can take on the function of re-creation, and at least some pains can be seen as the concomitants of growth, as "growing pains." Here it must be remembered that the aesthetical as such is not evil, nor does the fact that one must go beyond it imply that it is evil— it is simply neutral, or, as we would now say, it is ethically ambiguous. The fact that some people can find pleasure in cruelty does not mean that pleasure itself is bad but that, ethically, pleasure must be sought in something that does not violate an ethical obligation. Thus the ethical, when correctly chosen, really does *transcend* the aesthetical, in that it both preserves it by giving it a proper place in the ethical life and rescues it from its own limitations and destructive tendencies. Take the matter of moods. The ethical man does not stop having moods, or stop participating feelingly in a variety of environmental factors through a variety of moods. But he does not become the slave of the moods. One might say that he *has* the moods, rather than that the moods have *him*. And this is because his personality has a directed center and a continuity that is beyond the grasp or intrusion of mood, namely, the goal and striving of the ethical life.

6. Ways of Choosing the Ethical Wrongly

Something different from the above happens when the ethical is chosen in the wrong way, although of course we know by now that when the ethical is chosen in the wrong way then the ethical is not really chosen at all. Judge William describes several such cases, and the interesting thing from the modern point of view is that into the category of those who make the choice in the wrong way we must place existentialists of the Sartre and Heidegger variety, who place their main emphasis on the abstract freedom that comes to consciousness in this existential choice. They ignore the concrete determinants to such an extent that they can say (at least with Sartre) that man *has no nature as such,* but must create his own nature at the instigation of his freedom. The Sartrean man is so fascinated, so intoxicated by that freedom which he discovers in the act of choosing that he ignores the equally solid fact that he cannot become *anything* he chooses, but only what the actual components of his concrete self will allow him to become. For example, with all the freedom and will power in the world a man cannot *choose* to become a genius, or a member of a different race, even of a different family, or a man with an objectively different past. The fascination with freedom corresponds to the following case described in *Either/Or:*

The more significant the result which is to issue from the choice, the more dangerous are the byways, and here there appears a dreadful byway. When the individual has grasped himself in his eternal validity this overwhelms him by its fulness. The temporal vanishes from before his eyes. At the first instant this fills him with indescribable bliss and gives him a sense of absolute security. If then he begins to gaze upon this bliss, the temporal advances its claim. This is scorned. What the temporal can give, the more or the less which now presents itself, is so very unimportant in comparison with what he eternally possesses. Everything comes with him to a standstill, he has, as it were, reached eternity before the time. He relapses into contemplation, he gazes at himself, but this gaze cannot fill up the time. Then it appears to him that time, that the temporal, is his ruin; he demands a more perfect form of existence [in the Sartrean formulation, he demands to become

God]. . . . He has not chosen himself, like Narcissus he has fallen in love with himself. Such a situation has certainly ended not infrequently in suicide.[10]

Or one might say that like Narcissus he ignores his actual self because he is fascinated by an image of himself that reflects only one aspect of selfhood, the aspect of freedom. It is easy to see, if such is the situation of the Sartrean man, why it is so difficult for the modern existentialists of this type to proceed from their idea of freedom toward any positive ethical implications, for this empty abstract freedom has no continuity either with the past or with the future of a given individual. It makes responsibility an illusion, and it can find no common ground among contemporary individuals except that they all obstruct one another's freedom. But continuity in the individual, supplied by the striving for the highest good, is of the very essence of the ethical life, and universality is implicit in continuity also, the highest good being understood as that which demands itself of all men all the time.

Kierkegaard calls attention, through Judge William, to another case where the choice is made in the wrong way, that of the religious mystic, or at least that type of religious mystic whose object is to lose himself in the infinite. In choosing himself in his eternal aspect, he does it in such a manner as to isolate himself from all men, on the grounds that the highest good is the mystical union with God and that society or any proximate goals or even other human beings can act only as an obstruction to, or a distraction from, this highest goal. Such a life also lacks continuity, quite in the same sense as the aesthetic life.

It is appalling to read a mystic's lament over the dull moments. Then when the dull moment is past comes the luminous moment, and thus his life is constantly changing, it has movement indeed, but no development. His life lacks continuity. What really supplies the continuity is a feeling, the feeling of longing, whether this longing be directed towards what is past or towards what is to come. But the fact that a feeling fills the intervening space shows precisely that cohesion is lacking. . . . The whole world is a dead world for the mystic, he has fallen in love with God. . . . His inward action therefore does not consist in the acquisition of the personal virtues but in the development of the religious or contemplative virtues. But even this is too ethical an expres-

[10] *Either/Or*, II, 194.

sion for his life, and we must say that his real life is prayer. I will not deny that prayer, too, belongs to the ethical life, but the more ethically a man lives the more purposeful is his prayer. . . . It is not so with the prayer of the mystic. Prayer is all the more significant for him the more erotic it is, the more it is inflamed by a burning love. . . .

In my opinion one cannot acquit the mystic of a certain intrusiveness in his relation to God. Who will deny that a man shall love God with all his heart and with all his mind, yea, that he is not only to do this but that to do it is blessedness itself? From this, however, it by no means follows that the mystic is to disdain the reality of existence to which God has assigned him, for thereby he really disdains God's love or requires a different expression of it than that which God is willing to give. Here applies the serious saying of Samuel, "To obey is better than sacrifice, and to harken than the fat of rams."[11]

The mystic, at least the type of mystic here described, is an example of what happens when the individual tries to bypass the ethical in his pilgrimage through existence, even though this is done from what appears to be the highest motive, the desire for union with God. The mystic is impatient with existence, he can hardly wait to get it over and done with. In choosing himself abstractly as the drop of water which is to be mystically united with the divine ocean, he loses sight of his concrete self, or rather he disdains it, along with the whole temporal, finite realm, the historical life.

There are, of course, many ways in which one can choose oneself abstractly, thereby failing to make the choice ethically as far as the subsequent history of the self is concerned. The Communist devotee, for example, chooses himself abstractly as the tiny cog which is to work at its place in the machine of the partisan state. And he too, like the mystic, disdains every aspect of himself that does not contribute directly to his eternalization in identity with the machine's destiny, disdains especially all of the natural inclinations that might rise up in him to protest their exclusion from his abstract self. The Communist has his orders, which are his "highest good," and he needs the temporal to carry them out. Nevertheless, the temporal, and especially his own personal existence in time, remains opaque to him; it lacks transparency.

For it is a mistake to think that the abstract is the transparent. The abstract is the turbid, the foggy. . . . Only when in his choice a man has assumed himself, is clad in himself, has so totally penetrated

[11] *Either/Or*, II, 203-204.

himself that every movement is attended by the consciousness of a responsibility for himself, only then has he chosen himself ethically, only then has he repented himself, only then is he concrete, only then is he in his total isolation in absolute continuity with the reality to which he belongs.[12]

If the choice is made correctly, that is, concretely and in continuity with the past, the ethical stage in its ideality emerges. The ethical individual has *tasks,* instead of mere possibilities, and he himself, in all his particularity, is his task, the task to realize the highest good in and through this particularity. Thanks to repentance, which is the mode of accepting the evil that is past and cannot be undone, he also has continuity, transparency, and self-possession. Any talents he may have are, as it were, hints from the eternal as to which tasks he might make especially his own; they are not, as in the aesthetic life, accidental advantages by dint of which one may lead a "robber existence" relative to those less favored. The Judge grows quite rhapsodic as he describes the beauties of the ethical plan of life (in the second part of *Either/Or*). It is, he says, a very imperfect expression of the ethical to regard it as merely duty-performance, usually unpleasant, for thereby the connection between the good and the growth of personality is obscured. "The fault is that the individual is placed in an outward relation to duty. The ethical is defined as duty, and duty in turn is defined as a congeries of particular propositions, but the individual and duty stand outside of one another."[13] (Of course, if at this point he should be so confused as to insist that duty *should* be a pleasure, he would simply find himself back in the aesthetic stage, with all its bafflements, and find it necessary to start all over again.) But when the ethical is correctly understood as that which "stands in the most inward relation to my self," then this fragmentation into a congeries of particular propositions does not happen, and "the genuine ethical individual therefore possesses calmness and assurance because he has not duties outside of himself but in himself," a fact which makes him "infinitely secure in himself."[14]

[12] *Either/Or*, II, 208.
[13] *Either/Or*, II, 213.
[14] *Either/Or*, II, 213.

And, above all, time is his friend, the precious medium in which the tasks can be carried out. The growth of personality requires time.

The temporal therefore, if I may venture to say so, does not exist for God's sake, in order that in it, speaking mystically, He may test and try the loved one, but it exists for man's sake and is the greatest of all the gifts of grace. For man's eternal dignity consists in the fact that he can have a history, the divine element in him consists in the fact that he himself, if he will, can impart to this history continuity, for this it acquires only when it is not the sum of all that has happened to me or befallen me but is my own work, in such a way that even what has befallen me is by me transformed and translated from necessity to freedom.[15]

[15] *Either/Or*, II, 210.

VIII

The Pilgrimage Through Existence

Part Two: The End in Sight

1. *Approaching the Boundary of the Religious*

Judge William presents the ethical stage in such ideal terms that it is hard to believe that the ethical itself is not the happy ending of the story, the goal of the individual's pilgrimage where his self-hood can safely come to rest, with nothing but further self-perfection in the ethical tasks to occupy him till the end of his allotted gift of time. The very universality and inexhaustibility of the ethical demand—the fact that the highest good demands itself of *every* man and the fact that it is the *highest* good that thus demands itself —these two seem to guarantee the possibility of endless progress and to insure that in this stage one will never have to worry about satiation, or boredom, or waning zest, or lack of worlds to conquer. In the ethical stage the meaning of life becomes transparent as the struggle for the realization of the good that is inevitably to be crowned with some degree of victory, and the ethical individual himself becomes transparent to himself and to others. He has no secrets to hide from himself or others, and he has no difficulty in explaining or justifying himself to himself or to others. His life becomes an open book, and his ethical enthusiasm and steadfastness become an edifying example to others, especially to those still helplessly thrashing about in the quagmires and deceptions of the aesthetic stage.

Now this rosy state of affairs on the threshold of the ethical stage of life is the condition presupposed in all idealistic moral philosophies, as well as in the ethical teachings of most of the higher religions. The general idea is that man needs only to have set before his mind ideals sufficiently noble to kindle his desire to strive for them, and then the realization of them will follow as a matter of course, if given enough time. Hindrances there will be, coming perhaps especially from the "flesh," which is unwilling to go where the spirit wishes to lead it and which must be reasoned with and disciplined to follow—but all the greater will be the victory that overcomes such a built-in resistance to the realization of the self-ideal. The main thing is to keep one's eyes on the goal and never to let oneself be distracted or sidetracked.

On that level which concerns itself theoretically with what man ought to be and to do (theoretical ethics), the transition from the ethical to the religious is largely a matter of definition, depending on the extent to which the ethical goal itself is absolutized. Philosophically, objectively, ethics can be oriented in either a humanistic or a theistic direction. (It is a little difficult to see how ethics can be grounded in a purely naturalistic philosophy, in spite of the popularity of the varieties of so-called naturalistic morals in our day, and no doubt Kierkegaard would dismiss such views as not having reached the ethical category at all but being merely prudence-calculations or hidden forms of hedonism.) And if theoretical ethics can be oriented in either a humanistic or a theistic direction, the reason for this must be that some ideas of the highest good imply a moral deity "behind" the good, something whose will and behest the ethical stage attempts to fulfil, while other ideas of the highest good do not imply this but merely say that the ethical is justified by man's own will and demand on himself. Ideas, whether they correspond to reality or not, always have logical implications; therefore one might say that there are no ideas of the good for which one cannot find *some* religious implications (including negative ones) and there are no ideas of the deity for which one cannot find *some* ethical implications (including negative ones). On the theoretical level the ethical and the religious are inseparable in so far as they are parts of a continuous movement of thought from a doctrine to its implications and back again, or from the "if" to the "then" of an hypothesis. This is why Kierkegaard lumps the two categories together on the theoretical level to speak of "ethico-religious matters." On the level of theory, then, a change from the ethical to the religious stage would hardly be perceptible except as a definition—or redefinition—of the highest good in terms more theistic than humanistic; and perhaps also some religious obligations would be added to the ethical obligations, that is to say, the doctrines and practices of a particular religion would be adopted.

But in the realm of life—of existing—the change, if it really happens, does not happen as a redefinition of terms. It happens because the ethical individual, just to the extent that he is striving to realize the good with all his heart and strength, begins to discover hindrances whose nature and obduracy he would never have suspected had he not undertaken the ethical striving. Here once again existence itself rises up to resist the pilgrim, to put obstacles in his path, to drive him to despair—but, be it noted, ethical despair, which is a whole stage above aesthetic despair in the evolution or maturing of selfhood. And just as the change from the aesthetic to the ethical stage did not happen merely as the grasping of an intellectual conviction but as a spiritual crisis in which the individual rescued himself from the aesthetic despair by a leap into the ethical categories, so the transition to the religious will not really happen except as another spiritual crisis, another "rescue operation," and this time the leap is from ethical despair into religious categories. The individual will discover his need of God, not as a theoretical possibility, but as an existential necessity answering to the ethical predicament. However, since this transition represents as well the borderline between the humanistic and the theistic orientations of ethics, between what man can do by himself and what he needs God to help him to do (and even to do for him), Kierkegaard also expresses the limit of the ethical stage by saying that the *need* of God is man's highest perfection.

But now, what are these hindrances which only the ethically striving individual discovers? They are discrepancies, conflicts, and collisions, apparently both external and internal in origin, and so intricately compounded that they make the ethical situation sometimes ambiguous, sometimes utterly opaque to analysis. Externally, the ethical individual discovers discrepancies, at first perhaps only minor ones, between the ideal he is striving to actualize and the reality his ethical act brings into being. Something always seems to go awry, the shoe doesn't quite fit the foot, the excellent moral maxim doesn't quite fit the particular case, the act of justice always leaves some injured parties, the help given to one neighbor deprives another neighbor—and so on. In addition, the ethical individual discovers discrepancies within himself. These are not just matters of the flesh being weak (though this factor must not be despised) but also of the spirit being double-minded, desiring the good but at the same time desiring that the good should bring with it certain rewards. In the discourse *Purity of Heart* Kierkegaard describes the struggle of the ethical individual with his own double-mindedness, describes how he must constantly fight the "reward disease" in its thousand and one forms in order to purify his heart for the ethical tasks. Yet, just to the extent that he succeeds in purifying the ethical motivation, he becomes more refined in his ethical discernment, his conscience becomes more sensitive, and his sense of responsibility increases in scope and intensity. He sees wrongs and injustices where the ethically dull see none. More and more he experiences the "falling short" and discovers in the medium of existence the marks of finitude and the scars of sin, even though he may not think of them in those terms.

He discovers the discrepancy between the abstract and the concrete. Abstractly, the ethical demand is to do the highest good, to choose in any situation the alternative that promises to realize the best—but does existence obligingly present him with only black and white alternatives, so that only a blind man could fail to choose correctly? And who is so omniscient, so penetrating and far-seeing, as to be able to detect, in the very mixed and complex conglomeration of alternatives actually offered, the one which promises the best? And whose "best" is to be given preference? Is there not a real conflict among ethical obligations themselves, since the individual's responsibility is so many-sided? At the end of the previous chapter we observed how Judge William praises the ethical stage with almost a religious fervor, not hesitating to mention God in connection with the highest good; and yet there is no mention of the possibility of conflict between the duties toward marriage and other duties, those toward family, society, profession, and God himself. Nor is there any mention of the experience of falling short, of failures as well as victories, and the problems that accumulated failures create for the inner economy of the ethical self.

But perhaps that was only Kierkegaard's sly way of indicating something that the striving ethical individual only discovers for himself: the deception of language inherent in its abstract character, the fact that all talk about the ideal tends to promote a deception about the real, simply because it is talk and not action. The individual's ideas about the ethical may be absolutely perfect—but this will not help him, and it may even hinder him, "because speech is after all a more abstract medium than existence, and all speech in relation to the ethical is something of a deception. . . ."[1] In speech, especially in clear, well-turned speech, everything seems as if it were already accomplished, because it is perfectly expressed and perfectly understood. But in action, concrete reality asserts itself, and in retrospect every act always turns out to be not only less perfect but less comprehensible than the talk about it had led one to anticipate. Thus, if the object of ethics were really to secure a perfect verbal expression of the ethical goal, as in philosophical ethics, rather than to realize even a small part of that goal in action, it might happen that no one would get to the religious stage at all, because no one would reach the ethical despair which is its existential prerequisite.

The ethically striving individual also discovers the discrepancy between the universal and the particular. The ethical is the universal, for if anyone were left out of the obligation to do the good he would be, as it were, evicted from the category of man. How then is the particular to be understood ethically in relation to the universal? Is it something bad that must be got rid of, the sooner the better? Or is it something neutral and pliable that must be poured into the form of the universal good, like wax into a candle mold? In that case the individual would disappear, with or without struggle but with the intention that he *should* disappear, into the universal straight jacket, with all his particularity neatly strapped down and out of sight. He would become a mere specimen of the genus "ideal man." Yet if there is anything the ethically striving individual has learned in his struggles with himself and with others, it is that every case is different, that the individual is not a "case" at all but a unique concretion, that the abstract never quite truly represents or does justice to the concrete, and that the universal as a demand does not really know quite what to do with the particular or how to deal with it. On the other hand, how should the individual himself deal with it? How can he rescue his particularity as an individual from the all-devouring demands of the universal, except through a

---

[1] *Concluding Unscientific Postscript*, p. 414.

sort of divine sanction for his particularity, that is, through a personal religious relationship?

It is in questions and dilemmas such as these that ethical "maturity" is reached, the true ethical despair is approached, and the need of God begins to make itself felt. Not only does the individual need God to "cover" with his forgiveness the shortcomings he discovers in himself only through ethical striving, he also needs God to "cover" with his providence the conflicts and collisions in the ethical situation itself, since merely in order to persist in the ethical striving he needs the assurance that it is precisely in this imperfect medium of existence, and not in some imaginary ideal world, that God wants the ethical to be done. Martin J. Heinecken describes very clearly in modern terms the "bankruptcy of the ethical" in the following passage that indicates both the ethical despair and the need for God that appear on the limits of this stage:

All men in the pursuit of their vocation, if they take their duty seriously, become involved in conflicts where, no matter which choice they make, a breach of the universal ensues. . . . There is the policeman who kills in the course of his duty; there are the soldiers who drop bombs on innocent women and children; there is the judge who must set free the one who he is convinced is guilty, or condemn the one he knows innocent. There are the lawyer and the banker and the politician who in the pursuit of their professions can only through the blindness of pride suppose that they never violate any universal moral principles. It is only the moral prig, or the one satisfied with the evasions of a code-morality, or the one who has abandoned all moral principle, who can sleep with a clear conscience, glibly asserting that he has done nothing wrong when he decides to drop an atom bomb on Hiroshima. Anyone who operates a business in a brutal capitalist society without acknowledging the guilt of his own involvement is certainly deceiving himself. If he makes claims of absolute fairness and of never violating the demands of strict justice in giving to each his due, then he is blinded by his pride. If he means to extricate himself from his involvement in the society of which he is a part he tries the impossible. If he really takes seriously the demands of the ethical he will soon find himself hopelessly stymied. He too will find himself the victim of the despair common to all men. The law (the universal) would thus be the schoolmaster to bring him to Christ. As a forgiven sinner, he would have to be humble enough to do what his calling demands in the assurance of faith that this is the will of God *for him* with the sin involved covered by forgiveness, even though he will

undoubtedly thereby lay himself open to the criticisms of the moral-
ists. To do that which love demands in the moment is a strictly individual matter on which no man can sit in judgment but only the all-seeing
God.[2]

2. *The Ethical Superseded in "Fear and Trembling"*

Just as in the transition from the aesthetic to the ethical stage
the individual "acquired" himself, but did not *prove* anything, so
in the transition from the ethical to the religious stage, the individual "acquires" God, but still does not prove anything. No one
discovers a homunculus which he can point out as the eternally
valid self; no one discovers a something to which he can point
and say: behold, it is God. Objectively, the situation remains
simply uncertain, as before—there is nothing that can be proved
or disproved here. Subjectively, the leap brings about no more than
a new task of orientation, since the problem for the truth-seeking
individual, the person-becoming-truth, is never to prove anything
but always to express the correct relationships in his life. In the
ethical stage the correct relationships were described as the striving
to realize the universal good (or, as Kant has so well put it, to
act always so that the principle of one's action could be made into
a universal law). In the religious stage, the relationship to God
takes priority over the relationship to the universal good, so that
now the correct relationships can be described by saying that the
individual must try to maintain himself simultaneously in an absolute relationship to the absolute end and in a relative relationship
to relative ends.

Thus there arises the possibility of a collision which, says Kierkegaard, philosophy never dreamed of, the collision between ethical
obligation and the obedience to a direct religious command. This
is of course an exceptional situation, not likely to be encountered
every day, yet the fact that as a possibility this collision hangs
over every religious individual puts him in a state of *fear and
trembling*. In his book by that name, Kierkegaard has one of his
pseudonyms raise the question in a hypothetical sense: is a teleological suspension of the ethical possible? For if it is not, then
Abraham in his willingness to sacrifice Isaac should be called a

---

[2] *The Moment Before God*, An Interpretation of Kierkegaard (Philadelphia: Muhlenberg Press, 1956), pp. 255-256.

murderer, instead of being called the father of faith. Here again the situation is put in extreme terms, since killing is involved, and yet the same *kind* of problem arises in connection with such matters as marriage, family obligations, and choosing a vocation (it happened in Kierkegaard's own life in his relationship with Regina). At any moment the normally orderly ethical life of the religious individual may be interrupted by what might be called an order from a superior officer. In fact, the military analogy may help us here. Philosophy would say that God ought not to make any demands that might collide with the individual's ethical obligations, since philosophy's idea of God is generally not much more than ethical obligation writ large. But the religious point of view, using the military terms, could only be something like this: what kind of a general would it be who for his own purposes was not able to overrule the orders of the lesser officers or of the military rule books? Certainly the lives of all the religiously "great" individuals, the prophets and the saints, testify to such "interruption" from above, so the ethical cannot be the highest command that can be given to a religious individual. Yet the ethical is the orderly and the secure, and it should be noted that this interruption is a *suspension,* not an abrogation, of the ethical and that the suspension is teleological, purposeful, not arbitrary or whimsical. It is precisely because the ethical is *not* abolished, not strictly even superseded but only suspended while still pressing its claims, that the religious individual is thrown into a state of fear and trembling by the awesomeness of the decision he has to make.

The problem revolves once again around the relationship between the universal and the particular, which was discovered as a discrepancy in the ethical stage but now takes on more and more the character of the paradoxical. For to the extent that a person has succeeded in rescuing his particularity from being swallowed up in the universal or from being rejected as a bad thing—that is, to the extent that his particularity might be regarded as a good thing in the eyes of God—just to that extent, he can be sure, his particularity will not be allowed to him simply as a sort of luxury (perhaps as a reward for becoming religious!) but will become the very stuff of the religious relationship, that which is to be penetrated by the claims of God.

In the ethical stage, the individual who asserted his particularity over against the claims of the universal was in a state of temptation, in danger of becoming guilty by claiming exemption from the universal. But if it is possible as a particular individual to have a direct and absolute relationship to God, then the situation becomes reversed. "Faith is precisely this paradox, that the individual as the particular is higher than the universal, is justified over against it, is not subordinate but superior—yet in such a way, be it observed, that it is the particular individual who, after he has been subordinated as the particular to the universal, now through the universal becomes the individual who as the particular is superior to the universal, for the fact that the individual as the particular stands in an absolute relation to the absolute."[3]

The question is, "Is there such a thing as an absolute duty toward God?" and to answer it one must not make the mistake of confusing such a duty with just another (perhaps higher) ethical duty. One must not confuse a case like Abraham's willingness to sacrifice Isaac with the situation in which a higher ethical duty conflicts with a lower ethical duty, as when, let us say, duty to the nation conflicts with duty to the family. When Agamemnon sacrifices Iphigenia to appease the gods and save the national cause, we have the tragic hero, one who can justify himself by the very fact that everyone can understand him, sympathize with his conflict, and appreciate the sacrifice he makes as a father in subordinating the lower to the higher ethical demand. But Abraham is not a tragic hero, for his willingness to sacrifice Isaac is motivated not by a desire to serve the state but by his feeling that here is a test of his faith demanded by God. "With Abraham the situation was different. By his act he overstepped the ethical entirely and possessed a higher *telos* outside of it, in relation to which he suspended the former. For I should very much like to know how one would bring Abraham's act into relation with the universal, and whether it is possible to discover any connection whatever between what Abraham did and the universal . . . except the fact that he transgressed it."[4]

[3] *Fear and Trembling,* trans. Walter Lowrie (Princeton, N.J.: Princeton University Press), p. 82.

[4] *Fear and Trembling,* p. 88.

But the transgression of the universal is precisely that which makes it impossible for Abraham to justify himself to others, or even to talk about his act, to try to explain it. "So soon as I talk I express the universal, and if I do not do so, no one can understand me."[5] The religious individual caught in the tensions of this paradoxical situation, unable to explain himself to anyone by calling upon the universal, unable to use the universal to assure himself that he has not made a mistake about his relationship as a particular individual to God (for as a particular individual he exists in opposition to the universal)—this individual might try to help himself out (or at least philosophy might try to help him out) by calling to mind the *results* that his act, in the long course of outward history, may bring about. But here, as in all pragmatic solutions to existential dilemmas, one encounters the stubborn fact that the acting individual is simply not in a position to *know* what the results will be. And if there is any question of justifying or explaining an act in which much is at stake and much is to be risked —just such a great and heroic action as the individual might feel was directly commanded by God—then it must be remembered "that from the creation of the world it has been customary for the result to come last, and that, if one would truly learn anything from great actions, one must pay attention precisely to the beginning. In case he who should act were to judge himself according to the result, he would never get to the point of beginning. Even though the result may give joy to the whole world, it cannot help the hero, for he would get to know the result only when the whole thing was over, and it was not by this he became a hero, but he was such for the fact that he began.[6]

Results, then, will not help the religious individual—he may never live to see them, and in any case they are out of his control. Nor will the advice of others help him, for he could consult them only by appealing to the universal and declaring that he is proposing to transgress it by dint of having an absolute relationship to God as a particular individual. And yet he knows he may be mistaken. Nowhere does Kierkegaard imply that there is something infallible about the absolute duty toward God, or that simply because one

[5] *Fear and Trembling*, p. 89.
[6] *Fear and Trembling*, pp. 94-95.

acts in the belief that he is obeying a divine command one escapes the usual limitations of the human situation with respect to knowledge and the possibilities of error. The possibility of being mistaken is the very heart and core of the fear and trembling, accentuated by this isolation from others and from the universal, in the terrible aloneness before God. But therein lies the greatness, as well as the terror, of becoming the "knight of faith."

People imagine maybe that the individual can make himself intelligible to another individual in the same case. Such a notion would be unthinkable if in our time people did not in so many ways seek to creep slyly into greatness. The one knight of faith can render no aid to the other. Either the individual becomes a knight of faith by assuming the burden of the paradox, or he never becomes one. In these regions partnership is unthinkable. Every more precise explication of what is to be understood by Isaac the individual can give only to himself. And even if one were able, generally speaking, to define ever so precisely what should be intended by Isaac . . . , the individual nevertheless will never be able to assure himself by the aid of others that this application is appropriate, but he can do so only by himself as the individual. Hence even if a man were cowardly and paltry enough to wish to become a knight of faith on the responsibility and at the peril of an outsider, he will never become one; for only the individual becomes a knight of faith as the particular individual, and this is the greatness of this knighthood, as I can well understand without entering the order; but this is also its terror, as I can comprehend even better.[7]

Fear and trembling is a characteristic of the religious stage of existence; every religious individual has his own "Isaac," something ethically good and precious that he may be called upon to sacrifice for the sake of his religious calling as a particular individual. And is this paradoxical situation so unusual, so peculiar to Abraham or to the Old Testament notion of sacrifice? "In Luke 14:26, as everybody knows, there is a striking doctrine taught about the absolute duty toward God: 'If any man cometh unto me and hateth not his own father and mother and wife and children and brethren and sisters, yea, and his own life also, he cannot be my disciple.' This is a hard saying, who can bear to hear it? For this reason it is heard very seldom."[8]

[7] *Fear and Trembling*, pp. 107-108.
[8] *Fear and Trembling*, pp. 108-109.

As soon as one tries to mitigate the situation which creates the fear and trembling by removing the paradoxical from it, by saying for example that there cannot be an absolute duty toward God precisely because it might conflict with an ethical duty, then the whole situation collapses back into the ethical stage. God is just another word for the ethical, the ethical becomes the highest content of existence, God has no power over the individual, and the individual disappears into the universal. The religious stage is then an illusion or a purely cultural ornamentation of the ethical, since the ethical is not really transcended in the dimension of existence. Yet we have just seen how the ethical stage reaches its limit in ethical despair and the need for God. So it is as if another either/or were being pressed upon the individual here—either there is an absolute duty to God, or else the ethical despair cannot be overcome and the need for God cannot be fulfilled. If faith is possible at all, the absolute duty to God must be possible, and in addition the conflicts must be possible as well; the fear and trembling must be a real "burden" of the religious stage, not an illusion promoted by a mistaken view of the individual's particularity. To summarize:

The paradox of faith is this, that the individual is higher than the universal, that the individual (to recall a dogmatic distinction now rather seldom heard) determines his relation to the universal by his relation to the absolute, not his relation to the absolute by his relation to the universal. The paradox can also be expressed by saying that there is an absolute duty toward God; for in this relationship of duty the individual as an individual stands related absolutely to the absolute. So when in this connection it is said that it is a duty to love God, something different is said from that in the foregoing; for if this duty is absolute, the ethical is reduced to a position of relativity. From this, however, it does not follow that the ethical is to be abolished, but it acquires an entirely different expression, the paradoxical expression —that, for example, love to God may cause the knight of faith to give his love to his neighbor the opposite expression to that which, ethically speaking, is required by duty.[9]

3. "The Religious Suffering"—a Signal

It need not be hard for us to see why Kierkegaard stressed fear and trembling as one of the characteristics of the truly religious life. He had before his angry eyes the mediocrity, complacency,

---

[9] *Fear and Trembling*, p. 105.

and bourgeois respectability of Danish church life, where being a Christian was virtually identified with being a good husband and father (and perhaps alderman) and of course a pillar of society. To give an idea of the diametrical opposite to the fear and trembling in which the truly religious individual holds his God-relationship, and also to remind ourselves that we are not altogether in the position of no longer needing Kierkegaard's polemics against "respectable Christianity," I include here a bit of Climacus' unforgettable diatribe against the Danish idea of being a Christian:

How strange is the way of the world! Once it was at the risk of his life that a man dared to profess himself a Christian; now it is to make oneself suspect to venture to doubt that one is a Christian. Especially when this doubt does not mean that the individual launches a violent attack against Christianity with a view to abolishing it; for in that case it would perhaps be admitted that there was something in it. But if a man were to say quite simply and unassumingly, that he was concerned for himself, lest perhaps he had no right to call himself a Christian, he would indeed not suffer persecution or be put to death, but he would be smothered in angry glances, and people would say: "How tiresome to make such a fuss about nothing at all; why can't he behave like the rest of us, who are all Christians? It is just as it is with F. F., who refuses to wear a hat on his head like others, but insists on dressing differently." And if he happened to be married, his wife would say to him: "Dear husband of mine, how can you get such notions into your head? How can you doubt that you are a Christian? Are you not a Dane, and does not the geography say that the Lutheran form of the Christian religion is the ruling religion in Denmark? For you are surely not a Jew, nor are you a Mohammedan; what then can you be if not a Christian? It is a thousand years since paganism was driven out of Denmark, so I know you are not a pagan. Do you not perform your duties at the office like a conscientious civil servant; are you not a good citizen of a Christian nation, a Lutheran Christian state? So then of course you must be a Christian."[10]

This is what happens when the religious divides itself without remainder into the ethical, remaining still under the banner of religion but without any conception of a possible higher claim that might isolate the individual from the society thus conceived and even prevent him from realizing some of the ethical "goods," such as the rewards and responsibilities of marriage and good citizenship. But it was not always so. There was a time in the history of

[10] *Postscript*, p. 49.

Christianity when it was thought by many serious persons that the religious life could not be lived in the "world" at all, and required specially secluded retiring-places for its attempted realization. Kierkegaard uses the monastic movement as a point of departure for his discussion of another characteristic of the religious existence, that which he calls the *religious suffering,* or the *dying away from immediacy.*

The monastic movement must be given credit for recognizing that the problem of the religious individual's relationship to the "world" was a real one, and for attempting an actual, if somewhat naïve and institutional, solution to the problem. Unlike the Danish Christians just described, the medieval monk at least did not claim to have "gone farther" (than primitive Christianity), without actually having faced the problem at all. Lutherans especially were inclined to disparage monasticism, as if abolishing the monasteries had solved the problem that the monasteries were trying to solve and as if the much extolled "ordinary life" could be lived by a Christian without further ado, without any "difference," and without any difficulties.

I often think, when I look at Luther, that there is one very doubtful thing about him: a reformer who wanted to cast off the yoke—is a very doubtful matter. That is precisely why he was immediately taken in vain politically; for he himself has one side in common with politics, which is also true of his entire position: not to attack "the masses," but a particular ruler.

That is why Luther had such an easy fight. The difficulty lies precisely in suffering because one must make things more difficult for others. When one fights to throw off burdens one is of course understood at once by very many, whose interest it is to throw off the burdens. And consequently the real Christian sign, double danger, is absent.

In a sense Luther took the matter too lightly. He ought to have made it apparent that the freedom he was fighting for (and in that fight he was on the right side) led to making life, the spiritual life, infinitely more exhausting than it had been before.[11]

Let us examine some of the difficulties that make the religious life "infinitely more exhausting" outside of the monastery than in it and that produce what Kierkegaard calls *the religious suffering.* Objectively, theoretically, in the realm of pure thought, a man

[11] *Journals,* No. 1079, p. 384.

can pass from the ethical to the religious stage in the twinkling of an eye, in just the time it takes him to substitute a religious for an ethical concept of the absolute end or *telos*. He may think this out for himself in simply logical or metaphysical terms, such as that the highest good cannot be operative unless it is identified with the power that absolutely rules the world whatever appearances to the contrary seem to say—and in such matters thought can be very quick. But subjectively, existentially, the task now is to maintain himself simultaneously in an absolute relationship to the absolute *telos* and in a relative relationship to every relative *telos,* a task which, the would-be religious individual discovers, is not to be accomplished in the twinkling of an eye—nor can it be done once and for all, as in the realm of pure thought. Thus he knows, in his mind, that he ought to reserve the absolute relationship for God, and yet he repeatedly catches himself, in his immediate, daily life in the world, acting as if he were absolutely committed to any number of relative ends. Mentally he is a jump ahead of himself, and yet he knows he must close the gap. And closing the gap constitutes the religious suffering.

This suffering has its ground in the fact that the individual is in his immediacy absolutely committed to relative ends; its significance lies in the transposition of the relationship, the dying away from immediacy, or in the expression existentially of the principle that the individual can do absolutely nothing of himself, but is as nothing before God; for here again the negative is the mark by which the God-relationship is recognized, and self-annihilation is the essential form for the God-relationship. And this self-annihilation must not receive an external expression, for then we have the monastic movement, and the relationship becomes after all a worldly one; and the individual must not allow himself to imagine that it can be done once for all, for this is aesthetics. And even if it could be done at a stroke, because the individual is an existing individual, he will again encounter suffering in the repetition.[12]

But it must not be thought for a moment that "self-annihilation before God" means that the individual stops being a self, thereby regressing to the aesthetic stage where strictly speaking he did not as yet have a self. This over-simplification is one of the many possible misunderstandings of the requirements of the religious stage, one which many people are glad to snatch at because they are all eager to

[12] *Postscript,* p. 412.

get rid of the often burdensome task of being and becoming a self. Here, for example, is where some Oriental religions have gone astray, preaching that the self must be destroyed, must disappear as a drop of water disappears into the ocean of the infinite. But that is self-annihilation *into* God, not self-annihilation *before* God. No, it is just the other way around, paradoxically. It is precisely the individual self, in all its particularity and singularity and in all the fulness of its possibility—it is precisely this complete self that is to exist as nothing before God. And so also with the individual's activity. Becoming nothing before God does not mean quietism, refusing to act on the grounds that God will do all. On the contrary, it is just the striving, struggling individual in the full tilt of work at his tasks—and most of all the victorious individual who can point to achievements—who is to exist as nothing before God. "The religious does not preach indulgence, but proclaims that the greatest exertion is nothing—at the same time requiring it."[13]

Objectively, theoretically, in the realm of pure thought, the individual may experience no difficulty in understanding why he must become as nothing before God: so that God may become all in all in him, may use him as an empty vessel to fill with his grace, his will, and so on. "There is no contradiction in the idea that a man can do nothing before God except to become aware of this fact; for this is only another expression for the aboluteness of God . . ."[14] And we know that Christian devotional literature abounds in fervent poetical expressions of the religious individual's desire to be nothing before God so that God may be all in him, starting with "He must increase, I must decrease." The contradictions arise when this idea is introduced into the medium of existence. And if any witness to the difficulty of making the attempt is required, we need only remind ourselves of the historical attempts that have been made. Whether we examine the extremes of asceticism or the extremes of quietism, the Lutheran "faith-righteousness" at one end or the Roman Catholic "work-righteousness" at the other, a great deal of what we see strikes us somehow as mistakes, distortions of what the proper relationships should be. Yet dare we imply that we could do better if we tried and that all these other people were less sincere

---

[13] *Postscript*, p. 414.
[14] *Postscript*, p. 413, note.

or more stupid than we are? Is it not rather that the task of realizing the correct relationships is much more difficult, "infinitely more exhausting," than we or they imagined it would be?

So here is the religious suffering, the dying away from immediacy while remaining in it, the learning to live in this world as one who belongs to another world, the becoming detached from the things of this world without hating them. And all this is to be done without any calling of attention to oneself by means of "outward signs," and without any idea of meritoriousness. "Suffering as a dying away from immediacy is thus not flagellations and the like; it is not *self-torture*. For the self-torturer does not by any means express that he can do nothing before God, for he counts his acts of self-torture as being something."[15] Correctly, the correct relationships can be expressed only in inwardness, because "inwardness is the relationship of the individual to himself before God. . . ."[16]

Yet inwardness was exactly what the Hegelian philosophy was making impossible, Kierkegaard felt. Monasticism at least had appreciated that the "inner" and the "outer," the spiritual and the worldly, were not exactly commensurable, whereby the first could quite comfortably and adequately express itself in the second, and the Absolute could "exhaust itself in relative ends." The principle of mediation insisted that conflict and contradiction are only apparent, that all opposition can be resolved in a higher synthesis of the opposing factors. But when this principle is introduced into existence by an existing individual, the result is simply that he loses the absolute relation to the Absolute, since he cannot at the same time maintain the distinction and declare it to be illusory.

The majesty of the absolute relationship thus becomes an empty phrase, a showy introduction to life which remains outside it, a title-page not bound with the book. But the relationship to the absolute *telos* cannot pour itself exhaustively into the relative ends, because the absolute relationship may require the renunciation of them all. On the other hand, the individual who sustains an absolute relationship to the absolute *telos* may very well exist in relative ends, precisely in order to exercise the absolute relationship in renunciation.[17]

Thus, the proper way for the individual to express the incom-

[15] *Postscript*, p. 414.   [16] *Postscript*, p. 391.
[17] *Postscript*, p. 363.

mensurability of the outward with the inward is by *not* seeking a special form of outwardness to call attention to himself and to let the whole world know how his inwardness stands, how he is related to himself before God. But of course this "hidden" inwardness is the most difficult kind to maintain, because where there is no outward sign it is so easy to deceive oneself as to whether the inwardness is truly there and, if so, what its quality is. Here Kierkegaard is laying bare one of the most obdurate difficulties of the religious life—the spuriousness of an externalized piety, and yet the need for some outwardness and outward signs if only for communication. We all know that an obvious piousness generates instant suspicion about its genuineness, simply because it is so outward; we feel that the more genuine the religious existence, the less there would be a desire to make a public show of it. And yet there is the necessity of public worship and the need for teaching and bearing witness to the truth. In stressing the desirability of the hidden inwardness Kierkegaard certainly did not deny the need for these. He himself was a regular attender at public worship and a teacher and witness-bearer through his writings. He simply saw more clearly than most people do the perennial dilemma of the religious mode of existence: on the one hand, not to fall into the error of the monastics by seeking a worldly and even a meritorious expression for one's inward relationship to God: on the other hand, not to fall into the error of the philosophers by losing the precious inwardness entirely through abolishing the distinction. It is the old challenge to walk a knife-edge path between two opposite dangers—and that is the religious suffering.

This difficulty is also the witness of the negative—for as long as the religious suffering is there the individual may take comfort that he has the God-relationship, that he is repeatedly making the effort to re-establish the correct relations. Let the religious suffering disappear, and the God-relationship disappears with it. Kierkegaard does not deny that the religious individual has moments of joy. His point is just that these are *moments* and that the religious individual cannot have his life in moments only, with empty wastes in the intervals, for then he regresses to the aesthetic life. And the religious suffering does not disappear or dwindle through practice or through having lived out a long lifetime. If it really is the religious suffering and not some other kind of suffering (such as neurotic suffering, which is anything but religious), it lasts the whole lifetime and becomes more perceptive, more refined. The religious suffering is the symptomatic ache that accompanies, but also signals, the fact that existence is being transformed religiously.

4. *"Resignation" as a Test of Relationship*

We have already seen that in Kierkegaard's view of the religious stage "the relationship to the absolute *telos* cannot pour itself exhaustively into the relative ends, because the absolute relationship may require the renunciation of them all." By this realization one pays respect to the majesty and transcendence of God, even in the sphere of religious immanence, where as yet there is not the problem of a special revelation but where there is nevertheless a feeling that the infinite and eternal God must be something more than a summation of all finite and temporal realities. Well, then, how does the religious individual discover whether he is ready to renounce everything for the sake of the Absolute, should this be required of him? He finds this out by submitting himself and the entire spectrum of his finite and relative ends to the test of *resignation.*

Resignation as a strategy, or as an exercise in the relationship to the Absolute, may be regarded as another characteristic of the religious stage of existence still in the sphere of immanence, or what Kierkegaard calls "religiousness A." Resignation is not fatalism, though it may become that through a misunderstanding, as in the case of Mohammedanism, where the individual sloughs off the responsibilities of freedom and declares that whatever happens happens because Allah has willed it—and this can scarcely exclude the inward happenings. Nor is resignation an a priori asceticism toward some particular aspects of the immediate life deemed especially worldly or unspiritual. Resignation is not necessarily asceticism at all, and it is certainly not a concern over giving up things which are not good anyway. In resignation the question concerns one's willingness to give up, for the sake of the highest, things that are recognized as good in themselves and in their places, should this be required of the particular individual. In the extreme, the test of resignation is simply to ask oneself if one would be willing to be a martyr, should the appropriate occasion arise; in its mild, everyday form, it is to end every prayer, even the most heartfelt beseechings of God for something, with "nevertheless, not my will but thine be done."

In our current jargon, we might say that resignation is a device of the inward economy whereby the individual effects a reordering of his scale of values, such that the new relationship implied in the religious stage is reflected in it. In the ethical stage, it will be remembered, the individual first received the beginnings of some kind of order in his life, in that the shifting and momentary and unreliable hedonic values were placed in subservience to the prime ethical value, that of realizing the good, or, in Kantian terms, the categorical imperative. Now at first sight it would seem that the ethical goal is the highest goal possible for a human being, and so it does appear to all who contemplate the goal in abstract thought without setting about at once to realize it in existence. As soon as a person starts living the ethical plan of life instead of talking about it, he experiences the concrete falling short in particular cases, the repentance and guilt and need for forgiveness and renewal, all of which spell out the bankruptcy of the merely human powers, and he feels the need for divine help merely to persist in the ethical task. And as soon as he asks for and receives this help he is in the religious stage. But as soon as he is in the religious stage another re-ordering of his scale of values is called for, because now he has to play the game on God's terms rather than on his own. And even the goal, the highest good, must change, in order to correspond to what the highest good is in the eyes of the eternal rather than in the eyes of man, a goal that Kierkegaard always refers to as "the eternal blessedness."

The need for the test of resignation arises just because the individual who is now in the religious stage is not, however, transported to some heavenly plane but remains on earth, in the midst of the relativities of earthly life, trying to hold on to the lifeline to the infinite. How is he, from his earthly position, to know if he really has hold of it, or if he, in the confusion of all the clamoring relative ends, has not already lost it?

Existence is a synthesis of the infinite and the finite, and the existing individual is both infinite and finite. Now if for any individual an eternal happiness is his highest good, this will mean that all finite satisfactions are volitionally relegated to the status of what may have to be renounced in favor of an eternal happiness.[18]

But why *all?* Surely the infinite does not require him to commit suicide? No, it is just because he cannot tell in advance which particular one of the many "finite satisfactions" he may be required to give up in a future decision that he must keep himself in readiness to renounce any or all of them. All are *candidates* for renunciation, and it is by his willingness to place them in candidacy for renunciation that he finds out if he actually is in an absolute relationship to the Absolute.

He need only submit his entire immediacy with all its yearnings and desires to the inspection of resignation. If he finds a single hard spot, a point of resistance, it means that he does not have a relationship to an eternal happiness.
. . . But if as a result of the inspection, resignation finds nothing out of the way, it is a sign that in the moment of inspection the individual does have a relationship to an eternal happiness.[19]

And this kind of life, Johannes Climacus observes, can be pretty strenuous, more strenuous than sitting cosily in the midst of the relative ends and calmly contemplating the world-process as if from the divine standpoint. For the whole point is that one must not apply the test of resignation just once in a while, like an unfaithful servant who manages to have "his balances in order for the day of inspection. As soon as the audit is well over, he thinks, everything will again slip back into the old ruts."[20] To think about the absolute end just once in a while is to have a relative relation to it, whereby it becomes a relative end, because for an existing individual it is the relationship that counts.

So the task is "to exercise myself in the relationship to the absolute *telos* so as always to have it with me, while remaining in the relativities of life . . . "[21] And in case anyone thinks that this task would lead straight to the cloister, he needs to be reminded that (1) there is no meritoriousness in this task, as the monastic movement

[18] *Postscript*, p. 350.
[19] *Postscript*, pp. 353, 354.
[20] *Postscript*, p. 354.
[21] *Postscript*, p. 365.

mistakenly thought, and (2) there is no special outward expression to be sought for it, to call attention to the fact that one is not like other men. The whole thing is to take place in inwardness, in the individual's relationship to himself before God—"but let us not forget that inwardness without outwardness is the most difficult kind of inwardness, where self-deception is easiest . . ."[22]

How then does such a person live? Can we recognize him if we wish? We can if we are careful, for although he lives in immediacy like all others, he does not live in it in the same way.

The individual does not cease to be a human being, nor does he divest himself of the manifold composite garment of the finite in order to clothe himself in the abstract garment of the cloister. . . . In his immediacy the individual is rooted in the finite. But when resignation has convinced itself that he has acquired the absolute direction toward the absolute *telos*, all is changed, and the roots have been severed. He still lives in the finite, but he does not have his life in the finite. His life has, like that of other human beings, the various predicates of a human existence, but he is in them as one who is clothed in the borrowed garments of a stranger. . . . He is incognito, but his incognito consists in having an appearance entirely like others. Just as the dentist has loosened the soft tissues about a tooth and cut the nerve, so the roots of his life in the finite have been severed. It is not his task to give the tooth an opportunity to grow fast again, which would be mediation. . . . The individual does indeed remain in the finite, . . . but just as he deprived the finite of its unchecked vitality in the moment of resignation, so it remains his task to reinstate repeatedly the determination by which this was first accomplished. Let the world give him everything, it is possible that he will see fit to accept it. But he says: "Oh, well," and this "Oh, well" means the absolute *telos*. If the world takes everything from him, he suffers no doubt; but he says again: "Oh, well"—and this "Oh, well" means the absolute respect for the absolute *telos*. Men do not exist in this fashion when they live immediately in the finite.[23]

5. *The Two Types of Religiousness Idealized*

In connection with the subject of resignation, we must turn our attention for a while to the use to which Kierkegaard allowed one of his earlier pseudonyms (Johannes de Silentio in *Fear and Trembling*) to put it. The locus is the "Preliminary Expectoration,"

[22] *Postscript*, p. 364.
[23] *Postscript*, pp. 367-368.

which occurs between the "Panegyric" on Abraham and the analysis of ethical problems raised by Abraham's direct relationship to
God as expressed in his willingness to sacrifice Isaac ("Problem
I"). Johannes de Silentio tries to characterize, in a highly idealized
and imaginative form, one of the basic differences between what
he later calls religiousness A, or the religiousness of immanence,
and religiousness B, or the specifically Christian religiousness.

For his protagonists of the two kinds of religiousness, Johannes
uses two imaginary existential heroes, the knight of infinite resignation and the knight of faith. The point is to make a distinction
between what a man can attain by his own powers, in the practice
of resignation, and what he cannot attain by his own powers but
can attain only by virtue of faith in something that has been done
for him, namely (from a rationalist standpoint), by virtue of the
absurd. Following Hegel here, Johannes calls every attitude of the
self to the world a "movement" and speaks of the "double movement of infinity"—that is, of the infinite in man's self, first moving
away from the finite world in resignation in order thereby to come
to consciousness of itself, and, after that, moving back toward the
finite world again, in order to live in it. Thus, resignation is seen
to be only the first half of the "double movement of infinity." "The
infinite resignation is the last stage prior to faith, so that one who
has not made this movement has not faith; for only in the infinite
resignation do I become clear to myself with respect to my eternal
validity, and only then can there be any question of grasping existence by virtue of faith."[24]

Up to this dividing line between the two stages of religiousness
any man can arrive by dint of his own willing resignation of the
finite, becoming more and more sure of the infinite as a dimension
of his soul by virtue of all he is willing to give up for its sake. In a
more modern way of speaking we might say that even if all religion
were an illusion in that there really was nothing in the universe that
corresponded to the deep need for God in man, man could still
achieve a kind of melancholy dignity and triumph over the world
by asserting his independence of it and superiority over it by virtue
of his consciousness of the infinite. Or, to put it still another way,
this consciousness would become all that is left of the traditional

[24] *Fear and Trembling*, pp. 65-66.

idea of God, a kind of limit-concept of the infinite which one approaches precisely by moving away from everything finite. Such an immanent divinity can be reached by anyone who is willing to be a "knight of infinite resignation." But when it comes to getting the finite back again, or any part of it—the finite as constituting in its very finiteness part of God's intention for man—there is required the "absurd" act of faith in spite of appearances, which has since been almost caricatured as Kierkegaard's "leap into the arms of God."

The infinite resignation "is a purely philosophical movement which I dare say I am able to make if it is required, and which I can train myself to make, for whenever any finiteness would get the mastery over me, I starve myself until I can make the movement . . ."[25] Such a "philosophical" religiousness, however, is something quite different from the popular wish-fulfilment type of understanding of religion, wherein as a result of not getting what he wanted a man talks about having lost his faith; but "when one looks at the scale to see where he is, one sees, strangely enough, that he has only reached the point where he should make the infinite movement of resignation."[26]

But faith is not the active agent in resignation, faith, that is to say, in the meaningfulness and providential nature of the finite world. In resignation the active agent is the individual's love for the infinite, and "he whose soul has not this romantic enthusiasm has sold his soul, whether he got a kingdom for it or a paltry piece of silver. But by my own strength I am not able to get the least of the things which belong to finiteness, for I am constantly using my strength to renounce everything."[27]

By faith I make renunciation of nothing, on the contrary, by faith I acquire everything, precisely in the sense in which it is said that he who has faith like a grain of mustard can remove mountains. A purely human courage is required to renounce the whole of the temporal to gain the eternal; but this I gain, and to all eternity I cannot renounce it, that is a self-contradiction; but a paradox enters in and a humble courage is required to grasp the whole of the temporal by virtue of the absurd, and this is the courage of faith. By faith Abraham did not

[25] *Fear and Trembling*, p. 69.
[26] *Fear and Trembling*, p. 69.
[27] *Fear and Trembling*, p. 71.

renounce his claim upon Isaac, but by faith he got Isaac. By virtue of resignation that rich young man should have given away everything, but then when he had done that, the knight of faith should have said to him, "By virtue of the absurd thou shalt get every penny back again. Canst thou believe that?" And this speech ought by no means to have been indifferent to the aforesaid rich young man, for in case he gave away his goods because he was tired of them, his resignation was not much to boast of.[28]

So both the knight of faith and the knight of infinite resignation live in the finite, but with a difference. Neither enters the cloister, but the knight of infinite resignation lives in the finite like a stranger or foreigner in borrowed clothes. His is the sad superiority of the aristocrat traveling incognito, his the stoical endurance imposed by *noblesse oblige* on those who can never pretend to feel really at home in this far-from-best of all possible worlds. To one who has come to know the soaring bliss of the infinite, this world of finite matters is a wearisome multiplicity. Now the knight of faith also lives in the finite—but let us listen to Johannes de Silentio rhapsodize upon the difference:

The moment I set eyes on him . . . I myself leap backwards, I clasp my hands and say half aloud, "Good Lord, is this the man? Is it really he? Why, he looks like a tax-collector!" . . . I draw closer to him, watching his least movements to see whether there might not be visible a little heterogeneous fractional telegraphic message from the infinite, a glance, a look, a gesture, a note of sadness, a smile, which betrayed the infinite in its heterogeneity with the finite. No! I examine his figure from tip to toe to see if there might not be a cranny through which the infinite was peeping. No! . . . His tread? It is vigorous, belonging entirely to finiteness; no smartly dressed townsman who walks out to Fresberg on a Sunday afternoon treads the ground more firmly, he belongs entirely to the world, no Philistine more so. One can discover nothing of that aloof and superior nature whereby one recognizes the knight of the infinite. He takes delight in everything, and whenever one sees him taking part in a particular pleasure, he does it with the persistence which is the mark of the earthly man whose soul is absorbed in such things. He tends to his work. . . . In the evening he smokes his pipe; to look at him one would swear that it was the grocer over the way vegetating in the twilight. He lives as carefree as a ne'er-do-well, and yet he buys up the acceptable time at the dearest price, for he does not do the least thing except by virtue of the absurd. And yet, and yet I could become furious over it—for

[28] *Fear and Trembling*, p. 70.

envy, if for no other reason—because the man has made and every instant is making the movements of infinity. With infinite resignation he has drained the cup of life's profound sadness, he knows the bliss of the infinite, he senses the pain of renouncing everything, the dearest things he possesses in the world, and yet finiteness tastes to him just as good as to one who never knew anything higher. . . .[29]

So much for the two knights (an oblique reference to Don Quixote) who sally forth in the jousts of existence to represent Religiousness A and the paradoxical Religiousness B in the imagination of Johannes de Silentio. But, as the later description of the same stages by Johannes Climacus in the *Postscript* shows, these two fine figures are altogether too much idealized and exaggerated to correspond with anything one might meet in actual life, in the medium of existence. Here, stretched out on the rack of time, neither is the resignation so easily accomplished, in a moment, nor is it so easy to get the finite back again, even by virtue of the absurd. Even Abraham did not offer up Isaac and get him back without fear and trembling. Living so that "the finite tastes to him just as good as to one who never knew anything higher" is of course an *ideal* for the Christian believer, a kind of anticipation of the life in the Kingdom of Heaven. And indeed, if we wish to quote Scripture, we will find both kinds of religiousness represented in the New Testament. There are plenty of demands for renunciation, especially in the parables which teach of all that a man must be willing to give up for the Kingdom's sake, and in the calls to discipleship. On the other hand, there are also plenty of reminders of the goodness of the world—how every good and perfect gift is from above, how the father knows how to give gifts to his children, how all things are theirs. But a world that lives in a sickly relationship to the finite will not let the believer get away with this kind of life, this renouncing and receiving back from the hand of the Father, for to worldliness the claim of a right relationship to the finite by virtue of faith (according to which the finite *belongs* to God) is not a matter of indifference but an affront, a challenge against which it instinctively fights back. Therefore, as Kierkegaard stressed more and more in his later writings, the genuine imitation of Christ brings on a collision with the world. It brings the cross, if it is really an imitation of Christ.

[29] *Fear and Trembling*, pp. 53, 55-56, *passim*.

Nevertheless, the fact that the man of faith does occasionally reach this ideal, if only in moments, makes it possible for a casual observer to mistake him for the aesthetic individual, because the outward resemblance is in that moment very close—at least the resemblance to the aesthetic "beginner" in the early period of his enthusiasm and rapport with his surroundings. It is because of this resemblance that the romantics went astray in their attempts to bring back or to "save" the religious element in life. For by concentrating on the ideal only and by forgetting about the problems of inward appropriation and the religious transformation of existence, they mistook faith for one more immediate aesthetic emotion among others, something like an ecstatic union with nature-as-a-whole, or like Schleiermacher's immediate and unargued "feeling of dependence." But the immediacy of the aesthetic stage is immediacy "prior to reflection" whereas the religious immediacy, or seeming immediacy, is "after reflection," and is qualified by the fact that the properly believing individual is one who has, as it were, passed through and survived all the other stages—the aesthetical, the ethical, and the religiousness of infinite resignation. Even Johannes de Silentio, who is not a believer, can see that "faith therefore is not an aesthetic emotion but something far higher, precisely because it has resignation as its presupposition. . . ."[30]

6. *At the Boundary of Religiousness B*

But now let us return to Johannes Climacus' more sober and prosaic descriptions of the characteristics of the religious stage, still in the type he calls "A," the general religiousness. Thus far we have examined fear and trembling, the religious suffering as a dying away from immediacy, and the need for resignation as the "inspector-general" who sees to it that the proper relation to the absolute is maintained. Climacus himself deals with the question of why it is not possible for the religious individual to live like the knight of faith as eulogized in *Fear and Trembling*, and even not quite like the knight of infinite resignation who rejoices over the infinite he discovers in himself just to the extent that he renounces the finite things. Isn't it possible, for example, that the religious individual might also learn to rejoice over the religious suffering,

[30] *Fear and Trembling*, p. 67.

since it is a sign that the God-relationship is there, that the very goal of his pilgrimage through existence is in sight? And wouldn't this rejoicing over suffering necessarily cancel out or overcome the suffering itself? It would indeed, if only the individual could manage to stop existing and enter the realm of pure being, where all is finished and *becoming* is retroactively cancelled as counting for nothing. But if *becoming* counts for nothing, then the religious suffering counts for nothing, and there is after all nothing to rejoice over. But if religiously, *becoming* does count for something (not meritoriously, but before God something for which the individual must be thankful, in so far as it happens in him), then the religious individual is stuck in it. And just because he is in becoming, he

cannot effect the dialectical exchange which turns the suffering into joy. In the eternal happiness itself there is no suffering, but when an existing individual establishes a relationship thereto, this relationship is quite rightly expressed through suffering. If an existing individual, through knowing that this suffering means the relationship, were capable of elevating himself above the suffering, then he would also be able to transform his status from that of an existing individual to that of an eternal being; but this he will scarcely wish to attempt. [Unless, one might interject, he is a member of a mystical or pantheistic religion, in which case the union with the One or the All is exactly what he will attempt.] But if he cannot do this, he is again in the situation of suffering, because this knowledge must be held fast in the medium of existence. In the same moment the perfection of his joy will fail of being complete, as it must always fail when it must be had in an imperfect form.[31]

Confirmation of this state of affairs as the *Postscript* describes it comes from the manuals of religious discipline and from the lives of the saints. Wherever there are ecstatic experiences there is also a kind of sublime death-wish, the feeling that death in the elevated moment would be no loss, since it would prevent the return of the burdensome and by comparison arid business of living in the finite. Thereby arises a recognized type of spiritual temptation warned against in the classic religious literature, the *lust for the divine,* in which the religious individual cultivates the extraordinary experiences and disdains the ordinary, instead of humbly accepting both as the gifts of grace. On the other hand, some kinds

[31] *Postscript*, pp. 404-405.

of suffering that we read about in the New Testament are precisely in the nature of ecstatic experiences and should not be confused with the religious suffering, as when we read "that the Apostles when they were scourged went away rejoicing, giving thanks to God that they were accounted worthy to suffer for Christ's sake. . . . No, when the individual is secure in his God-relationship and suffers only outwardly, then this is not religious suffering."[32]

There remains one more characteristic of the immanent religiousness to be noted, and in some ways it is the most important, since it is the "wall" or the exhaustive limit of this stage. This is the *consciousness of guilt* as a totality-determinant or qualitative characteristic of existence. And how is it that only the religious individual becomes conscious of this characteristic of existence, instead of some actual criminal or law-breaker? Just because he strives for the highest, not in order to obtain some advantage at odds with the law, but in order to introduce the eternal into the medium of existence. And so, as Climacus observes in one of his many recapitulations, the investigation appears to be moving backward instead of forward. For just at the moment the individual has been rescued from the aesthetic trap and set upon his feet with his stride firmly directed along the hard but glorious ethical road that leads to the realization of the highest good, there occurs a *but,* a delay. And this very delay is the beginning of guilt. The reason for this is again that in existence time cannot be abstracted from, that time matters, that

time is concrete, and even while the individual deliberates he is ethically responsible for his use of time . . . . even at the instant when the task is clearly set there has been some waste, for meanwhile time has passed, and the beginning was not made at once. Thus things go backward: the task is presented to the individual in existence, and just as he is ready to cut at once a fine figure (which only can be done *in abstracto* and on paper, because the loose trousers of the abstractor are very different from the strait-jacket of the exister) and wants to begin, it is discovered that a new beginning is necessary, the beginning upon the immense detour of dying from immediacy, and just when the beginning is about to be made at this point, it is discovered that there, since time has meanwhile been passing, an ill beginning is made, and

[32] *Postscript*, p. 405.

that the beginning must be made by becoming guilty and from that moment increasing the total capital guilt by a new guilt at a usurious rate of interest.[33]

But this going backward is nevertheless a going forward if we allow that penetrating deeper into existence is a species of going forward, like penetrating into a jungle, as I have implied all along by calling Kierkegaard's individual a pilgrim. And of course in the matter of acquiring guilt-consciousness, as in all the other characteristics, there are bypaths, ways of going wrong or going about it in the wrong way. Thus, the religious individual will never arrive at the correct or truthful consciousness of guilt as a total qualification of existence if he should avail himself of several easy "outs" lying ready to hand. The most obvious of these is to lay the blame for the guilt on existence itself, or on the one who placed him in the embarrassment of existence, the earthly or the heavenly father—it does not much matter which. We may note, for example, that this is what is done in some Oriental religions, as well as in Manichaean heresies, where the "blame" is in effect removed from the individual and placed upon the evilness of "matter," or upon the involvement of the individual in an impersonal, fateful change-ability, such as the Wheel of Kharma. Much of modern literature reflects the diffuse sense of guilt that affects all the more sensitive elements in our society, along with varying degrees of the tendency to blame this fact on existence itself, on the very fact of being born, which (as in Kafka) resembles waking up in the middle of a trial to find oneself the accused. And of course with the general lessening of the consciousness of the eternal in man, it is possible to give all sorts of *ad hoc* explanations for this feeling of generalized guilt, attempting thus to shake it off by attributing it to a plethora of antecedent childhood and family conditions.

Yet it is strictly speaking only the eternal element in the makeup of man which, by virtue of the fact that it always sees a higher possibility in every actuality, makes the individual see the guilt of falling short and makes him accept it as his own guilt, since any attempt to blame something else for the guilt is only a new form of guilt, the guilt of irresponsibility toward existence. Responsibility toward existence is the basis of the whole endeavor of ethics,

[33] *Postscript*, p. 469.

as well as of the general religiousness, without which the whole thing collapses back to the aesthetic stage, to the not-yet-self of the hedonist. So the religious individual discovers the total guilt to be a solid, massive fact across his path and learns to live with it, much as Columbus discovered America across his path on the way to the Indies—he had hardly suspected such a discovery when he started out, but once America was found, it was useless to try to argue it away. "In every-day life the total guilt, as a thing which is generally presupposed, is gradually so taken for granted that it is forgotten. And yet it is this totality of guilt which makes it possible that in the particular instance one can be guilty or not guilty."[34] Every attempt to find an "easy way out" of the consciousness of guilt by blaming it on something nonhuman is a deliberate or unwitting denial of the eternal in man, and simply results in sinking the selfhood of man back to the pre-ethical stage, where it exists in unaccountable action and reaction with the environment.

Another "easy way out" is the comparative or quantizing conception of guilt, in which the individual adds up, as it were, all of his finite and particular guilts up to that particular point in his life to make a trial balance and with this balance to see how he compares with his fellow-men. He always comes out pretty well on such a reckoning—even very well, by police standards, since he can always find so many who are so much worse off than himself in that respect. But getting relief from guilt by counting the population of jails is hardly a device to be recommended for spiritual growth. The eternal does not operate by police standards, not even by society's standards. The eternal has no truck with comparative standards but is its own standard, and therefore "it is precisely unethical to have one's life in the comparative, the relative, the outward, and to have the police-justice, the court of conciliation, a newspaper, or some of Copenhagen's notables, or the rabble of the Capital, as the court of last resort in relation with oneself."[35]

Still another "easy way out," although it would appear anything but easy, is the attempt to make satisfaction for the guilt by some self-inflicted penance or by any propitiatory act to appease the

[34] *Postscript*, p. 471.
[35] *Postscript*, p. 472.

clearly felt divine wrath against one's shortcomings. How much of the history of religions could be written under this category! And, in our own times, under this category one can hardly resist thinking of the motivation behind so much large-scale philanthropic dona- tion of money by tycoons of industry, so quickly discerned as "con- science money" by the resentful workers. Or, of the motive behind so much social uplift work on the part of many only slightly less in need of uplift. This way out is "easy" nonetheless, no matter how many millions of dollars are involved, or if only some personal self-denial is involved, for it succeeds in cutting down to measure the nature of the guilt, or, as Kierkegaard says, in "finitizing" the guilt, thus making it seem as if after all the guilt could be got rid of, provided only that one could give enough or do enough. But, says Climacus, the highest expression for this guilt, the expression that shows absolute respect for the Absolute, is the constant re- membrance of it, the eternal recollection of guilt—not any naïve and well-meant effort to do away with it in small pieces. For al- though the desire to do penance is witness to the fact that the guilt-feeling is there as it should be, the idea that it can be got rid of by penance merely shows that the individual is not using *the eternal* as his standard, in comparison with which the smallest guilt is just as shattering as the greatest. As for the forgiveness of sins and the atonement that are preached by Christianity, these cannot be appealed to by religiousness A, which does not have the Christ as its presupposition, but only by religiousness B, which has the Absolute Paradox as its presupposition—and in that case the guilt factor receives another twist of meaning. It becomes more sharply defined as sin.

7. The Conditions for Entering Religiousness B

The eternal recollection, or the constant remembrance, of guilt is the wall or limit of the first stage of religiousness, because it represents "as far as you can go" religiously without calling upon a messiah, or a savior, to do something for you. Just as at the point of transition from the ethical to the first religious stage it could be said that the need for God was man's highest perfection, so here at the limit of the general religiousness it might be said (the positive being measured by the negative) that the need for a savior is the religious individual's highest perfection. But, of course, it is one thing to say that this need exists in the highly developed or advanced religious individual (and to trace the expressions of this need in the actual practices of so many religions), and it is quite another to assert or claim that this clearly felt need has been answered in history with the appearance of Jesus of Nazareth, in and through whom God himself gave the answer. One is talk about the need, and the other is talk about the answer to the need; and between them lies all the difference between psychological description and theological assertion.

Climacus calls the general religiousness "the religion of immanence," since he claims that this type of religious existence could have occurred in paganism (even if it didn't) and can and does occur in the more spiritual forms of the world's religions, and can and does occur now in Christianity, where it can be the religiousness of all who are not "decisively Christian." By this last assertion I think he means that it can be the religiousness of all those who, although they have their religious existence in relation to the Christian Church and in terms of its traditional practices and dogmas, have not yet reached the point where they personally feel the need of a savior and find this need answered in Jesus Christ. There are, after all, elements in Christianity that keep the religious individual busy, other than the atonement and the forgiveness of sins, and Kierkegaard does not wish to imply that these other things are not important. What I do think he wishes to imply is that, while these other aspects of Christianity have certain "equivalents" in other religions and in paganism (for example, ethical teachings and spiritual practices), neither the other religions nor the most enlightened paganism has any equivalent for Jesus Christ as the answer to the religious individual's need for an atoning savior and the promised forgiveness of sins. That is why he calls this "the specific thing in Christianity" and the religiousness that includes it "decisively Christian" and "the religion of transcendence," since this type of religiousness does take the religious individual beyond what the religion of immanence has to offer. Christianity, one might say, is richer by this factor, the atoning and forgiving savior; and yet it is in the very nature of spiritual development that Christianity must include many who call themselves Christian but who are not yet in a position to appreciate this richness nor to avail themselves of it, to appropriate its blessings, because they have not yet lived deeply enough in the religiousness of immanence to reach its exhaustive limit, the feeling of the need for the atoning savior. And then there are also conditions to be met, as we shall soon see.

But for the religiousness of immanence there are no conditions to be met, and therefore there is no reason why it should not occur in a noble form of paganism or in any of the other "higher" religions, as they are called with good reason. They are "higher" religions just in so far as they encourage or permit a type of religious existence for the religious individual similar to that described in the previous sections of this chapter, making allowance for the variety of cultural ways in which it can be expressed. And they are "higher" in so far as they have advanced beyond superstition and magic and the manipulation of the deity for selfish ends to the recognition of the importance of ethical obligation, however the latter may be conceived in theological or mythological terms. Climacus does not claim that the religiousness of immanence *commonly* occurs in these other religions, but that there is nothing to prevent its occurring within them, in the case of particularly advanced religious individuals.

Philosophically, the religion of immanence would perhaps be called "religious idealism" by us, since it rests on nothing more than a certain view of human nature, the traditional view of philosophical idealism that man is a mixture of the finite and the infinite, the temporal and the eternal, and that his salvation consists in realizing or cultivating (as far as possible in the impure medium of existence) the infinite and eternal at the expense of the finite and temporal. These latter constitute "immediacy"—and this one must "die away from" in order to realize the "highest good," which first presents itself as the goal of ethics but is gradually seen to be the mask and lure of the Eternal, demanding and drawing to itself the corresponding quality in man. There is nothing to stop anyone from undertaking this self-transformation, and there are no external conditions to be met, such as a relationship to a historical event. And, basically, there are no internal deterrents, except weakness or flabbiness in the individual's love toward the Eternal. Surely it is not impossible to conceive of Greek rationalism as a plan of salva-

tion in these terms. Driven by the Heavenly Eros, man seeks to
liberate himself from the lower passions that enthrall and enslave
him, and to unite himself with the visions of the eternal ideas and
forms, especially Beauty-itself, Truth-itself, and Goodness-itself,
and in this elevation and union to find his salvation, his eternal
happiness. At any rate, Climacus certainly does use the term
"paganism" in a very broad sense while pointing out "the specific
thing in Christianity":

Existing religiously, one can express one's relationship to an eternal
happiness (immortality, eternal life) outside of Christianity, and this
has surely been done; for of religiousness A one may say that, even
if it has not been exemplified in paganism, it could have been, because it has only human nature in general as its assumption, whereas
the religiousness which has the dialectical in the second instance [that is,
which raises the problems that Christianity does in demanding that the
individual must become related to the God-man in history] cannot
have been before itself, nor even after it has come, can it be said to
be able to have been before it was. The specific thing in Christianity
is the dialectical in the second instance, only not, be it noted, as a task
for thought . . . , but relating itself to the pathetic as an incitement
to new pathos.[36]

With "the specific thing in Christianity" we are brought back
to the thought-experiment which was the subject matter of *Philosophical Fragments* and to which Kierkegaard's long disquisition
on subjective appropriation is the "postscript." It will be remembered that there Greek rationalism was compared and contrasted with "another view," which is now identified as "the specific thing in Christianity," the contrast being made as sharp as
possible by means of several "dialectical contradictions." These
contradictions, on which religiousness B rests, are as follows, to
recapitulate: (1) that the individual expects "an eternal happiness
in time through a relationship to something else in time," (2) "that
an eternal happiness is based upon something historical," which
can be known only by approximation; and (3) "that the historical
fact here in question is not a simple historical fact, but is constituted by that which only against its nature can become historical,
hence by virtue of the absurd."[37]

[36] *Postscript*, p. 496.
[37] *Postscript*, pp. 505, 508, 512 (section headings).

All these contradictions, the thoughtful Christian believer is aware, are implied in the believing relationship to the Christ, but he believes nevertheless. This does not mean that he has suddenly decided to despise understanding or to espouse the view that stupidity or muddle-headedness are special qualifications for becoming a Christian. No,

the believing Christian not only possesses but uses his understanding, respects the universal-human, does not put it down to lack of understanding if somebody is not a Christian; but in relation to Christianity he believes against the understanding and in this case also uses understanding . . . to make sure that he believes against the understanding. Nonsense therefore he cannot believe against the understanding, for precisely the understanding will discern that it is nonsense and will prevent him from believing it; but he makes so much use of the understanding that he becomes aware of the imcomprehensible, and then he holds to this, believing against the understanding.[38]

Here again is a clear answer to those who object to Kierkegaard as being an "irrationalist," as though he recommended the believing of nonsense as the path to salvation. It is precisely the person who uses reason to the utmost who discovers its limits when he recognizes the incomprehensible—and the incomprehensible is not the same as nonsense. Nor does the believing Christian think that his faith has put him into an especially favored vantage point, as compared with that of an unbeliever, from which to glimpse the solution to metaphysical puzzles. Rather, he "takes the mystery of faith seriously and is not duped by the pretense of understanding, but is aware that the curiosity which leads to glimpsing is infidelity and betrayal of the task."[39]

Religiousness B brings with it not only the encounter with the incomprehensible, namely, the mystery of the Incarnation, but also certain other implicates which make it repellent from the standpoint of religiousness A, although it is only the person who has lived religiousness A to the utmost who is able to know that he needs that which only religiousness B offers: the forgiveness of sins through an atoning savior. Thus, there is set up an attraction-repulsion relationship between the A-type of religious individual and religiousness B, which Climacus describes as "heightening the

[38] *Postscript*, p. 504.
[39] *Postscript*, p. 505.

pathos," as arousing, in fact, the highest pathos of which existence is capable. Only the person who has lived religiousness A—in resignation, in fear and trembling, in suffering the dying away from his immediacy, and in becoming aware of guilt as a total determinant of life—is in a position to know by his own experience, not by doctrine or by hearsay, his need of a savior. And yet the terms on which the savior is offered demand that he break his continuity with the past, with his own understanding of himself in the past, and even with his understanding of his God-relationship in the past, demand that, in fact, he become "a new creature," someone else than he thought he was. For this reason he is both drawn and repelled. "As great as his pathetic tension is in relation to his eternal happiness, so great also will be his Socratic fear of the danger of error."[40] In all humility before the fact, how many friends each of us could name who did not become Christians because their Socratic fear of error far outweighed their feeling of the need for a savior!

Whereas religiousness A is democratic and universalistic, not only inviting everyone ("Ho! everyone that thirsteth!") but assuring him that he is eligible, religiousness B "is discriminative, selective, and polemical: only upon a definite condition do I become blessed, and as I absolutely bind myself to this condition, so do I exclude every other man who does not thus bind himself."[41] So obnoxious to all natural ways of thinking is the doctrine here touched upon, the doctrine of election, that it is offensive to both the democratic and the aristocratic spirits, for just as election does not chummily and gregariously include everyone, so it is also no respecter of persons and is quite capable of excluding the most superior individuals. An aristocracy of the religious it certainly does not create, except as a misunderstanding. "This discrimination imparts to the Christian a certain resemblance to one who is fortunate through favor, and when it is so conceived selfishly by a Christian we have the desperate presumption of predestination."[42] One can almost see Climacus (who, we remember, is merely thinking through the implications of becoming a Christian) back away from the doctrine

[40] *Postscript*, p. 346.
[41] *Postscript*, p. 516.
[42] *Postscript*, p. 516.

of election as he comments on the difficulty of accepting its implications, even when misunderstandings have been removed.

To have one's own eternal happiness based upon an historical fact makes the Christian's happiness or good fortune recognizable by suffering, so that the religious determinant of being God's elect is as paradoxically contrary as possible to being a Pamphilius of fortune, precisely because the elect, though he is not the unfortunate man, is not in the plain understanding of the word the fortunate; no, it is a thing so difficult to understand that for everybody but the elect it must be enough to drive one to despair. Hence the notion of being the elect is so disgusting when one aesthetically wishes to be, for example, in the place of an Apostle. The blessedness which is contingent upon an historical situation excludes all who are not in this situation, and of them there are countless numbers who are not excluded by their own fault but by the accidental circumstances that Christianity has not yet been preached to them.[43]

Just as repellent for thought as the idea of becoming the elect is the break with the past required by the new existence medium, which is the consciousness of sin. Christianity does offer the boon of the atonement and the forgiveness of sins, but first of all it takes the liberty of convicting all men of being sinners. Sin is a far more serious offense than guilt, and it has a retroactive effect on the individual's understanding of his past such that he must break with it. (Here again we must remember that in Climacus' way of speaking, in the dialectical approach, the positive is always recognizable and measurable by the negative.) The Christian is blessed, to be sure, with the highest blessing there is, but only on condition that he never forget that he is a forgiven sinner. And a forgiven sinner is something different from a guilt-conscious idealist. Guilt is merely the falling short of an ideal aspect of human nature as such, the falling short of the eternal in man, whereas sin is more nearly something like active opposition, rebellion against a holy, transcendent, and yet loving God who has the right and the power to demand everything of a man. "Hence the individual is unable to acquire Sin-Consciousness by himself, as he can guilt-consciousness; for in guilt-consciousness the identity of the subject with himself is preserved, and guilt-consciousness is an alteration of the subject within the subject himself; sin-conscious-

[43] *Postscript*, p. 516.

ness, on the other hand, is an alteration of the very subject himself, which shows that outside of the individual that power must be which makes clear to him the fact that in coming into life he has become another than that he was, has become a sinner. This power is the Deity in time."[44]

Sin-consciousness could not have occurred in paganism, nor does it occur in the non-Christian religions (some of which, however, have reached guilt-consciousness and have invented devices for dealing with it). But once it has come into the world, when Christ comes and gives it to the believer, there comes with it also the consciousness of the sin of the whole race, of sin as the common denominator of humanity, and this is another repellent factor of isolation for the believer.

These repellent factors, which include the believing against the understanding as well as the several isolating factors, give rise to the possibility of *offense,* "whether this be more closely defined as the offense which suffers, or as the offense which mocks at the paradox as foolishness."[45] We have already noted how profoundly Kierkegaard was affected by the saying of Christ, "Blessed is he who is not offended in me," and how vividly he imagined the concern of Christ over the fact that this one thing he could not do: he could not remove the possibility of offense. Yet offense is basically the correct name for what happens in a person who cannot accept the Christ because of these repellent factors, as well as for what has happened in one who has had the passion of faith and has lost it. "But this again is the sharpened pathos [of religiousness B]: to have constantly a possibility which, if it comes to pass, is a fall just so much the deeper as faith is higher than all the religiousness of immanence."[46]

8. On the Boundaries—Irony and Humor

This, then, is the end of the pilgrimage through existence. Further than what Christianity in this specific sense teaches about the meaning of existence one cannot penetrate either in depth or in height, and all other interpretations are a return to some previous

[44] *Postscript,* p. 517.
[45] *Postscript,* p. 518.
[46] *Postscript,* p. 518.

stage in the course of the pilgrimage. On looking back over the road by which the pilgrim came, one must admit that a great deal of ground was covered and that there were many resting places on the way, where many a pilgrim came to a stop if he could not or did not wish to go further. It was of course part of Johannes Climacus' intention all along to show, in relation to the problem of becoming a Christian, "how much must have been lived before the problem can have any significance for the individual. . . ."[47]

If in the course of following this progression of the individual through the stages it has sometimes seemed to the reader that all these categories and characteristics are much too abstract and too simple a way of ordering and classifying the infinite variety of actual individuals, it must be remembered that the same would be true for *any* intellectual schema for understanding people. Kierkegaard himself was aware of this fact, and warned against expecting to find in life, among one's friends, say, any obvious and pure exemplars of any stage. People are simply not that consistent; but even if they were, there is plenty of room for variety in the manner in which they can express the stage they have reached. For even where there is so much as a moderate attempt at consistency, the furthest stage reached always contains within itself, telescoped as it were, all the previous stages in their properly subordinate degree of importance. Only the purely aesthetic individual could be single-valued—all the others being hierarchically structured—and even he finds it hard to be consistently hedonistic! If, however, we should happen to spot a "purely ethical" individual, that is, one who had suppressed all of the aesthetic factors in his life as being anti-ethical, we could be pretty sure that he represented an aberration. Furthermore, when we remember that this entire matter of the stages takes place in the individual's inwardness and remind ourselves that inwardness and outwardness are not exactly commensurable, it becomes obvious how extremely difficult, how risky, it is for one individual to try to pinpoint the stage that another individual is in. Indeed, only a veritable Sherlock Holmes of human nature would be able to spy out and track down the clues by which human beings ordinarily betray the values they actually live by. Kierkegaard, to be sure, rather fancied himself in

[47] *Postscript*, p. 342.

that role (he called himself "a spy in the service of the highest"),
but his *purpose* in delineating the stages was not that we should
all become spies upon the existential progress of our neighbors,
but that each individual should use this schema for a better
understanding of himself, for "self-examination," and, always, for
edification.

And yet he also permitted himself a few generalizations about
people in general. By far the largest number of people, he said,
live unthinkingly in the aesthetic stage, with only enough of the
ethical factor added to act as a deterrent on the unlimited pursuit
of pleasure by themselves and others, enough, that is, to maintain
a certain respect for the law. They remain in this stage because
thinking itself is unpleasant to them, and usually only some calam-
ity, or crisis, or collision with others, will force them to think about
themselves and to ask *why,* for example, the ethical should be
allowed to outweigh the aesthetic (as the very existence of en-
forceable laws in any land presupposes). The reflective person, on
the other hand, does not wait for the police officer to spell out
to him the difference between obligation and pleasure, but performs all such collisions, along with far more subtle ones, in the
imagination.

Nevertheless, as if the three stages—and their telescoping in the
individual who passes through them—did not allow of sufficient
variety of attitudes, Kierkegaard describes two more attitudes, lying
on what he calls the "confinium," or the boundary line, between
each two of the stages. On the boundary between the aesthetic and
ethical stages he places the attitude of irony, and on the boundary
between the ethical and the religious stages he places the attitude
of humor. I can indicate them here by only the briefest sketch.
They are both "fence-sitting" attitudes. In each case the individual
uses criteria taken from the higher stage to criticize the behavior
of individuals in the lower stage, without being himself sufficiently
committed to the higher stage to realize the impertinence of criticism coming from one so far from the goal of the higher stage
himself. He understands the criteria but lacks the seriousness of
applying them first of all to himself.

Thus, the ironic individual is always in the act of pointing out
that things are not as they ought to be, that people do not behave

as they ought to, and he uses satire, or ridicule, or heavy-handed sarcasm, or barbed wit, to drive home the nature of the discrepancy he finds. Yet whence does he get the idea that people and their relationships ought to be any different from what he in fact finds them to be? From the ethical sphere, which alone is concerned with the ideality of man and which assumes that man not only should, but can, remold himself to correspond with the highest good. The ironist either secretly or openly carries about with him some picture of an ideal man, which, used as the yardstick, constantly reveals to him the shortcomings of actual men and the hypocrisy of those who pretend to live by the ideal. Irony is an adjunct of humanism, for it certainly would make no sense to become ironic about nature, or about the animals, which presumably cannot be any *different than they are*. (This fact does not prevent, in our day, all sorts of "naturalistic" social philosophers and social critics from growing quite ironic over social conditions and behavior they dislike.) "Irony arises from the constant placing of the particularities of the finite together with the infinite ethical requirement, thus permitting the contradiction to come into being."[18]

The ironist may be, and often is, an ethicist in disguise—but not necessarily so. He may indeed be the ethical individual who is merely using irony as the incognito for his ethical passion, but he may also be an individual who has misunderstood the ethical requirement as being that he should transform the whole world, whereas the first ethical requirement is that he should transform himself. His goading and criticism of the world then takes on a dubious character if he still does not go over into the ethical sphere, that is, get off the fence. The presence of irony in a man therefore is not a guarantee that we are dealing with a hidden ethicist, but only a possibility that such is the case. We may also be dealing with a person who is lacking in existential seriousness and does not apply to himself the same strictures that he applies to others, and whose irony therefore really issues from a conviction of his own superiority.

The situation is analogous in the case of humor. Both irony and humor operate with a discrepancy, a contradiction, an incon-

---

[18] *Postscript*, p. 448.

gruity, for such is the essence of the comical—but humor can be distinguished by the fact that it is less angry, less self-righteous, less hard and intolerant, than irony. Humor might be called a sadder and wiser version of irony, sadder and wiser in the ways of men, for it is a whole existential stage beyond irony and has thus acquired some insight into the difficulties of the ethical. And again, humor may be the incognito for the religious individual, but not necessarily. A humorist who has not yet reached the religious stage, but is only on the verge of it, constantly

sets the God-idea into conjunction with other things and evokes the contradiction—but he does not maintain a relationship to God in terms of religious passion *stricte sic dictus*, he transforms himself instead into a jesting and yet profound exchange-center for all these transactions, but he does not himself stand related to God. The religious man does the same, he sets the God-idea into juxtaposition with everything and sees the contradiction, but in his inmost consciousness he is related to God.[49]

But why, on the other hand, does the religious individual need an incognito? In order to guard his religious inwardness against being childishly and self-importantly converted into a worldly outwardness and especially into that pious prattling that characterizes the "immediately religious" or the "awakened" individual.

An immediate religiosity rests in the pious superstition that it can see God directly in everything; the "awakened" individual has impudently made arrangements for God's presence wherever he himself happens to be, so that as soon as you catch sight of him you may be sure that God is there, because the "awakened" individual has Him in his pocket. Religiosity with humor as its incognito is therefore a synthesis of absolute religious passion (the inwardness being dialectically produced) with a maturity of spirit, which withdraws the religiosity away from all externality back into inwardness, where again it is absolute religious passion.[50]

9. Cautions About Understanding the Stages

There is, then, no lack of variety of attitudes allowed for in Kierkegaard's valuative interpretation of existence delineating the successive possibilities in the individual's spiritual development. I should like at this point to warn the reader against interpreting the

[49] *Postscript*, p. 451.
[50] *Postscript,* pp. 451-452.

schematic diagram of the stages (found on the frontispiece of this book) in any hard and fast or literal manner. There is always the danger, in making any diagram at all, of the likelihood of making something appear simple which is in fact far from simple— and yet, the sole excuse for any diagram as an aid to thought is that it provides a rough sketch, a simplification. According to Kierkegaard, reality cannot even be *conceived*, that is, exhaustively represented by concepts, so it is hardly to be expected that reality could be adequately represented by a diagram. For example, my diagram does not reveal the fact that the actual transitions from one stage to the next are qualitatively different from one another, since each one has to take into account "how much has been lived through" up to that point. Similarly, the diagram leaves the relationship between humor and the specifically Christian religiousness (religiousness B) somewhat unclear. Kierkegaard himself spoke sometimes as if humor were the last borderline position prior to Christianity, other times as if it were the last border before the general religiousness (religiousness A). This is because he was writing in a situation in which very few people made any distinction between the specifically Christian categories and the general religiousness, the "dissolving tendency" being to let the former sink and disappear into the latter. In my diagram, then, humor can still be considered as "prior" to religiousness B, but only if religiousness B is thought of as containing religiousness A within itself in a transcended and amended form. I offer this diagram only with the hope that it may help the reader to summarize and visualize the Kierkegaardian stages, knowing well that they could be schematized in many different ways.

But even when all due precautions have been observed, the present-day reader still may not know quite how to take the Kierkegaardian stages—whether to take them as a psychology of religion, including the psychology of the individual, or as a philosophy of religion, including a general philosophy of value. They represent something of all of these, but in so far as they are a psychology, the vocabulary is not nearly neutral enough; it is in fact loaded with ontological and theological implications. And in so far as they constitute a philosophy, then which philosophy? Surely not the Hegelian philosophy! We have to admit that the difficulty of

fitting Kierkegaard's thought into any of the traditional cubby-
holes provided in the compartmentalization of knowledge constitutes
its originality, and explains its germinal influence on subsequent thinkers. By straddling psychology and philosophy, stubbornly allowing neither the one nor the other to issue in merely
objective knowledge, another "theory about something," he calls
attention to the prior reality which is the presupposition of both—
the concrete individual who must after all be present before psychology and philosophy have anything to talk about. As a result,
Kierkegaard's psychological observations acquire an ontological
dimension, a reaching down into the very core and passional center
of what it means to be a human being, that arouses the distrust
of the objective, "scientific" psychologist; on the other hand, his
philosophical concepts of the ethical and the religious acquire a
psychological dimension, a laying bare of the struggling individual
in whom these concepts have their source, that provokes the disdain of the logic-seeking abstract philosophical thinker.

The terminological difficulty remains, but it would be a mistake
to see in Kierkegaard's thought just another variety of anti-Hegeli-
anism (of which there are many). Rather, it is his hacking out of
an area somewhere between psychology and philosophy (over the
objections of both), where one can talk about the human being in
a new way, the human being as he is to himself in his struggle with
reality, that entitles Kierkegaard, if anything does, to be called
the father of modern existentialism. He would probably disown
some of his imputed offspring, but, all the same, it is in this area
that present-day existential analysis and psychoanalysis carry on
their work, still earning for themselves the distrust and disdain of
the two flanking disciplines. And, since neither scientific psychology
nor abstract philosophy could supply him with a vocabulary suitable for this area, he hammered one out of Hegelianism, making
use of the dialectical opposites (time-eternity, existence-essence,
finite-infinite, immanent-transcendent, and so on) but letting them
stand simply as opposed to one another, unmediated, unreconciled,
unsynthesized. He saw no "movement" whereby these opposites
yearned to come together in an annihilating yet preserving embrace, except as a mental exercise which changed nothing in reality,
since these were just abstractions from different aspects of reality.

On the other hand, he needed the dialectical approach, because he thought it could do better justice to the complexity and conflict of human existence than undialectical thinking, which could see no opposition anywhere but only a continuous flow of causes and effects, and made conflict nearly unthinkable. As a result, he bequeathed to subsequent existential thinkers a set of words that made it possible once again to talk about the human being as something distinct from nature and distinct from pure ideas, a vocabulary to take the place of words like "soul" and "spirit" which had become so discredited and devaluated in the secular-technological culture coming into dominance. In a way, he made a new humanism possible—he had to make it possible, in order to show how Christianity went beyond humanism. To take only two examples, he gave the words "existence" and "truth" a set of specifically man-oriented meanings that made it impossible to reduce their referent, the human subject, to a natural object in the same class with animals, plants, and stones (and thus comprehensible in the same categories as they). "Existence" became the massive concreteness of the specifically human way of being in the world, not just existence or nonexistence as the presence or absence of an object in space, or as the distinction between fact and fiction. And "truth" became not just the fitting of ideas to objects, or ideas to ideas, by an "X," but the specifically human mode of truth-as-relationship, truth as produced by the human subject in the reality of his selfhood.

Finally, the need for this new-old terminology was forced on Kierkegaard also by the deterioration, through misuse and overuse, of the classical theological terms in the language of the church. For instance, he allows Climacus to explain in the *Postscript* why he had not availed himself of the traditional Christian terminology when setting up the "thought experiment" of the *Fragments*:

That Christianity was the content of the hypothesis experimentally developed in the *Fragments*, the piece did not say. This silence was an attempt to gain a breathing-spell, a freedom from immediate entanglement with all sorts of historical, historico-dogmatic, introductory, and ecclesiastical questions concerning what Christianity really is. . . .

Hence, in order to obtain a little peace for the weary Christian terminology, a rest of which it may stand greatly in need, unfathomable and calmly profound as it is in itself, but made breathless and almost unmeaning in current usage; and in order to avoid if possible being entangled in the crush, I chose to suppress the name of Christianity, and to refrain from using the expressions which repeatedly find themselves tossed about and perplexed in current speech. The entire Christian terminology has been appropriated by speculative thought to its own purposes, under the assumption that speculative thought and Christianity are identical.[51]

More specifically, Climacus thought that if he had used such terms as Incarnation and Atonement, it would immediately have been assumed by the reading public that he was using them in the sense of their Hegelian interpretation. Or, even more fuzzily, it would have been assumed that everybody knows what these great Christian terms mean because everybody is a Christian. The problem was to find a point of departure in the history of thought where as yet it could not be assumed that everybody knew what Christianity was, and then to define Christianity in those terms. "For this reason I had recourse to paganism, and to Greece as the representative of the intellectual, and to Socrates as its greatest hero. After thus having made sure of paganism I sought to find as decisive a difference as was possible."[52]

Christianity contrasted with humanism is the content of the *Fragments,* and the content of the *Postscript* is an introduction to the problem of becoming a Christian when the point of departure is *in* humanism, an introduction which Climacus himself says is "not historical but psychological, calling attention to how much must have been lived,"[53] how much of existence must have been worked through, how much the quality of selfhood must have been transformed, before the individual is ready for Christianity. It is a psychological account (with ontological overtones) of the "preparation" in humanism for the Incarnation, somewhat on the order of recent studies of the Old Testament which try to show the "preparation" in the Hebrew religiousness for the coming of the Gospel. As such it invites the reader to self-examination regarding his own preparation—in his own terms and times—in the matter of becoming an individual, becoming religious, and becoming a Christian.

[51] *Postscript*, p. 324.
[52] *Postscript*, p. 329.
[53] *Postscript*, p. 342.

IX

Anxiety, The Exile From Eden

1. How to Discuss Original Sin

Kierkegaard subtitles his essay on anxiety "a simple psychological deliberation oriented in the direction of the dogmatic problem of original sin." It was published at the same time as the *Fragments* and is rightly considered a companion volume, for both works are concerned with the same problem, but from different angles. The problem is to make as clear as possible the distinction between Christianity and humanism. The *Fragments* does this from the philosophical standpoint; *The Concept of Dread* goes at it from the standpoint of the psychological understanding of human nature which the two views (Christianity and humanism) presuppose.

Today we are witnessing another revival of humanism, and this new humanism is a protest against scientific and technological totalitarianism; in some cases it is quite eager to enlist the support of religion in its fight against the political-scientific management of whole peoples at the expense of the "human values," such as freedom, justice, individual worth, religious and cultural self-expression. It is to be expected that there will always be revivals of humanism, with or without alliances to religion, because these revivals are a reaction against exclusive emphasis on some one factor that is a part of humanism itself. The pesent new humanism objects to the view of man as a technician or engineer in control of his environment and even of his own nature as a social and economic animal. It merely wishes to restore balance by reaffirming the "neglected" values that go to make up a truly human animal, namely, the aesthetic, ethical, and religious values. In a sense the new humanism is an effort to restore the Greek view of man as a well-rounded, temperate, reasonable being, engaged in perpetual quest of self-knowledge and self-perfection.

In the discussion that follows it will be well to keep in mind that it is this Greek view of man that Kierkegaard has in mind when he talks about "paganism." Greek humanism was to him paganism at its best, and paganism at its best was nothing to sneer at, especially when compared with the superstition and thraldom of paganism at its worst. But in the matter of making clear the distinction between paganism and Christianity, it was necessary to give paganism (at its best) a twofold assessment. It was first of all necessary to secure an expression for the difference between Christianity and paganism in its form prior to the coming of Christianity into the world. And, secondly, it was necessary to define paganism *within* Christianity, or what paganism becomes when it has Christianity to contend with.

The first or pre-Christian paganism should always be delineated in the most ideal terms. One must bring to light how high and how noble were the possibilities within paganism, what excellencies were displayed in its best representatives, what specific ideals for emulation it set before men. If this is not done, if paganism is simply dismissed with contempt, how can it ever be made clear what it was that paganism lacked even at its best, in order that Christianity might claim to be a more excellent way and to be "the truth"? And anyway, it would surely be foolish to rant against the pre-Christian pagans for not discovering by their own wits what required historical revelation by God in the matrix of an especially prepared historical people to be taught to mankind. Pre-Christian paganism has the right (as much as any of the Oriental religions, for example) to be judged by its best, not its worst, representatives. As an apologist for Christianity, Kierkegaard saw that it would be much too cheap a victory merely to claim its superiority over paganism at its worst, over the superstition and magic and idolatry that are found in all lands, in all ages, under many auspices. No, Christianity must be tested against the best rivals that can be found, and so Kierkegaard never tires of praising the Greeks for going as far as they did in the attempt to define the human ideal in terms of the good life or the catalogue of human virtues, and also for their attempts to live in accordance therewith.

But it is a different story when we are talking about paganism inside, alongside, or in opposition to, Christianity. Paganism becomes something quite different when it has to live not by its strength as an ideal but by the power of its various degrees of implied or actual rejection of Christianity. These attitudes may range from the happy, ignorant, innocent paganism of children, all the way (in the finest of shadings) to desperate, demonic opposition to Christianity, the latter attitude of course having been impossible in pre-Christian paganism. In any case, paganism loses something of its happy-go-lucky zest, its charming, Greek-like youthfulness, and becomes thoroughly ambiguous within itself as a preparation, or as an early stage, leading to—what? The pagan inside Christianity becomes the "natural man"—that is to say, the unregenerate man, the not-yet-saved man. It would have made no sense to call the Greek pagan the unregenerate man, when the very thought of regeneration, of a new birth, was absent from the Greek idea of man. However, now that Christianity is here, it is just as useless and guiltily evasive for man to hanker nostalgically after the remembered happy paganism of the Greeks as it is for a grown man to hanker nostalgically after the same remembered qualities of his childhood.

If Christianity has succeeded in giving paganism a bad conscience, it can be only because Christianity has discovered something which was actually there all the time, although hidden and unacknowledged in the pagan conception of man—something which paganism ignored and which it cannot even now acknowledge without repudiating itself or else increasing its own guilt in complicity with this "something." This "something" is of course sin, along with the consciousness of sin and the way in which the consciousness of sin operates retroactively on the concepts of human nature and the human race in the dogma of original sin.[1] Original sin is the great divide that separates Christianity from humanism both ancient and modern—but we must instantly add that it is original sin as understood by Christianity, not by

---

[1] Original sin may be distinguished from particular sins both historically and structurally. Historically, the word "original" reaches back into the history of the human race and into the biography of the individual to describe how the "first" (that is, originating) sin came into being, how the quality of sinfulness makes its appearance in human existence. In that case original sin has the meaning of "the fall." Structurally, the word "original" has the ontological connotations of a basic trait of human nature that makes particular sins possible. In that case original sin has the meaning of the "flaw," or the marring of the image of God in man.

humanism, that forms the great divide. Post-Christian humanism understands that there is something unexplainable called original sin, but it always has an explanation ready anyway—either that the Christian dogma is unintelligible and can be safely ignored, or that the manifestations of particular sins can be conveniently placed in humanistic or naturalistic categories. Thereby the problem is brought back to where we started, namely, what is it then that Christianity discovered which paganism was not able to discover for itself?

In *The Concept of Dread* Kierkegaard sets himself the task of discussing the doctrine of original sin in such a way as to make it intelligible, yet without reducing it to something else or explaining it away so that there would turn out to be no such thing after all. Just in order to attack this problem, then, he had first of all to clear a space, to find a universe of discourse in which the discussion could take place without being self-defeating. The discussion could not take place within "modern philosophy" (that is, the school of Hegel) because this school had brought about endless confusion by introducing various time-honored Christian words—"reconciliation," for example—into epistemology and logic, all in the name of "going further" than Christianity. But what sort of an advance was it to talk about speculative knowledge —and especially about the identity of the knowing subject and the thing known—as a "reconciliation"?

That thought possesses reality was the assumption of all ancient philosophy as well as of the philosophy of the Middle Ages. With Kant this assumption became doubtful. Suppose now that the Hegelian school had really *thought through* Kant's scepticism . . . and then reconstructed the earlier view in a higher form, in such wise that thought does not possess reality by virtue of a presupposition—is then this consciously produced reality of thought a reconciliation? In fact philosophy is merely brought back to the point where in old days one began, in the old days when precisely the word "reconciliation" had immense significance.[2]

And when, in addition to this, "having got the word 'reconciliation' introduced, they now hint that logic is properly the doctrine about the *logos*," and when they have introduced "movement"

---

[2] *The Concept of Dread*, tran. Walter Lowrie (Princeton, N.J.: Princeton University Press, 1944), pp. 10-11.

into logic by means of the dynamism of the "negative," and when finally in the Hegelians' so-called ethics it turns out that the "negative" is also the "evil"—what will be the upshot? "That language will presumably have to celebrate a great sabbatical year, in order to be able to begin with the beginning."[3] At any rate, this is not the universe of discourse in which to discuss original sin, for this philosophy is either an overrefined paganism, or it is sheer confusion.

Nor can the discussion take place in the realm of ethics, for ethics is the science of the ideal, and to the ideal, sin and original sin present themselves only as an obstacle. Christian ethics takes account of the reality of sin as an obstacle, but only as an obstacle that is presupposed to have been overcome. Sin can have no place in the delineation of the Christian ideal as a goal of action.

So that leaves psychology, a science concerned with human nature, and sin and original sin could perhaps be discussed as something in human nature—a psychological propensity, let us say. This is what Kierkegaard settles for—but with the warning that even psychology is not properly oriented to deal with sin, in a way to do it justice. For here the danger is that psychology would "explain it away" by putting it in the same class with any number of other propensities or characteristics of human nature, thus making it into something unavoidable, something for which man cannot be held accountable. The only thing psychology can do that leads us in the proper direction is to describe some attribute of human nature which makes sin possible, and even likely—but not necessary. "That human nature must be such that it makes sin possible, is, psychologically speaking, perfectly true; but to want to let this possibility of sin become its reality is shocking to ethics and sounds to dogmatics like blasphemy. . . ."[4] Sin and original sin are concepts that belong properly only to dogmatics, but dogmatics cannot discuss them "psychologically" because it cannot allow itself the disinterested or curious neutral mood of investigation into "how it happens that," "how man must be constructed in order that," and so on. Dogmatics posits sin, but in the same breath posits it as the thing condemned, the thing above all to be avoided,

[3] *Dread*, p. 11.
[4] *Dread*, p. 20.

so the attitude of dogmatics can only be polemical. The discussion, then, must take place on the borderline between psychology and dogmatics, the psychological treatment proceeding "in such a way that it has *in mente* and before its eye the dogma of original sin."[5]

2. The Fall from Innocence

The task Kierkegaard set himself, then, was to define and describe that property or attribute of human nature, of the human psychological structure, out of which sin could appear as the "qualitative leap," that is to say, not by a casual necessity, as if the sin were already inherent or immanent in the antecedent condition, but by a sort of "bad" freedom, or free "fall," so that the sin appears as the new or emergent quality, not predictable and not determined in terms of the antecedent condition alone. Such a property or attribute must have above all the character of ambiguity, being in itself neither good nor bad but capable of going in either direction, and it must be tied up with the specifically human structure—it must not be a characteristic that man shares with the animals to any extent, such as fear or anger. Such a characteristic is to be found in the psychological condition or state variously described as anxiety, anxiousness, worry, concern, or apprehension in the face of an unknown—the German *Angst*. Since in this chapter I shall be referring to Lowrie's translation, and he decided to use the word "dread," I will use it also, but with the advice to the reader that he can get the full connotations out of Kierkegaard's remarks only by supplementing this word with clumsy collections of words that are trying to say the equivalent thing. "A passive anxiousness in the face of an undefined threat" would perhaps be a fair approximation to the meaning of the Danish and German word *Angst*. And our psychoanalytic terms "diffuse anxiety" and "anxiety state" also convey some of the connotations here intended by the word "dread," though naturally this dread is at a level of intensity not high enough to be considered psychopathic. Unfortunately, the word "dread" can be a transitive verb ("I dread cold winters"), which makes it seem almost synonymous with fear, but it is the noun denoting a state of being in dread that must be kept in mind here, supplemented by the con-

[5] *Dread*, p. 13.

notations of anxiety, worry, and even fearful fascination, in order not to miss the rich possibilities of "the concept of dread" in Kierkegaard's analysis.

Only when the concept of dread is understood in its relation to the total structure of the human person is it possible to make sense out of the dogma of original sin and out of such a vivid story describing how sin first came into the world as the Genesis account of Adam. This story is of course an account not of what happened once upon a time, but of what happens in all men. Adam is not only the "first" man and the representative man, he is also the representative of every succeeding man as the "first" man, that is, as one who must begin at the beginning. To himself every man is the "first" man, in addition to being merely a representative of the human race, and if the "event" of being human happens to him at all, it will happen to him as originally as it did to Adam and as it does to every other man. Whatever explains how sin originates in each man must therefore explain Adam, and vice versa.

To explain Adam's sin is therefore to explain original sin, and no explanation is of any avail which explains original sin and does not explain Adam. The deepest reason for this is to be discovered in the essential characteristic of human existence, that man is an individual and as such is at once himself and the whole race, in such wise that the whole race has part in the individual, and the individual has part in the whole race.[6]

In other words, what is proposed here is a kind of recapitulation theory in the realm of the spirit. We are familiar with the biological theory to the effect that ontogeny recapitulates phylogeny: the development of the individual embryo goes through a series of stages that bear a rough resemblance to the phylogenetic stages in the development of the entire animal kingdom. It is improbable that Kierkegaard ever heard of this theory, and it is certain that he had nothing in mind which is as determined by necessity as a biological process; nevertheless, I believe the analogy is a proper one. Kierkegaard counted it as a perfection, not a defect of human existence, that each individual is privileged, in terms of spiritual determinants, to be both himself and the race as considered in its strictly human (beyond animal) development.

[6] *Dread*, p. 26.

Every individual has the same perfection. . . . Every individual is essentially interested in the history of all other individuals, yea, just as essentially as in his own. Perfection in oneself means therefore the perfect participation in the whole. No individual is indifferent to the history of the race, any more than is the race to that of any individual. While the history of the race goes on, the individual regularly begins afresh, because he is himself and the race, and hence in turn his is the history of the race.[7]

The difficulty about understanding original sin is that a quality is posited, sinfulness, which seems to presuppose itself, and yet it is out of a state of innocence that the first sin emerges. The first sin then bears the weight of being not only a sin, but of being also that by which the quality of sinfulness first comes into the world. And this is precisely the case in Adam and in every subsequent man.

With the first sin came sin into the world. Exactly in the same way is this true of every subsequent first sin of man, that with it sin comes into the world. The fact that it was not there before Adam's first sin is (in relation to sin itself) an altogether accidental and irrelevant reflection which has altogether no significance, and is no justification for making Adam's sin greater or the first sin of every other man less.[8]

It is no use, for example, trying to make Adam's sin appear more awful by eulogizing the state of innocence in which he lived, painting poetic fancies about the Garden of Eden and the state of *rapport* that existed between Adam and nature, Adam and Eve, Adam and God. This would only appear to exonerate the first sin of every subsequent man, for *he* is born into no such paradise. Kierkegaard objects to the tendency of nineteenth century theology to identify innocence with immediacy and then to add, Hegel-wise, that it is the characteristic of immediacy to be annulled (*aufgehoben*), for this obscures the fact that when innocence is "annulled," it is "annulled" by the guilt of sin and not by a "characteristic of immediacy." In fact, innocence is *not* the immediacy whose destiny it is to be annulled, and one should not yearn wistfully for the recovery of its imagined perfection, for as soon as it is lost a different kind of perfection is the goal of man. To wish for innocence is therefore a waste of time and a new guilt, as well as a means of obscuring the real situation of man.

[7] *Dread*, p. 26.
[8] *Dread*, p. 28.

The account in Genesis gives also the right explanation of innocence. This is by no means the pure being of immediacy, but it is ignorance. The fact that ignorance regarded from without seems as though designed to become knowledge is entirely irrelevant to ignorance.[9]

This ignorance, which is the primal innocence, could very well endure as a state, so we should not be in such indecent haste to get it annulled. We should ask next what is the spiritual state of man in the condition of ignorance which is the primal innocence. Kierkegaard's psychological view of man is that man is a synthesis of the bodily and the soulish, the synthesis being constantly performed in and by a third factor, the spirit. This view, incidentally, is not so different from that which psychoanalytic psychology entertains, for the latter regards man as a psychosomatic entity, and it distinguishes in that entity a single factor responsible for conscious integration of the total experiences. This factor, variously called the ego, the self, the person, or the ego as it is influenced in later life by the self-ideal or the super-ego, would correspond to Kierkegaard's "spirit," and the psychosomatic experiences, the raw materials which it tries to integrate, to Kierkegaard's "bodily-soulish" factors. In the state of ignorance which is the primal innocence, the spirit is not yet awake and functioning, but it is there in a state of dreaming, and it is dreaming about itself as a possibility without becoming a reality just yet.

In this state there is peace and repose; but at the same time there is something different, which is not dissension and strife, for there is nothing to strive with. What is it then? Nothing. But what effect does nothing produce? It begets dread. This is the profound secret of innocence, that at the same time it is dread.[10]

At this point the writer of *The Concept of Dread* feels he must remind the reader that dread is not to be confounded with "fear and similar concepts which refer to something definite, whereas dread is the reality of freedom as possibility anterior to possibility. One does not therefore find dread in the beast, precisely for the reason that by nature the beast is not qualified by spirit."[11] I take "freedom as possibility anterior to possibility" to mean that if man

[9] *Dread*, p. 34.
[10] *Dread*, p. 38.
[11] *Dread*, p. 38.

is to become a creature that has more than one possibility, has that which we call "the freedom to choose between alternatives," there must be a structure of sufficient complexity to permit several alternative actions, and just this structure, this presence-of-several-possibilities, is what gives rise to anxiety in relation to the future, that is, dread. If there were only one possibility, there would be nothing to worry about, nothing either to avoid or to attain, a state of blissful unconcern we like to imagine for the animals. But man, even in his most animal-like or vegetative condition, is not an animal only, and he cannot escape feeling his destiny to become free and to be spirit, even if he feels it only as a dread or anxious-ness for the future that both beckons and repels. "Dread is a *sympathetic antipathy and an antipathetic sympathy*."[12]

We know that dread is by no means an unvaryingly unpleasant experience, as witnessed by the eagerness with which children lap up "dreadful" stories and with which both children and adults pursue the "thrills" of chase and horror in the theater. Such indulgence for an adult already has a certain element of guilt in it, which is either not acknowledged or is waived aside for the sake of the catharsis or the recreation achieved. But,

the dread which is posited in innocence is, in the first place, not guilt; in the second place, it is not a heavy burden, not a suffering which cannot be brought into harmony with the felicity of innocence. If we observe children, we find this dread more definitely indicated as a seeking after adventure, a thirst for the prodigious, the mysterious. . . . This dread belongs to the child so essentially that it cannot do without it; even though it alarms him, it captivates him nevertheless by its sweet feeling of apprehension.[13]

This ambiguity of dread is just what makes it the correct psychological antecedent for sin, especially for the first sin. It does not explain sin by predetermining it, but it sets the stage for it.

Innocence has now reached its apex. It is ignorance, but not an animal brutality, but an ignorance which is qualified by spirit, but which precisely is dread, because its ignorance is about nothing. Here there is no knowledge of good and evil, etc., but the whole reality of knowledge is projected in dread as the immense nothing of ignorance.[14]

[12] *Dread*, p. 38.
[13] *Dread*, p. 38.
[14] *Dread*, p. 40.

When Adam hears the prohibition about eating from the tree of knowledge of good and evil, it must be assumed that to him the prohibition is an enigmatic one requiring only obedience rather than understanding, since only after eating of it could he understand what good is or what evil is. This consideration discredits the interpretation that it was the prohibition itself that tempted him to desire the fruit, for he does not even know what freedom is, or what disobedience is. "The prohibition alarms Adam [induces a state of dread] because the prohibition awakens in him the possibility of freedom . . . the alarming possibility of *being able*. What it is he is able to do, of that he has no conception. . . ."[15] Similarly, of the threatened punishment, "thou shalt surely die," Adam, like a child, has no conception, only the vague notion that it must be something terrible. "The terrible becomes in this instance merely dread; for Adam has not understood what was said, and here again we have only the ambiguity of dread. The infinite possibility of being able draws closer for the fact that this possibility indicates a possibility as its consequence."[16]

Then comes the fall, not the possible but the actual fall, which psychology does not explain (unless it were to be considered an explanation to say that whatever is possible must become actual, which is not true even in nature).[17] The fall results in the fact that two qualities enter the world, sinfulness and sexuality. Sexuality is something other than sexual differentiation, which the animals have and which man in the state of innocence has, but in ignorance of sexuality. Sexuality is sexual differentiation as a problem for the spirit, for man cannot have sex as the animals have it, a blind vital instinct. Adam and Eve discover sexuality and shame or modesty in the same instant, and sew themselves aprons. As soon as the spirit (the ego in its integrating function) is there, the entire psychosomatic spectrum becomes a task for the spirit to integrate into itself, and sexuality represents the extreme of sensuousness that must be taken into account by spirit. And, as soon as sin is present, sensuousness takes on a dread-inducing quality which of course it did not have when man was in innocence, because now there is

[15] *Dread*, p. 40.
[16] *Dread*, p. 41.
[17] See p. 239 for a discussion of "the dizziness of freedom" in which the fall takes place.

the anxious consciousness that sensuousness *may* become sin, and this dread applies most of all to sexuality as the extreme of the sensuous.

3. The Snowballing Effect

The difference between Adam and every subsequent man is characterized best by the *incremental* character of dread. Anxiety *grows*. As soon as sinfulness enters the world, whether by the symbolic first sin of Adam or by the actual first sin (undoubtedly lost or repressed from childhood memory) of the subsequent man, dread is increased both in strength and in the new consciousness of dread which sin itself brings with it, that is, the anxiety in the face of the new possibilities that having sinned implies by way of guilt or punishment or continuance in evil. We may call this the snowballing effect of dread. Thanks to this effect, the later individual is born into a different kind of world from that of the earlier individual, a world in which sinfulness has already acquired considerable power in its permeation of the entire human situation, including all man-to-man, man-to-God, and man-to-nature relationships, and therefore a world in which dread has increased correspondingly in strength and consciousness. This of course is what it means to be a historical individual and to participate in the history of the race. But in fact the whole world, the creation itself, takes on a different significance by dint of the fact that sin has entered it and continues to enter it through the acts of men, and that anxiety is increased. Kierkegaard says that to discuss this objective effect of dread is not the business of psychology because it is really an assertion of dogmatics; nevertheless, he makes use of Rom. 8:19 to remind us of how Scripture is aware of the situation. There the "anxious longing of the creation" is mentioned,[18] and, "if there can properly be any question of anxious longing, it follows as a matter of course that the creation is in a state of imperfection."[19] It is as if the entry of sin into the world through man, of this freedom that is a misuse of freedom, "cast over the whole creation a reflection of possibility and a shudder of complicity. . . .

---

[18] "For the creation waits with eager longing . . ." (RSV). The above is Kierkegaard's own translation of this phrase from the Greek.
[19] *Dread*, p. 52.

Surely this dread in the creation can rightly be called an objective dread. It was not produced by the creation but was produced by the fact that it is seen in an entirely different light which was shed upon it when by Adam's first sin sensuality was degraded to signify sinfulness and is constantly so degraded in so far as sin continues to come into the world."[20]

This interpretation, however, "parries the rationalistic view that the sensual itself is sinful. After sin has come into the world, and every time sin comes into the world, the sensuality becomes sinful; but what becomes was not beforehand what it became."[21] From this complicity and blame the creation longs to be delivered, a deliverance promised in the dogma of the atonement. As Paul goes on to say, "We know that the whole creation has been groaning in travail together until now; and not only the creation, but we ourselves, who have the first fruits of the Spirit, groan inwardly as we wait for adoption as sons, the redemption of our bodies. For in this hope we were saved" (Rom. 8.22-24, RSV). About such a promise psychology as such can have nothing to say, only about dread as a precursor of sin.

On the subjective side the increment of dread, which is the difference between the earlier and the later individual, shows itself as the increase in the self-consciousness of dread, that is, dread becoming more aware of itself *as* dread in the individual and more aware that the "nothing" of dread might be a definite something. There may even be conscious attempts to deal with the dread by getting it to pass over into a definite fear of a specific object, and then to deal with this fear by means of courageous and intelligent *action*. There is, for example, the time-honored priestly function of channeling the tribe's diffuse anxiety into fear of the gods, who can then be propitiated by appropriate acts. The well-known fact that *action* affords a temporary relief from the gnawing of anxiety is what transforms the permanent anxiousness inherent in the very structure of man into a temptation to action at any cost, even the guilty action. But this temptation is no exoneration for man. Dread, even in its incremented historical form, is still not yet guilt, nor can it be said to "push" the man into guilt. "Therefore, even though

[20] *Dread*, pp. 52-53.
[21] *Dread*, p. 53.

the dread become more and more reflective, the guilt which breaks forth in dread by the qualitative leap retains nevertheless the same accountability as that of Adam, and dread retains the same ambiguity."[22]

Meanwhile, the greater reflective consciousness of dread there is, the more it seems as if the "nothing" of dread could be pinned down to a definite something. In fact, it can be pinned down to something fairly definite, but even then it retains the characteristic of negativity which makes it both elusive and threatening. Let us imagine a man faced with the need to make a decision which would lead to this or that action. It is important, first of all, that we should not define man's freedom moralistically as the freedom to decide between good and evil, for this narrow concept of freedom ignores both the complexity and the ambiguity of existence. As if each situation calling for action presented only two clear-cut alternatives, one good and one bad, and as if there were any acts totally devoid of ethical implications! Freedom is the "being able" of man, the "having possibility." The more freedom, the more dread, because the more possibility. Why should this be so? Why shouldn't freedom glory in its possibilities, the more the better, instead of being delivered by them into dread? Because there is another side to man, his finitude, which is just as real and just as deserving of consideration as his freedom.

A man deciding on an action is faced with two opposite fears of "nothing" whose combined effect on him increase the anxious tension between his freedom and his finitude. On the one hand, there is the dread or anxiety that, in actualizing certain possibilities by means of the action, he may jeopardize his own future, not to mention his life itself, by the unpredictable reality he thus brings into being. The "nothing" here stands for *the unknown,* especially the unknown as his own future which he by his own act brings upon himself. On the other hand, there is the dread or anxiety that by *not* actualizing certain possibilities he is limiting his own stature as a person, he is frustrating the freedom that is in him and wants to realize itself in action. Here the "nothing" stands for *frustration,* limitation, the dwarfing or crippling of the self. The anxiety about the first nothing, the unknown, holds him in indecision and checks

²² *Dread*, p. 54.

action. But the anxiety about the second nothing, the restriction of selfhood, tends to drive him out of indecision into action and therefore back into the clutches of the first nothing, the fear of the unknown. The first anxiety is the expression of his finitude, his inability to foresee and determine all the consequences of his act, while the second anxiety is the expression of his freedom, which feels itself frustrated and contradicted when possibilities are not realized. That the action which finally does break out of this mounting tension could easily be one which the man himself considers a wrong act is easily understandable in psychological terms, but in ethical terms it is no exoneration for the man, for he himself, the freedom in him, acknowledges after he has recovered from this "anxiety attack" that he need not have succumbed. Kierkegaard describes this situation in a now almost classical passage:

One may liken dread to dizziness. He whose eye chances to look down into the yawning abyss becomes dizzy. But the reason for it is just as much his eye as it is the precipice. For suppose he had not looked down.

Thus dread is the dizziness of freedom which occurs when the spirit would posit the synthesis, and freedom then gazes down into its own possibility, grasping at finiteness to sustain itself. In this dizziness freedom succumbs. Further than this psychology cannot go and will not. That very instant everything is changed, and when freedom rises again it sees that it is guilty. Between these two instants lies the leap, which no science has explained or can explain. He who becomes guilty in dread becomes as ambiguously guilty as it is possible to be. Dread is a womanish debility in which freedom swoons. Psychologically speaking, the fall into sin always occurs in impotence. But dread is at the same time the most egoistic thing, and no concrete expression of freedom is so egoistic as is the possibility of every concretion. This again is the overwhelming experience which determines the individual's ambiguous relation, both sympathetic and antipathetic. In dread there is the egoistic infinity of possibility, which does not tempt like a definite choice, but alarms . . . and fascinates with its sweet anxiety. . . .[23]

Nevertheless, dread is the expression of the spiritual stature of man, of the advance that human nature has made over animal nature, at whatever cost in the way of emotional and mental struggle. Dread may be called the pervasive condition which makes man aware that his exile from nature is a consequence of having gone

[23] *Dread*, p. 55.

beyond nature, beyond the Eden-like existence of the animals. To
say this is not to romanticize the animals. Certainly the animals
experience fear, and we know that they have specific fear-reactions
built into their nervous systems. But as far as we know an animal
does not experience dread over the fact that by its actions it may
become something less than an animal, or fail to be the best animal
of its kind, or be tempted to become something more than an
animal. All this is reserved for man in relation to what it means to
be a man. Freedom brings with it a responsibility toward existence
which is felt by man both as a fear of failure to do the best with it
and as a temptation to do something fantastic with it (" the egoistic
infinity of possibility"), both of which spell the end of the innocent
ignorance and irresponsibility of animals (and children). Once the
possibility of spirit is there, it will give man no peace, and precisely
this "no peace" is anxiety or dread. His only hope is in a different
kind of happiness from that of animals and children, in the perfection of spirit.

The snowballing effect of dread, the "more" of it in the historically later individual, is due as much to the increased spiritual awareness of the dangers that threaten spirit as it is to the accumulation
of knowledge of good and evil in the world. Thus the knowledge
that sensuousness *may* become sinfulness (in history it is over and
over again observed to become that in particular instances, though
not in all) creates a dread of sexuality, because of the intensity
of the erotic in it. It is as though the spirit, as soon as it realizes
that its task is to synthesize or integrate the psychic and the somatic, would like to make things easier for itself by somehow getting rid of the most obstreperous vitality at the somatic end of the
spectrum, that is, sexuality. For example, Kierkegaard thought that
in the foremost representatives of the Greek view, the presence of
sexuality in man was felt as an embarrassment. In spite of the cult
of beauty and of the body, the strategy of Greek rationalism was
to draw men's *eros* away from these merely physical manifestations
to the heavenly or intellectual *originals* of beauty, and to woo men
away from acting according to passion toward acting according to
reason. It struck the Greeks as a contradiction that man, who is
destined for the life of reason, should nevertheless have sexuality,
or, since he has it, that he should take it seriously. "Hence the

highest pagan expression is that the erotic is the comical."[24] By attacking sexuality with the weapon of irony, thereby making it seem ridiculous, the Greek rationalist expressed his perception of it as a threat to the spirit, and at the same time made it a scapegoat on which to lay the blame for the failure of man to live by the light of reason. It was the animal passions that blinded and overpowered men—hence the Greek rationalists did not take either marriage or women very seriously (for example, romantically) for fear of making themselves ridiculous.

On the other hand, in Christianity the spirit tries to make things easier for itself either by declaring through an ethical misunderstanding that the sexual itself is sinful or by appealing prematurely to the state of spiritual perfection when sex will make no difference.

Here the erotic is not ironically neutralized but suspended, because it is the tendency of Christianity to lead the spirit further. When in bashfulness the spirit is in dread and fear of arraying itself in the generic difference, the individual suddenly leaps away, and instead of penetrating it ethically grasps an explanation drawn from the highest sphere of spirit. This is one side of the monastic view, whether that is more particularly characterized as ethical rigorism or as a life in which contemplation is predominant.[25]

Monasticism assumes that in the spirit sex makes no difference, yet it spends so much of its energy striving against sex that finally sex takes on the meaning of sinfulness. The fact is that Christianity does define spirit in its perfection, that is to say, in its infinity, as a state in which sexuality is absent (not repressed, but simply not there). "A perfect spirit cannot be conceived as sexually differentiated. This is in harmony with the doctrine of the Church concerning the character of the resurrection, in harmony with its notion of angels, in harmony with the dogmatic definitions of the person of Christ."[26] But it is no use pretending that man is now, in this life, an angel, and no use pretending that sex is not there, and no use for the spirit to try to make its job easier by such evasions or such wish-projections onto the present of a future state of perfection.

[24] *Dread*, p. 62.
[25] *Dread*, pp. 63-64.
[26] *Dread*, p. 71.

Once the sexual is posited as the extreme point of the synthesis, it is no use ignoring it. The task is of course to win it into conformity with the destiny of the spirit. (Here lie all the moral problems of the erotic.) The realization of this task is the triumph of love in a man in whom the spirit has triumphed in such a way that the sexual is forgotten and only remembered in forgetfulness. When this has come about, then sensuousness is transfigured into spirit and dread driven out.[27]

4. *The Anatomy of Anxiety*

As history goes on, the "nothing" which is the object of dread achieves a variety of concrete expressions that represent attitudes of freedom toward that which is dreaded, attitudes not only of individuals but of whole peoples more or less—whole cultures. Thus the Greeks can be characterized in their general cosmic attitude as being in dread of fate. Fate was for them the "nothing" of dread, it was a combination of necessity and chance whose spokesman is the oracle. The Greek had to consult the oracle, knowing its utterance would be just as ambiguous as dread is and as fate is, being one moment necessity, the next moment chance. "In this fact lies the profound and inexplicable tragic of paganism. The tragic, however, does not lie in the fact that the utterance of the oracle is ambiguous, but in the fact that the pagan could not forbear to take counsel of it. He is in relation to it and dare not refrain from consulting it."[28]

But it is just the hypostatizing of chance and necessity in the idea of fate that prevents the concept of guilt and sin from emerging in proper form in paganism. This is corroborated by the fact, or rather the contradiction, that in paganism it is possible to become guilty by fate, as in the Oedipus legend or as in the explanation of the "flaw" in the character of the great man by means of the frivolous notion of the jealousy of the gods. For guilt and sin to emerge as distinctive concepts there must first be the idea of the single individual and his accountability as a single individual. Nothing in the nature of the world or of the past, nothing in the very nature of things, must be permitted to obscure the individual's significance in this respect if guilt is to assume its deepest meaning for the spiritual life of man.

[27] *Dread*, pp. 71-72.
[28] *Dread*, p. 87.

The Oriental religions deal with this situation in a way that is not basically different from the Greek way, although it may seem so superficially. Instead of doing away with guilt directly by means of fate, they do away with the individual; for them, to be an individual *is* the basic guilt of man, and yet it is also his fate. The Jews, on the other hand, had the right conception of guilt as presupposing the accountable individual and as presupposing even the accountable nation, composed of such individuals. Judaism had the Law, defining that for which Judaism was held accountable, and in Judaism therefore the cosmic negativity of dread took on the form of being in dread of becoming guilty under the Law. The Jew knew what he had to do, knew that he would sooner or later fail and become guilty, knew that he needed help (but not whether it would come), and so he resorted to the concept of *sacrifice* and, more significantly, to the repeated sacrifice by the priestly cult.

To the oracle of paganism corresponds the sacrifice of Judaism. . . . The Jew has recourse to the sacrifice, but that is of no help to him, for what properly must help him would be that the relation of dread was annulled (*aufgehoben*) and a real relation posited. Inasmuch as this does not come to pass, the sacrifice becomes ambiguous, a fact which is expressed by its repetition, a further consequence of which would be a pure scepticism with respect to the act of sacrifice itself.[29]

Surely such scepticism (about the efficacy of a sacrifice that must continually be repeated) is at least part of the ground for the prophetic protest in the Old Testament against priestly elaboration of the sacrificial ceremonial, and the looking forward to a Messiah who would come and redeem his people. However, such a redemption is not to be had for the wishing; it must wait upon the Incarnation. But when the Incarnation comes, it posits guilt *as* sin, and "only with sin is atonement posited; and its sacrifice is not repeated."[30]

With Christianity it would then seem that the great negativity, the "nothing" which is the object of dread, must be sin. And this is true—Christianity does require the individual to be in remorse over every particular sin and in dread of entering into new sin. But Christianity also brings something with it that makes it just as

[29] *Dread*, p. 93.
[30] *Dread*, p. 93.

sinful to wallow in dread and remorse as it is to be devoid of dread
and remorse entirely—and that is the forgiveness of sins. Ethically,
what is demanded of the individual is a positive act, and, because
there is a proper dread of sin and error, every such act must be
undertaken in "fear and trembling." But if dread should try to get
the upper hand, to paralyze the person with anticipated possible
sins and future remorses, forgiveness stands by with its proffered
help to break the spell of dread. The tendency to wallow voluptuously and self-importantly in remorse, a tendency by which dread
(of sin) attempts to enthrall and debilitate the individual, is
analogous to the aforementioned tendency of egoistic freedom to
wallow voluptuously in possibility. Now if the individual will not
help himself by means of the proffered forgiveness and thus drive
dread away in each case through a positive action grounded in
faith, Christianity then charges him with taking the atonement in
vain and making light of the forgiveness of sins. And, when, in
spite of all, the individual still persists in not letting himself be
helped, then we have the beginning of something quite the opposite
of the dread of sin, we have dread of the good, the possession of
the spirit from below, the demonic.

The demonic has its own varieties and nuances of expression,
arising from the many different ways in which freedom can be lost
after it has been partially established in the synthesizing function
of the spirit. In the demonic mode of experience a part of the
person separates itself from the rest and "goes over to the enemy,"
maintaining its strength and rebellion precisely by the amount of
*un*freedom it can cause in the still-integrated part of the person.
Kierkegaard presents a catalogue of symptoms that would now be
called the signs of neuroticism, listing them under two general
headings—freedom lost somatic-psychically, and freedom lost
pneumatically, that is, in the spirit itself. Under the first heading he
gives such examples of compulsive behavior as "an exaggerated
sensibility, an exaggerated irritability, nervous affections, hysteria,
hypochondria, etc. . . . "[31] Under the second heading he places
all those spiritual sins which are expressions of the fact that the
person is not willing to live out the truth with his whole being.

[31] *Dread*, p. 122.

The content of freedom, intellectually regarded, is the truth which makes man free. But precisely for this reason is truth in such a sense the work of freedom that it is constantly engaged in producing truth. . . . truth exists for the particular individual only as he himself produces it in action.[32]

If he is not willing to do this, it means that some part of him is in an unfree relation to the truth, is in dread of the good that the truth might bring about in him or through him in action. And to the extent that he is in dread of the good he is demonic. The correct expression for the relationship between the demonic and truth is found in Jas. 2:19: "Even the demons believe—and shudder." Thus the demonic in a man, as the secret dread of the good, is able to express itself in such quite ordinary traits as "indolence, putting the thing off till another time, as curiosity which comes to nothing more than curiosity, as dishonest self-deception, as effeminate softness which relies upon others, as an affectation of aristocratic indifference, as stupid bustle, etc."[33]

Most pervasively, the demonic expresses itself as a kind of misplaced levity, an absence of seriousness about oneself just at the point of inwardness where, if seriousness is missing, all else is meaningless. Macbeth is a murderer, "yet everyone who has lost inwardness can with good reason say, 'The wine of life is drawn,' and can say too, 'There's nothing serious in mortality, all is but toys'; for inwardness is precisely the fountain which springeth up unto eternal life, and what issues from this fountain is precisely seriousness."[34] The man who laughs off the thought of eternity as "taking oneself too seriously" is in dread of the good; he does not want to let the good get its grapnel hooks into him, he easily finds a hundred ways of escape—and just this is the bondage of the demonic, that by his own "free" act he continually escapes the good.

When faith is present, dread is not abolished but is dealt with, in each case, in a positive, faith-grounded way. To abolish dread, that deep anxiousness which is the symptom of his responsibility toward existence, would be to abolish the spiritual structure of man, to make him either an angel or a beast. But when faith is present, dread is not allowed to become neurotic, to debilitate the man, to get him in its power to the point of making him impotent.

[32] *Dread*, p. 123.   [33] *Ibid.*   [34] *Ibid.*, p. 130.

And, more positively, when faith is present, dread is used educatively by the individual to apprise himself of his real situation, of the possibilities that are closed to him as well as those that are open, those that are a waste of effort to worry about and those that could easily be much worse than they are. All these educative aspects of dread or anxiety are brought out in the long "be not anxious" passage in Matthew 6.

But to use anxiety educatively one must be honest toward existence, that is, one must be willing to acknowledge the terrible as well as the wonderful possibilities in it instead of complaining about life because it does not consist of the wonderful possibilities only.

When such a person, therefore, goes out from the school of possibility, and knows more thoroughly than a child knows the alphabet that he can demand of life absolutely nothing, and that terror, perdition, annihilation, dwell next door to every man, and has learned the profitable lesson that every dread which alarms . . . may the next instant become a fact, he will then interpret reality differently, he will extol reality, and even when it rests upon him heavily he will remember that after all it is far, far lighter than the possibility was.[35]

5. "The Age of Anxiety"

In view of the foregoing analysis of anxiety, it cannot any longer appear to us as an accident that the present age, which produced the most sudden and astounding proliferation of knowledge in the entire history of the human race, came in due course of time to think of itself as the Age of Anxiety. For knowledge multiplies possibility, and possibility, the "being able" of man, produces the "dizziness" of freedom-in-conjunction-with-finitude which is the structural anxiety of the human mode of existence. This phenomenon of knowledge also illustrates the incremental character of anxiety in history. Awareness of anxiety increases in the course of history not only because man continually places more and more knowledge between himself and the Eden-like ignorance which alone could eradicate his anxiety, but also because his own history shows him and will not let him forget his actual misuses of possibilities in the past, their continuing consequences in the present, and the pall of dread they cast over the future. Whereas at the beginning of the modern age each new advance in knowledge,

[35] *Dread*, p. 140.

especially in knowledge leading to the "control" of nature, was hailed as a triumph of the human spirit and a promise of deliverance from nature's dangers, now, after the history of two scientific wars and the permanent threat of scientific annihilation, the question "What will they think of next?" is no longer asked out of curiosity and pride, but anxiously, in an ambivalence of hope and horror. And, not unexpectedly, there is also a tendency to put the blame for this anxiety on knowledge itself—all that knowledge lying around in heaps, like unguarded storage dumps of dynamite!

But it is not only anxiety before the threat of possible annihilation that is increased by the many new possibilities opened up by increased knowledge. There are, after all, many good and constructive possibilities inherent in knowledge also, and it is the nonuse of the good possibilities to anything like their full extent that produces another kind of anxiety with every increase of knowledge, the anxiety of becoming guilty by doing nothing. To the mind of the ethical individual, knowledge, simply as knowledge, increases responsibility and therefore culpability. We need only think of the situation in medicine, for example the discovery of the polio vaccine, to see how new knowledge creates culpability where there was none before. Before the vaccine was available, when anyone contracted this disease it was like being struck by lightning—what could be done? Now that the vaccine is here, an element of negligence enters the picture, and with it comes the anxiety of the uneasy conscience which only the stupid can escape and the callous shrug off. And this is true of all the good possibilities of knowledge that remain unused—at least it is true for the ethical individual, who is aware that the good demands to be *done* and that the individual cannot be related to the good except as he produces it in action. And now that, thanks to the knowledge of communication, all problems present themselves on a world-wide scale—the news services pouring out their continuous stream of disasters, continually reminding us of the disparity between the knowledge available and its unused good possibilities (for instance, starvation, when knowledge for both food production and population limitation is available)—it is small wonder that a kind of diffuse anxiety of the guilty conscience adds itself continually to the increment of anxiety about imminent destruction.

And then there is also the question of meaning for the intellectual which was discussed in Chapter II—the fact that the sudden
increase in knowledge does not simplify but instead aggravates
the problem of finding meaning in the totality, so that modern man
in general—but the modern intellectual in particular—actually
"suffers" from too much knowledge. The sudden avalanche of
scientific knowledge refuses to fall into any simple pattern that
spells out an obvious meaning for man, and though this fact may
profitably turn him toward himself for finding the meaning of life,
it nevertheless acts as an obtrusive presence—one more among
the difficulties and complexities of existence that arouse in him the
anxiety about chaos as the threat of ultimate meaninglessness. The
multiversity of his world does not strike the man in a state of ignorance (for instance, the young person and the primitive or
simple adult) as chaos but as mystery, arousing fear and wonder
and perhaps the confidence that more knowledge would dispel the
mystery. But when there *is* all this knowledge, and still the mystery
refuses to yield up its secret—then there is the threat of ultimate
chaos, which arouses anxiety.

So modern man has discovered the hard way, historically, that
the increase of knowledge brings with it the increased consciousness of anxiety, and now the question is what to do about it. Certainly if man were not destined to become spirit and if anxiety
were just an unpleasant feeling one should try to get rid of, the
obvious solution would be—back to Eden! Back to the blissful
ignorance of innocence, the joyful absence of accountability that
even now exonerates children, back to the South Sea Islands where
striving is unknown, anxiety is minimal, and where anthropologists
can find hardly a handful of neurotics! And this solution is being
tried, in more ways than the tourist traffic shows. The catalogue
of neo-primitivisms in all parts of our culture bears witness not
only to their proponents' disgust with overrefinement and sophistication, but also to the longing for primal innocence, carelessness,
spontaneity, rapport with nature, childlikeness, and other nostalgically idealized preanxiety states made possible by ignorance.

However, if back-to-Eden is not a very practical solution in the
midst of a technological civilization that few will give up, there are
other ways in which modern man is trying to reduce the all-per-

vasive increase of palpable anxiety. There is the solution of pinning the blame on freedom—or at least on too much freedom—and then of reducing anxiety by voluntarily relinquishing sizable portions of freedom to authority, an option that has been carefully analyzed by Erich Fromm in his *Escape from Freedom*.[36] But whoever forfeits freedom forfeits his selfhood, and by allowing others to make his decisions for him he exchanges the anxiety of freedom for the despair of not having a self—a solution that could occur to man only when his dehumanization had reached the point where not having a self was considered a small loss.

Then there is the solution that proposes to reduce anxiety by means of the cultivation of the fine arts. Art gives us at least premonitions, glimpses, intimations of order, which have the effect on us of "tranquilizing the soul." Why not use the products of the creative imagination to reduce the anxiety of meaninglessness—in the words of a poem by Wallace Stevens, "Tranquilizing with this jewel/The torments of confusion"?[37] And indeed why not, if the proper object is to get rid of the anxiety produced in us by chaos, that "slovenly wilderness," that "ubiquitous concussion"?[38] Unfortunately, art takes a sly and terrible revenge on those who try to use it in this way, in this contemporary "rage for order." For if the artist in his own life experiences the anxiety of meaninglessness and if he does not wish to become a refined charlatan, he finds himself cornered by the paradoxical task of inventing new forms not to make order out of chaos, but to express chaos, and his products therefore evoke the anxiety of chaos far more vividly and stirringly than any scientific treatise on the subject.

Finally there are the ways of attacking anxiety pragmatically and scientifically as a problem to be solved. These range all the way from pills and nerve-operations and alcohol and entertainment, through the tranquilizing use of religion, to psychotherapy proper, all under the assumption that anxiety must be *reduced* by whatever means can be found. Yet if anxiety is the necessary

[36] Fromm, *Escape from Freedom* (text ed.; New York: Rinehart, 1941).

[37] "Homunculus et la belle étoile," *Collected Poems of Wallace Stevens* (New York: Knopf, 1954), p. 27. Copyright 1923, 1931, 1954 by Wallace Stevens.

[38] Stevens did not necessarily hold to this theory but merely depicted it as one possible function of imagination in our time.

though painful condition for the development of the sipirt in the individual, only neurotic anxiety should be reduced, and then not because it is anxiety but because it is an unrealistic, twisted, unprofitable anxiety which debilitates the individual instead of helping him by showing him where the real dangers lie. Only those psychotherapists who are aware of the function of "normal" anxiety in the individual's "becoming," that is, his growth in selfhood, also perceive the possible dangers in the many-sided contemporary efforts to reduce anxiety. For example, Rollo May, a therapist who uses both Kierkegaard's concept of anxiety and modern existential analysis to extend the scope of psychoanalytic theory and practice, has this to say about the curious need sometimes to arouse anxiety in the patient in order to get him to take himself seriously:

The therapist is doing the patient a disservice if he takes away from him the realization that it is entirely within the realm of possibility that he forfeit or lose his existence and that may well be precisely what he is doing at this very moment. This point is especially important because patients tend to carry a never-quite-articulated belief, no doubt connected with childhood omnipotent beliefs associated with parents, that somehow the therapist will see that nothing harmful happens to them, and therefore they don't need to take their own existence seriously. The tendency prevails in much therapy to water down anxiety, despair, and the tragic aspects of life. Is it not true as general principle that we need to engender anxiety only to the extent that we already have watered it down? Life itself produces enough, and the only real, crises; and it is very much to the credit of the existential emphasis in therapy that it confronts these tragic realities directly.[39]

Kierkegaard says that the man who boasts he does not know anxiety is simply revealing his spiritlessness. The more spirit, the more anxiety, because the more awareness there is that something precious is at stake. Without anxiety, or even with the wish to be without anxiety, there is no seriousness, nothing precious is threatened because nothing *is* precious. Everything is in a state of deadly continuity; boredom and staleness prevail, and man "even before he is dead . . . can almost take his place in a gallery of wax figures."[40] But the chief thing is to let oneself be educated by anxiety,

[39] Rollo May, Ernest Angel, and Henri F. Ellenberger (eds.), *Existence, A New Dimension in Psychiatry and Psychology* (New York: Basic Books, Inc., 1958), p. 89.
[40] *Dread*, p. 145.

not overwhelmed by it, so that anxiety becomes "a saving experience by means of faith." The anxiety-of-freedom-before-possibility is a school that wishes to teach us what is precious and what is not, what it is wise to be anxious about and what not (as in Matthew 6, where anxiety about food and clothing is compared with seeking the Kingdom of God and his righteousness). Not backward to Eden, but forward to the Kingdom of God—that is the lesson which anxiety, our exile from Eden, is trying to teach us.

X

Despair and Faith: Radical Sickness
and Radical Cure

1. Spiritual Health and Spiritual Sickness

What has been said in the previous chapter about anxiety, that it is a structural element in the very nature of man, that it is a corollary of the conjunction of freedom and finitude in man, and that it is something which the spirit must learn to deal with "if he would not go to perdition either by not having known dread or by sinking under it"[1]—all this is not true of the subject of Kierkegaard's second psychological investigation, despair. Anxiety is "normal" when it is not so unrealistic as to be pathological, but despair is a sickness even when it is prevalent enough to be called normal and even when it is unconscious. Despair presupposes a certain structure in man (especially when that structure is regarded teleologically, that is, from the standpoint of what the self by its very nature is intended to become), but, far from being an inevitable part of that structure, despair is rather a malfunctioning of it, a deformation or crippling sickness that prevents it from becoming what it is intended to become.

Is it possible to discover, just by looking at the structure of man, what he is intended to become? It is, provided we include all factors. Man, if regarded merely as a synthesis or integration of two factors (the finite and the infinite, the temporal and the eternal, necessity and freedom, body and mind—whichever way we want to view and label the two factors), is not yet a self. The two factors merely "relate themselves to the relation. . . . If on the contrary the relation relates itself to its own self, the relation is then the positive third term, and this is the self."[2] The distinction here is between what we would now call self-consciousness, and personhood proper, which must include, in addition to self-consciousness,

[1] *The Concept of Dread*, p. 139.
[2] *The Sickness unto Death*, pp. 17-18.

self-relatedness. Now this self-relatednes must either be autonomous or it must not be autonomous, being in the latter case dependent on "the Power which constituted it." Right at the start of *The Sickness unto Death* Kierkegaard points out the great divide between a humanistic and theistic interpretation of man. Either man can make a self out of himself by constantly relating himself to himself in every other relation, or he can make a self out of himself only by including in every act of self-relation the relation to the power on which the entire constellation of relationships is dependent, that is, God. Kierkegaard's own answer is contained in his definition of despair, which is first of all a sickness in the spirit, a mis-relation of the factors just described. This sickness can take three forms: (1) not being even conscious of having a self, which is a sort of subliminal or unconscious despair; (2) being in despair because of not wanting to be oneself; and (3) being in despair because of wanting to be or because of insisting on being a certain kind of self. Now if man were an autonomous being, quite capable of making a self out of himself, (3) would obviously not be a form of despair, but would be his proper function and fulfilment as a human being. Nevertheless, Kierkegaard emphatically regards this as a form of despair, on the grounds that "the self cannot of itself attain and remain in equilibrium and rest by itself, but only by relating itself to that Power which constituted the whole relation."[3] To make the autonomous attempt is to court despair, and furthermore "if by himself and by himself only he would abolish the despair, then by all the labor he expends he is only laboring himself deeper into a deeper despair."[4]

I should like to point out that if one were in the mood for it (and if one were certain that Kierkegaard was not listening) one could, by piling up empirical evidence from the case histories in the psychoanalytical literature in support of this third form of despair, regard it (if true) as an empirical argument for the reality of God. That is to say, the third form of despair, if it actually occurs, would seem to argue that man cannot become a true self without including God in the relationship and founding the whole relationship on him. However, like all such "empirical" arguments

[3] *Sickness*, p. 18.
[4] *Sickness*, p. 19.

it has only a presumptive force, and one need only prick this balloon with the needle of scepticism to see it explode—for where is it written that man *should* become a self in the sense in which Kierkegaard uses the term? At any rate, this sceptical alternative does not prevent Kierkegaard from defining the standard of man's psychological health as that condition in which despair is absent: "This then is the formula which describes the condition of the self when despair is completely eradicated: by relating itself to its own self and by willing to be itself the self is grounded transparently in the Power which posited it."[5]

In order to keep the goal constantly before our eyes, Kierkegaard has arranged that the psychological formula for spiritual health is at the same time an operational formula for Christian faith. Having faith means that the self accepts its real self as given to it by God, is willing to be *that* self before God, and considers the making of that particular self (rather than some other, wished-for self) into what God intends it to be as its special task and calling from God. Thus, a humble and realistic acceptance of oneself in the sight and under the direction of God is the secret of spiritual health and the only *radical* cure for despair. Anything short of this is just symptom-dosing, not a radical cure. But the universal sickness of mankind is precisely that man does not want to be what God wants him to be. Man is in his very nature stamped by the destiny God has provided for him in making him man—the high privilege of becoming spirit, of becoming a self and of having a self, in the image of God, after the manner revealed in the Christ. Man shows his unwillingness to be what God wants him to be by the endless variety of ways in which he either refuses to be spirit at all or tries to be spirit in the wrong way, that is, in every possible way except in the way God intends for him. The utter hopelessness of this enterprise is exactly the reason why it is called despair and why being in despair can be compared to a sickness—it is man's sickly, diseased yearning for the impossible, and his resentful, petulant rejection of the real and of the possible in which there is hope. To be in this condition is to be in a living death, a hopeless living that cannot even hope in death since physical death itself is no assuagement for it, as it can be for a physical disease.

[5] *Sickness*, p. 19.

2. The Universality of Despair

Although a superficial appraisal would seem to show that people as a rule despair over *something,* some hope unrealized or wish unfulfilled or object unattained or even what they call a crushing misfortune, something purely external which overtakes them, nevertheless the real despair always has to do with the self. The despairer cannot face the new situation or the disappointment, but more exactly he cannot face *himself* in it, cannot endure to be the one to whom the disappointment or disaster has happened. "For in the fact that he despaired of *something,* he really despaired of himself, and now would be rid of himself."[6]

Kierkegaard gives as an example the ambitious man, like Caesar Borgia, whose motto was "Either Caesar or nothing." Such a man is dictating to providence, laying down the terms on which he is willing to exist (as we all do in a lesser way, with our lesser ambitions). What happens, then, when such a man does *not* become Caesar? He despairs, and he does so for the very reason that he does not become "nothing," the alternative he himself demanded. He still remains a self, but a self that he rejects in the shame and anger of his disappointment. "This self which, had he become Caesar, would have been to him a sheer delight (though in another sense equally in despair), this self is now absolutely intolerable to him. In a profounder sense it is not the fact that he did not become Caesar which is intolerable to him, but the self which did not become Caesar is the thing that is intolerable; or, more correctly, what is intolerable to him is that he cannot get rid of himself."[7]

On the other hand, if he had become Caesar, he still would not have become himself but merely would have found a pleasant way to get rid of that unwanted self which is forced upon his attention if he does not become Caesar. "Essentially he is equally in despair in either case, for he does not possess himself, he is not himself."[8] And so it is also in another example Kierkegaard gives, the case of the young girl in love who believes she is in despair over "something," that is, her lover, because he died or was unfaithful to her— in any case, because she lost him. Such despair, however, is only

[6] *Sickness,* p. 27.
[7] *Ibid.*
[8] *Ibid.*

the beginning of despair. The true despair, when the disease has properly declared itself, is over herself. "This self of hers, which, if it had become 'his' beloved, she would have been rid of in the most blissful way, or would have lost, this self is now a torment to her when it has to be a self without 'him'. . . . "9

So the formula for despair in all its different forms is to be in despair over oneself and in that despair to will to be rid of oneself. In the parlance of a more recent psychology, despair is the attempt to substitute an idealized, imaginary self for one's real self, precisely in order not to have to be, or to admit that one is, the real self, that particular *given* which one has been saddled with by "nature" without the slightest regard for one's own wishes in the matter. It is the "givenness" that is offensive when the relation to the Giver is negative, and in defiance the self tries desperately to be a self of its own choosing. Hatred of the real self is thus a hidden form of the hatred of God. Whether the self calls God "nature" or "the family" or the "Power that constituted the self," every relationship that starts from this antagonistic relationship involves the self deeper and deeper in despair no matter how active and positive it may outwardly appear, for this is basically a contest of right and power between man and God; which of them has the right and power to create a self? It is a desperate conflict, since every gain by the despairing man must be counted a loss.

That self which he despairingly wills to be is a self which he is not (for to will to be that self which one truly is, is indeed the opposite of despair); what he really wills is to tear his self away from the Power which constituted it. But notwithstanding all his despair, this he is unable to do, notwithstanding all the efforts of despair, that Power is the stronger, and it compels him to be the self he does not will to be. But for all that he wills to be rid of himself, to be rid of the self which he is, in order to be the self he himself has chanced to choose. To be *self* as he wills to be would be his delight (though in another sense it would be equally in despair), but to be compelled to be *self* as he does not will to be is his torment, namely, that he cannot get rid of himself.[10]

When despair is thus defined—as, in its most intimate nature, a despair over one's real self, a hopelessness in regard to what one

---

9 *Sickness*, p. 28.
10 *Sickness*, pp. 29-30.

really is, and, theologically speaking, the most radical disbelief that even God could do anything hopeful for this reality that one is— then it is not so difficult to understand why despair is very nearly the universal disease of mankind. "At any rate there has lived no one and there lives no one outside of Christendom who is not in despair, and no one in Christendom, unless he be a true Christian, and if he is not quite that, he is somewhat in despair after all."[11] Such a view is neither pessimistic nor gloomy nor exaggerated. "On the contrary it is uplifting, since it views every man in the aspect of the highest demand made upon him, that he be spirit."[12]

We are ordinarily prevented from seeing the cogency of this view—and of its realism—by our persistent tendency to regard despair as a conscious feeling of hopelessness over *something,* some condition or situation outside of, not part of, the despairer's own spiritual state. We keep thinking in terms of external arrangements; for instance, we think of removing the occasion of despair in order to cure the despair, or we think of compensating for the disappointment with something else, or we think of distracting attention from the despair by turning to positive pleasures and enjoyments. All such maneuvers assume that spirit is an immediate relation between the self and the world (the "reaction" or "conditioned reflex" of behaviorisitic psychology) and that despair is therefore merely a mistake, an unsuccessful attempt, or an unfortunate setback, in that kind of immediate, stimulus-response relationship. But spirit is no such immediate relation between the self and the world, and therefore despair, the sickness of the spirit, cannot be an immediate mis-relation. Accordingly, "there is no such thing as 'immediate' health of the spirit."[13] Immediate happiness as the goal of life for most people, and "even that which, humanly speaking, is the most beautiful and lovable thing of all, a feminine youthfulness which is sheer peace and harmony and joy . . ."[14]—all this is hidden despair, because immediate happiness is not a characteristic of spirit. Rather, "the dearest and most attractive dwelling-place of despair is in the very heart of immediate happiness."[15]

[11] *Sickness,* p. 32.
[12] *Sickness,* p. 33.
[13] *Sickness,* p. 37.
[14] *Sickness,* p. 37.
[15] *Sickness,* p. 38.

Immediate happiness is for children. But we have seen in the analysis of the aesthetic stage what happens to an adult person who pursues it as his only goal, we have seen how the hidden despair in it comes out into the open and how it mires him in the swamps of pleasure hunting if he does not take the hint despair is trying to give him—that he is destined to be spirit. So it is no recommendation, from the standpoint of spirit, to boast that one has never known despair.

But precisely this is the common situation (as the physician of souls will doubtless concede), that the majority of men live without being thoroughly conscious that they are spiritual beings—and to this is referable all the security, contentment with life, etc., etc., which precisely is despair.[16]

Those who at least admit to the experience of despair are generally the more profound natures to start with, either that, or else they have been "helped" by the vicissitudes of life to become aware of spirit. And about these vicissitudes it is also necessary to be cautious, to notice what they consist of and what they lead people to do with themselves. The hardships are just as ambiguous as the joys of life if they do not lead to spirit. Kierkegaard is the friend of sufferers, always ready and standing by with the "gospel of sufferings," but only in order to bring the boon of spiritual growth out of sufferings, never to weaken the sufferer with a misguided pity. His parting shot on the universality of despair is thus no bemoaning of the general misery of mankind, but the spurring on of man to that which is available to everyone even in the midst of human want and misery:

Ah, so much is said about human want and misery—I seek to understand it, I have also had some acquaintance with it at close range; so much is said about wasted lives—but only that man's life is wasted who lived on, so deceived by the joys of life or by its sorrows that he never became eternally and decisively conscious of himself as spirit, as self, or (what is the same thing) never became aware and in the deepest sense received an impression of the fact that there is a God, and that he, he himself, his self, exists before this God, this gain of infinity, which is never attained except through despair.[17]

[16] *Sickness*, pp. 39-40.
[17] *Sickness*, p. 40.

3. One Way to Analyze the Symptoms

Having defined the sickness of the spirit and also its correlative in the standard of health, and having indicated briefly its incidence or prevalence in the population as an almost universal, chronic state of the human species, Kierkegaard turns next to a more specific delineation of its symptomology.

And here, if we would benefit from his description, we must first divest ourselves of a natural modern prejudice against the terms in which he chooses to present the description, what he calls "factors" and their relation and mis-relation. Those of us who have had to accommodate ourselves to several different kinds of terminologies in the field of psychoanalysis ought by now to be sufficiently "above the storm" to be free from any absolutistic claims for one particular set of terms or categories in which the dynamism of dynamic psychology is described. Obviously, if there is to be a description of the human soul that goes beyond mere labeling of the whole regarded as some kind of substance (e.g., a "monad"), there must be some kind of distinguishing and naming of parts (an anatomy), plus a schema, map, topology, or simply a picture showing how the parts function separately and in relation to one another and the whole. Such a schema was Freud's Id-Ego-Superego arrangement, for example, and another was Jung's shadow-*anima-persona* schema and the "psychological types" it generated. That still others are possible and plausible and have been set forth by more recent workers in the field should merely warn us against the futility of thinking that any one schema could tell the whole story. In this field we must simply concede that there are different ways of describing the same thing, or at least different aspects of the same thing with different emphases. We must allow to each investigator his own terms, if only he can show us something in his terms which we can recognize in ourselves as true, even if we are disposed to think of it in somewhat different terms.

Kierkegaard himself helps us toward this tolerance of different descriptions by offering us at least two ways in which the forms of despair may be viewed. First there is what might be called the "succotash" view: so much corn and so many beans go to form the ideal succotash. As soon as anything is thought of as a synthesis of two factors, the succotash view is a possible way of describing the correct or incorrect proportions between the two factors. "The forms of despair must be discoverable abstractly by reflecting upon the factors which compose the self as a synthesis."[18] But a second and even more important way of describing despair is to ignore the component factors and to concentrate on how the quality of despair changes or, rather, intensifies, depending on what degree of consciousness (consciousness by the despairing self that its condition *is* despair) accompanies it, and how the self reacts defensively and offensively to this consciousness. This view might again be called (as in the previous chapter with regard to anxiety) the snowballing effect, because the growth and intensification of despair is due to the self's own efforts to fight the despair, which in turn increase the consciousness, which in turn increases the efforts, and so on.

Turning first to the "succotash" analysis, we remember that in Kierkegaard's terminology the self can be regarded as a synthesis of two opposing factors, finitude and infinitude, which the self relates to each other and to itself and "whose task is to become itself, a task which can be performed only by means of a relationship to God."[19] This means that the task is for the synthesis to become concrete, while not allowing one or the other factor to become dominant in the concretion, for as soon as one or the other factor is allowed to take over, the self is not itself and is then by definition in despair. So how is this synthesis to be accomplished? According to Kierkegaard, "the development consists in moving away from oneself infinitely by the process of infinitizing oneself, and in returning to oneself infinitely by the process of finitizing."[20]

In this analysis, despair can be characterized as the wrong proportion of the two factors. There is the despair of infinitude, which is due to the lack of sufficient finitude in the synthesis, and there is the despair of finitude, which is due to not enough infinitude in the synthesis. Infinitude is the expanding factor, finitude the limiting factor, in the composition of the self. When there is too much infinitude the self suffers from immersion in the

[18] *Sickness*, p. 43.
[19] *Sickness*, p. 44.
[20] *Sickness*, p. 44.

fantastical and the limitless. It sees itself in imagination as the idealized self. Its feeling, will, and knowledge become fantastical by wallowing in the many possibilities of selfhood presented by the overactive imagination, for the imagined self can be many kinds of self, but the real self only one. Imagination is the organ of infinitude, the expanding factor, or the future-projecting factor, but the danger to the self is that the imagination so captivates the self that it becomes fantastical, and "the fantastical is that which so carries a man out into the infinite that it merely carries him away from himself and therewith prevents him from returning to himself."[21]

Thus, when the person's *feeling* becomes fantastical through the expanding medium of imagination, then the self, instead of feeling its own feelings, becomes more and more volatilized until it becomes "a sort of abstract sentimentality which is so inhuman that it does not apply to any person, but inhumanly participates feelingly, so to speak, in the fate of one or another abstraction, e.g. that of mankind *in abstracto*."[22] We have as an example the sentimental idealism of those who try to "love mankind," those whose feelings are moved by visions and ideals of what man should be like, or might be like, if only particular people were different from what they actually are.

When *knowledge* becomes fantastical through the expanding medium of imagination, instead of the self appropriating knowledge so that "the increasing degree of knowledge corresponds with the degree of self-knowledge" (since "the more the self knows, the more it knows itself"),[23] the fantastical knowledge then becomes "a kind of inhuman knowing for the production of which man's self is squandered, pretty much as men were squandered for the building of the Pyramids, or as men were squandered in the Russian horn-bands to produce one note, neither more nor less."[24] We know that this is in fact what Kierkegaard thought the new scientific knowledge, as well as the Hegelian world-historical knowledge, was, for both were a kind of knowledge that is drunk with power

[21] *Sickness*, p. 46.
[22] *Sickness*, p. 46.
[23] *Sickness*, p. 47.
[24] *Sickness*, p. 47.

and fascination, and is gained at the expense of reducing to nothing and finally forgetting the meaning or value of the actual individual self.

When the *will* becomes fantastical through the expanding medium of the imagination, the self is still more volatilized through shrinking from the concrete—the self is so lost in the willing of huge, abstract projects and in the fascinated contemplation of what it wills, that it puts off by means of endless procrastination, distraction, and dissipation, with any excuse at all, the small, prosaic first thing that must be done toward the realization of the project being willed. We think here at once of the daydreamer with big ideas, a science student, for instance, who dreams of winning the Nobel Prize in chemistry but cannot bother to learn the Periodic Table. Or, the literary student who dreams of writing the great American novel but will not start by writing a good theme for English 101.

In all these cases imagination is a snare, and yet imagination is the indispensable organ of infinitude, the expanding factor in the self. This imagination, without which man could have no dealings with the divine, can nevertheless lure him into vanity and futility, as we already know from the Bible, where man is reproached for his "vain imaginings" and where God even repents himself of having created man when he sees "that every imagination of the thoughts of his heart was only evil continually."[25] But the answer is not eradication of imagination, Kierkegaard tells us, for this leads to despair of another kind. The answer to this problem lies in keeping the imagination in the closest, most intimate contact with the growing edge of the self, where the imaginable is at every moment disciplined and directed by the presently real and the proximately possible. Kierkegaard's formula here is that the self must

constantly become concrete in the same degree that it is abstract, in such a way that the more it is infinitized in purpose and resolution, the more present and contemporaneous with itself does it become in the small part of the task which can be realized at once, so that in being infinitized it returns in the strictest sense to itself, so that what is *farthest* from itself (when it is most infinitized in purpose and resolution) is in the same instant *nearest* to itself in accomplishing the

[25] Gen. 6:5.

infinitely small part of the task which can be done even today, even at this hour, even at this instant.[26]

This is his formula for the "becoming" of the self when it is *properly* performing the synthesis of infinitude and finitude instead of succumbing to the heady effects of the imaginings themselves, thus turning them into vain imaginings, vain in the sense of both futile and conceited. For it is the despair of infinitude when "the self thus leads a fantastic existence in abstract endeavor after infinity, or in abstract isolation, constantly lacking itself, from which it merely gets further and further away."[27]

The opposite mis-relationship is the despair of finitude, which is due to the lack of infinitude in the composition of the synthesis. "The lack of infinitude means to be desperately narrow-minded and mean-spirited."[28] Here the self is lost in another way: by becoming entirely finitized, by not daring to be self except in the most commonplace, conventional, and worldly fashion in which pretty much everyone imagines he is a "self." "Despairing narrowness [the lack of infinitude] consists in the lack of primitiveness. . . ."[29] By primitiveness Kierkegaard means the originality, the particularity, which in every man is intended to become the uniqueness of a self. Every man is as it were originally a unique "fragment," and a rough and angular fragment at that; the process of becoming a self should be as when a diamond-in-the-rough is changed into a precious stone by a clever gem grinder who takes advantage of all the special and peculiar angles in the original stone—*not* as when, through perpetual milling about with other stones, the primitive angularity and peculiarity is worn off and finally ground smooth like a pebble indistinguishable from all the other pebbles on the beach. Here the basic fault is not lack of imagination (as one would expect from the analysis of the preceding form of despair), but cowardice—because all the imagination in the world will not help a man who will not venture, who allows himself to be molded and "defrauded" by the "others."

By seeing the multitude of men about it, by getting engaged in all sorts of worldly affairs, by becoming wise about how things go in this

---

[26] *Sickness*, pp. 47-48.
[27] *Sickness*, p. 48.
[28] *Sickness*, p. 49.
[29] *Sickness*, p. 50.

world, such a man forgets himself, forgets what his name is (in the divine understanding of it), does not dare to believe in himself, finds it too venturesome a thing to be himself, far easier and safer to be like the others, to become an imitation, a number, a cipher in the crowd.[30]

Here we have the conformity ideal and the "other-directed" person described by sociologist David Riesman[31] as something new on the American scene.

This conformity ideal Kierkegaard considers to be despair, one of the most insidious forms of despair just because it so easily gets itself accepted as success. "The despair which not only occasions no embarrassment but makes one's life easy and comfortable is naturally not regarded as despair."[32] But that is what makes it dreadful, and "the world has of course no understanding of what is truly dreadful."[33] That a man can lose himself by learning the ways of the world, by becoming perfectly adjustable to its demands, by offering it no hindrance, no difficulty, from the direction of his infinitude, is regarded by the world as no loss at all. "So far from being considered in despair, he is just what a man ought to be."[34]

Along somewhat similar lines, modern psychoanalysis talks about the "shrinking of the self in withdrawal from tough reality for fear of being rebuffed." That this kind of behavior is encouraged by the world, that is, by family or by society or by the body politic, for the sake of its own smooth and uninterrupted functioning, is ironically confirmed by proverbs, old saws, wise sayings. Kierkegaard says that almost all proverbs turn out to be recipes for shrewd or safe behavior. He gives as an example the proverb which says a man ten times regrets having spoken for once he regrets his silence.

And why? Because the fact of having spoken is an external fact, which may involve one in annoyances, since it is an actuality. But the fact of having kept silent! Yet this is the most dangerous thing of all. For by keeping silent one is relegated solely to oneself, no actuality comes to

[30] *Sickness*, p. 51.
[31] In *The Lonely Crowd* (New Haven, Conn.: Yale University Press, 1950).
[32] *Sickness*, p. 51.
[33] *Ibid.*
[34] *Ibid.*

a man's aid by punishing him, by bringing down upon him the consequences of his speech.[35]

Elsewhere Kierkegaard has spoken of the need to get men back into the medium of existence where God could educate them. Here it becomes a little more clear what it means to be educated by God through existence: to be "helped" by the very punishment that life hands out. But only if one will dare, will venture, will reject the world's shrewd and cowardly advice of "nothing risked, nothing lost." Something *is* lost, a mere nothing in the eyes of the world but the very thing toward which God would help one with His education through existence:

And yet, by not venturing, it is so dreadfully easy to lose that which it would be difficult to lose in even the most venturesome venture, and in any case never so easily, so completely as if it were nothing . . . one's self. For if I have ventured amiss—very well, then life helps me by its punishment. But if I have not ventured at all who then helps me?[36]

Such is the despair of finitude, to be so stuck fast in it that one can hardly turn to the place from which help could come, to infinitude.

Still following the succotash view (the self regarded as a synthesis of two opposing factors), Kierkegaard gives another analysis, under the rubric of possibility-necessity. The self needs both possibility and necessity to become actual, to become itself. A thing that has been determined needs no possibility, and never had any. Pure possibility is the domain of God, with whom all things are possible. When there is too much possibility, the self "tires itself out with floundering in the possible . . . . more and more things become possible, because nothing becomes actual. At last it is as if everything were possible—but this is precisely when the abyss has swallowed up the self."[37] We can think here of the fairly familiar example of the young person on the threshold of life, whose economic condition makes it unnecessary for him to earn his livelihood. Such a person is so open to possibility that very often, in spite of talents or interests he may have, nothing definite

[35] *Sickness*, p. 52.
[36] *Sickness*, p. 52.
[37] *Sickness*, pp. 54-55.

comes of it, simply because there was nothing he *had* to do. But
such a person could be helped by finding the necessary within
himself, by becoming "aware that the self he is, is a perfectly
definite something, and so is the necessary."[38] Then he would
have a command to obey, a limit to which to submit himself in
order to become actual.

On the other hand, when the life situation is a trap, a slavery,
a routine, a prison, we have the despair due to lack of possibility,
a much more common and understandable condition for most of
mankind. In this situation, says Kierkegaard, it is only a question
of the strength which the self will summon to fight for possibility
—whether he will fight with human strength, so that defeat comes
when (humanly speaking) no more possibility exists, or with the
strength of God, in the faith that with God all things are possible.
Possibility is to the self what oxygen is to breathing, and a man
who will not fight for breath will die. That is what prayer is,
essentially—the spirit fighting for the breath of possibility that
will keep it alive.

For in order to pray there must be a God, there must be a self plus
possibility, or a self and possibility in the pregnant sense; for God *is*
that all things are possible, and that all things are possible *is* God; and
only the man whose being has been so shaken that he became spirit by
understanding that all things are possible, only he has had dealings with
God. The fact that God's will is the possible makes it possible for me
to pray; if God's will is only the necessary, man is essentially as speech-
less as the brutes.[39]

A person without possibility either becomes a fatalist, to whom
everything seems equally necessary, or he becomes a Philistine,
to whom everything seems equally trivial since everything is
viewed as the probable, the likely, the expected, the usual.

4. *Another Way to Analyze the Symptoms*

We turn now to Kierkegaard's second way of describing the
symptomology of despair, which I have called the snowballing
effect. "With every increase in the degree of consciousness, and in
proportion to that increase, the intensity of despair increases.

[38] *Sickness*, p. 56.
[39] *Sickness*, p. 63.

. . ."[40] There is thus a spectrum or gradation of despair, which is proportional to consciousness and ranges from a minimum to a maximum.

The devil's despair is the most intense despair, for the devil is sheer spirit, and therefore absolute consciousness and transparency; in the devil there is no obscurity which might serve as a mitigating excuse, his despair is therefore absolute defiance. This is the maximum of despair. The minimum of despair is a state which (as one might humanly be tempted to express it) by reason of a sort of innocence does not even know that there is such a thing as despair. So when consciousness is at its minimum the despair is least; it is almost as if it were a dialectical problem whether one is justified in calling such a state despair.[41]

We have already noted the near-universality of despair, and of course the sickness has its widest prevalence in the human race in the form of unconsciousness-of-being-in-despair. This fact is nothing to be proud of, for it is simply a by-product of the widespread intellectual and spiritual laziness of mankind. By and large, people prefer to live under delusion and in the thraldom of the senses, rather than to bestir themselves to discover truth and relate themselves to it. Here Kierkegaard offers an image which ties in the whole idea of spiritual development with his conception of the stages:

In case one were to think of a house, consisting of cellar, ground-floor and *premier étage*, so tenanted, or rather so arranged, that it was planned for a distinction of rank between the dwellers on the several floors; and in case one were to make comparison between such a house and what it is to be a man—then unfortunately this is the sorry and ludicrous condition of the majority of men, that in their own house they prefer to live in the cellar. The soulish-bodily synthesis in every man is planned with a view to being spirit, such is the building; but the man prefers to dwell in the cellar. . . . He loves that to such a degree that he becomes furious if anyone would propose to him to occupy the *bel étage* which stands empty at his disposition—for in fact he is dwelling in his own house.[42]

The cellar-dwellers in the house of the spirit are people who live in purely aesthetic categories, the open or crypto-hedonists, and we know from our examination of the aesthetic stage that these

[40] *Sickness*, p. 65.
[41] *Sickness*, pp. 65-66.
[42] *Sickness*, pp. 67-68.

categories can of course include the highest sort of intellectual and worldly attainment. Paganism in history, modern paganism, and even paganism within Christendom have shown us repeatedly what prodigious works man can produce and still be in despair:

It would also be a prodigious stupidity to deny that pagan nations *en masse*, as well as individual pagans, have performed amazing exploits which have prompted and will prompt the enthusiasm of poets; to deny that paganism exhibits examples of achievement which aesthetically cannot be sufficiently admired. It would also be foolish to deny that in paganism lives have been led which were rich in aesthetic enjoyment, and that the natural man can lead such a life, utilizing every advantage offered with the most perfect good taste, even letting art and learning enhance, embellish, ennoble the enjoyment.[43]

But it is only by the ethico-religious standard of what spirituality is that such lives can be judged to be in despair, not by any aesthetic concept of despair which they may have. The cellar-dwellers must be judged by the life that is possible on the top floor.

Every human existence which is not conscious of itself as spirit, or conscious of itself before God as spirit, every human existence which is not thus grounded transparently in God but obscurely reposes or terminates in some abstract universality (state, nation, etc.), or in obscurity about itself takes its faculties merely as active powers, without in a deeper sense being conscious whence it has them, which regards itself as an inexplicable something which is to be understood from without—every such existence, whatever it accomplishes, though it be the most amazing exploit, whatever it explains, though it were the whole of existence, however intensely it enjoys life aesthetically —every such existence is after all despair.[44]

What an indictment of the nineteenth century and of most of twentieth century existence so far, is contained in this one sentence! To be able to explain everything externally (science), enjoy everything aesthetically (culture), produce anything (technology), manage everything (social engineering), and yet to be inwardly opaque, unaccountable, unaware that one is from God and exists before God—that is the characteristic modern despair, characteristically unconscious in all but a few modern men, in all but a few theologians, novelists, and poets.

[43] *Sickness*, p. 71.
[44] *Sickness*, p. 72.

As evidence of the fact that paganism did not have the correct concept of spirit, Kierkegaard cites the attitude of ancient wisdom toward suicide: it was taken lightly and, in some of the pagan schools of philosophy, even praised as a high act of rational courage. But if the right idea of spirit is present and man is conscious of himself before God as spirit, suicide is decidedly sin: "to break out of existence in this way is rebellion against God."[45] One cannot say then that the suicide committed by pagans was despair; rather, it was the pragmatic solution by the individual of his life problem in a manner that assumed it to be of concern to no one but the individual himself. Yet just this omission of God from the situation showed the presence of the form of despair which is unconscious of being spirit and of having a self before God. "One cannot say, therefore, that the self-slaughter was despair, which would be a thoughtless hysteron proteron; one must say that the fact that the pagan judged self-slaughter as he did was despair."[46]

When despair reaches the point of *consciousness* of being despair, there arises then the additional complication of whether or not the self also has the *correct concept* of despair. For this raises, Kierkegaard observes, the ticklish point as to whether it is really possible to be in despair and at the same time to be so clear about oneself that one has the correct concept of despair. "How far complete clarity about oneself, as to whether one is in despair, may be united with being in despair, whether this knowledge and self-knowledge might not avail precisely to tear a man out of his despair, to make him so terrified about himself that he would cease to be in despair . . ."[47]—that is the delicate dialectical puzzle, which fortunately need not occupy us here (though it is really the limiting case to which this study points), since it concerns only the abstract, ideal case of perfect clarity and perfect self-understanding of which real life offers almost no examples. "Real life is far too multifarious to be portrayed by merely exhibiting such abstract contrasts as that between a despair which is completely unconscious, and one which is completely conscious of being such."[48] Real life

[45] *Sickness*, pp. 72-73.
[46] *Sickness*, p. 73.
[47] *Sickness*, p. 75.
[48] *Sickness*, p. 75.

is a matter of partial glimpses and half obscurities, of consciousness one moment and distraction the next, and of actual ambivalence with regard to self-knowledge.

There is a mixture of love and fear in all of man's attempts at
self-clarity. He wants to know, and at the same time he fears to
know, so that it is always a delicate question how much of his
obscurity about himself is willed and how much is at that point
purely circumstantial. We all know people who can't stand the
pains of introspection—they are too "busy" or too "healthy" or
too "sensible" for such morbid self-concern, such waste of time.

It is important to observe that in Kierkegaard's concept of the
self and in his idea of God, perfect self-knowledge would lead to
knowledge of God, or, rather, knowledge of the *self-before-God*.
As J. V. Langmead Casserley has pointed out, this viewpoint definitely places Kierkegaard in the Augustinian tradition. "Kierkegaard also follows Augustine in his realization that all self-consciousness is at bottom creature-conscious. 'The exceptional is a
particular relation to God.' 'It is the God-relationship that makes
a man a man.' We have not plumbed our self-consciousness to its
depths until we have discovered, at the very heart of it, our responsibility to the Other, who transcends our self-consciousness and
yet is known in our self-consciousness, whose existence self-consciousness apprehends and whose nature it partly discerns by
analogy with its own most intense and profound experiences."[49] But
of course Kierkegaard, in contrast to Augustine, was more interested in the psychology of spirit than in a "metaphysics of self-
consciousness," as Casserley calls this line of Christian thinking.
Therefore he pounces on the question, not what the self-knowledge
ideally leads to, but why it is that man tries to avoid this self-
knowledge. Why? Precisely because man obscurely suspects that it
might lead to God-knowledge, knowledge of the self-before-God,
and to that very "responsibility to the Other" from which he seeks
to escape! This is exactly what makes despair so dialectical—that
the *will* is involved in it. And blindness to the saving truth is at
any moment the most ambiguous compound of wilful ignorance
and innocent ignorance. "For in fact there is in all obscurity a

⁴⁹ Casserley, *The Christian in Philosophy* (New York, Scribner's, 1951),
p. 155.

dialectical interplay of knowledge and will, and in interpreting a man one may err, either by emphasizing knowledge merely, or merely the will."[50]

5. Types of Early Despair

The opposite of obscurity is transparency—here to be taken in two senses, both as the self "seeing through itself" in the sense of seeing through its own evasions and dodges, its wilful ignorance, and as the self "seeing through itself" as through a window to the Other, moving through real ignorance toward knowledge. The latter sense is what Kierkegaard meant by saying that only through the utmost subjectivity does one reach the true objectivity— the otherness, priority, and independence of God.[51] The former sense is the heightening of self-consciousness as the self becomes aware of what despair really is and also aware that in spite of all plausible evasions, its condition is despair every moment that it is not healed in the relationship of faith. For we recollect that "the opposite of being in despair is believing; . . . the formula which describes a condition in which no despair at all exists . . . is also the formula for believing: by relating itself to its own self, and by willing to be itself, the self is grounded transparently in the Power which constituted it."[52]

There are two ways of falling short of the formula for the healing faith, once one has some degree of consciousness of what despair is and knows he is in despair. Kierkegaard calls them the despair of weakness and the despair of strength, or the despair of the weak-willed and the despair of the strong-willed, or even "womanly" and "manly" despair. Nowadays we would probably prefer terms something like "withdrawing" and "aggressive" to describe the contrasting types of despair, and would not call them despair at all but "defense-techniques" or "strategies" for dealing with whatever is threatening or hostile toward an individual. In any case, the contrast between the two types is only relative, for "no despair is entirely without defiance: in fact defiance is implied in the very expression, 'not to will to be.' "[53] Nevertheless, in this relative con-

---

[50] *Sickness*, p. 76.
[51] In the *Journals*, No. 1042.
[52] *Sickness*, pp. 77-78.
[53] *Sickness*, p. 78.

trast the despair of weakness is the despair of not wanting to be the self that one is, while the despair of strength is wanting to be a self of one's own choosing and making, a self-made self—as encouraged by the you-can-be-anyone-you-want-to-be approach of modern popular success-psychology.

We are already acquainted with the aesthetic man who lives in immediacy, whom Kierkegaard here describes as

merely soulishly determined, his self or he himself is a something included along with "the other" in the compass of the temporal and the worldly, and it has only an illusory appearance of possessing in it something eternal. Thus the self coheres immediately with "the other," wishing, desiring, enjoying, etc., but passively; even in desiring, the self is in the dative case, like the child when it says "me" for I. Its dialectic is: the agreeable and the disagreeable; its concepts are: fortune, misfortune, fate.[54]

In this passage "the other" refers to the world, not to the God that appears at the depth of subjectivity. It is the outside world, the environment, the not-self; it is that to which modern psychology says the self is either well- or ill-adjusted, according to whether its prevailing state is pleasant or unpleasant. But, according to Kierkegaard's psychology, this state of being at the mercy of the environment, whether positively or negatively, whether in desiring it or in recoiling from it, is a state in which there exists as yet no self in the sense of spirit, since a self which could perform the feat of "adjusting itself" in relation to either the positive or negative features of the environment would be both active and partially transcendent over against the environment. This would be a self aware of having some degree of control or management over its own reactions, hence also aware of an element of the eternal in itself (as set off from the passing show, the flux of events and sensations that washes up against the self and tries in a million ways to get a "rise" out of it).

Now the question is: how does this dawning of transcendence, this beginning of a feeling of independence from "the outside" or the "not-self," arise? It arises precisely through the immediate self's survival of the frustration. "Now then there *happens,* befalls (falls upon) this immediate self something which brings it to despair;

⁵⁴ *Sickness,* pp. 80-81.

in no other way can this come about, since the self has no reflection in itself, that which brings it to despair must come from
without, and the despair is merely passive."[55] The frustration, the
disappointment, the loss, whatever it is that the immediate self was
willing to swear it could not live without—that, nevertheless, it
now lives without. After the frustration occurs, it is only a question of intelligence, really—of how much the self is willing to
learn about itself from this lesson administered by life itself through
that particular frustration. But this is just the lesson that most of
mankind wishes not to benefit from, through a kind of spiritual
stupidity. The immediate man calls it despair when he loses something temporal, whereas the real despair is that he may easily lose
the eternal by not paying attention to the lesson hidden in the loss
of that which he valued so much. What usually happens, instead of
the valuable lesson being learned, is that the immediate man, or
the immediacy in him, lays down its ultimatum—it declares that
if it cannot have thus-and-so, it will die. And sure enough, when
the desired item is denied to it, immediacy "despairs and swoons,
and thereupon it lies quite still as if it were dead, like the childish
play of 'lying dead'; immediacy is like certain lower animals which
have no other weapon or means of defense but to lie quite still
and pretend they are dead."[56]

But then time passes, sooner or later the circumstances change,
and either the wish is granted or it is not. If he gets his wish the
immediate man rises from playing dead and picks up exactly where
he left off, as fit as a fiddle, being in no way changed by this
experience. If he still does not get his wish, he either learns to be
himself and to accept himself without the wished-for item (the
solution of faith), or he rejects himself in any number of different
ways (the situation of despair).

In the latter case, the man's situation is now more correctly
described as despair, because now a self is involved, along with
the question of how the self is related to itself (whether by means
of rejection or acceptance), whereas in the case of immediacy there
was not enough transcendence of the environment to give the man
an awareness of the self as a continuing thing toward which he

[55] *Sickness*, p. 81.
[56] *Sickness*, pp. 82-83.

can have an attitude. However, as soon as a self is there to be thought about, the liability to despair increases, because now it is not just some external blow of circumstance that can cause the man to be in despair, as in pure immediacy; now, merely thinking about the self and accepting or rejecting it in particular circumstances, even in "good" circumstances and "good" happenings, can cause the despairing situation (literally, the hopeless situation) to obtain.

What is being discovered here by the evolving spirit is the stubborn fact that self-acceptance is not nearly so easy to bring about in actuality as the glib advice of today's psychological counselor would seem to imply. Yes, you must accept yourself with all your limitations, that is the true road to happiness. The theory of happiness is there, and the patient may even understand what he is supposed to do, and want to do it. But, in practice, "accept yourself with all your limitations" usually means, "blind yourself to your limitations—after all, no one is perfect and you are probably better than any number of people you could think of." And thus, in practice, self-acceptance is achieved at the expense of self-knowledge. The two do not seem to get along with each other very well. There is actually a tension between them: the more self-knowledge shows me to myself in my true colors, the less easy it is for me to accept myself. Or, conversely, it is only with the assistance of certain illusions about myself or certain distractions away from myself that I can accept myself, although then there is a real question whether it is myself that I accept. The object is to *become transparent,* but this is infinitely harder to do than to say; in fact, it turns out to be the hardest thing of all, which can in the end be done only with the assistance of God, only by means of his prior acceptance of me. And it is the difficulty—the doing rather than the saying or understanding—that really stops people. They start out in youth to win both self-knowledge and self-acceptance, a fact that is manifested in the struggle of youthfulness by the various early forms of despair, but as soon as they come up against some real difficulties, especially difficulties within themselves, they veer away toward worldly wisdom, which regards despair as a form of late adolescent growing pains one will "naturally" grow out of. However, nothing happens "naturally" in the

category of spirit. Rather, as a result of listening to worldly wisdom, the spirit is *arrested,* and "the majority of men do never
really manage in their whole life to be more than they were in
childhood and youth, namely, immediacy with the addition of a
little dose of self-reflection."[57]

This description, in the terms Kierkegaard uses, just about covers
the modern psychological ideal of the "well-adjusted personality,"
an individual who lives mostly in immediate interaction with the
environment, both social and natural, and who has just enough
transcendence, enough "self" and "self-control" to be able to
"make a sensible adjustment" when the environmental impact is
painful. In making the sensible adjustment, he avails himself of
the practical wisdom he gets from his friends and relations, or from
his psychoanalyst, on how to be what is called "normal," that is,
on how to be, in Kierkegaard's terms, an *arrested spirit.*

It is impossible to represent truly this sort of despair without a certain
admixture of satire. The comical thing is that he will talk about having
been in despair; the dreadful thing is that after having, as he thinks,
overcome despair, he is then precisely in despair. It is infinitely comic
that at the bottom of the practical wisdom which is so much extolled
in the world, at the bottom of all the devilish lot of good counsel and
wise saws and "wait and see" and "put up with one's fate" and "write
in the book of forgetfulness"—that at the bottom of all this, ideally
understood, lies complete stupidity as to where the danger really is
and what the danger really is. But again this ethical stupidity is the
dreadful thing.[58]

It will be recalled that in *Either/Or* Judge William tells the young
man that his trouble is that he will not despair in earnest—that he
merely despairs now and then, or up to a point, or merely flirts
with despair, but then again returns to the earthly things for
refreshment, distraction, fascination, and enjoyment in the hope
that things will get better, the time of trouble will pass, his luck
will turn, etc., etc. Exactly what the practical wisdom of the
world advises him to do!

The danger, then, according to Kierkegaard's psychology of
spirit, is that the individual will become well-adjusted too soon.
Much too soon, long before he has had a chance to learn, by way

[57] *Sickness,* p. 92.
[58] *Sickness,* p. 90.

of struggle with himself and with "the other," who he is and why he is, the individual discovers some clever little strategy or technique for self-defense against the onslaughts of people and things and events. Here lies the genesis of all future neuroses. It is not that strategies of self-defense are in themselves neurotic; they are quite indispensable to a certain stage of growth. But the manner in which the person becomes dependent on them, habituated to their comfort, and finally encapsulated in their rigid walls, determines the degree and kind of neurosis that later develops. The opposite of the neurotic development, but obviously not the "normal" course, which, as we have seen, leads to the arrest of spirit, is that the individual, by "seeing through" his own defenses and then by "seeing through" the whole trap or prison which is constituted by the need for defenses, gradually outgrows or manages to throw off one defense-mechanism after another until he stands naked before God in that defenselessness which paradoxically turns out to be the only invincible armor against the assaults of life. He grows in spiritual stature by submitting himself continually in examination before such questions as: Against what am I trying to defend myself? How can this assault (disappointment, humiliation, frustration) really hurt me—my true, eternally valid self— if it reveals some truth to me and is trying to teach me something? How can the truth hurt me at all? Whom am I trying to fool about myself, with my defenses? And whom is it worthwhile trying to fool if I can't always fool myself, and if I can never fool God? To undergo and to answer to this kind of self-examination is to become a self that is at once transparent and strong, needing no defense against the world.

6. Types of Advanced Despair

Speaking in the broadest terms, then, what is usually described as the neurotic development would best fit in under Kierkegaard's second form of despair: despair at not wanting to be oneself, or the despair of weakness. The very fact that defenses are needed in this form of despair shows that weakness is at the bottom of it, that is, weakness of selfhood. Nevertheless, there must be enough consciousness of what selfhood is, ideally, to enable the person to reject that self he knows himself to be. Thus, when the disappoint-

ment from the outside strikes him, he at first despairs over "it."
But as soon as his self reflection is aroused, as soon as he applies
to the situation his at least partial understanding of what a self
should be, namely, that a self should not be so dependent on mere
external happenings—then he despairs over himself for having
despaired over "it." From this thought it is only a step to the
thought that the ideal self should not be dependent on *any* earthly
thing—and thus he discovers the eternal aspect of the self, by
abstracting infinitely from all earthly things. To be sure, he discovers this infinite self negatively, by virtue of the fact that he has
fallen so far short of it, and yet he knows it is there as a possibility. So the next step is to realize that his despair over himself is
really despair over the eternal in himself—over its ability to help
him. This is the despair of weakness in advanced form. "The despairer understands that it is weakness to take the earthly so much
to heart, that it is weakness to despair. But then, instead of veer-
ing sharply away from despair to faith, humbling himself before
God for his weakness, he is more deeply absorbed in despair and
despairs over his weakness."[59]

This form of despair can now also be described as self-hate,
or better, self-disownment. "Just as a father disinherits a son, so
the self is not willing to recognize itself after it has been so weak."[60]
But, unfortunately, the person cannot get rid of himself by returning to the earlier forms of despair, to the distraction and self-forgetfulness of immediacy, to the "busyness" of the "normal" or
arrested spirit, because he now carries with him the idea of what
a self should be, along with his falling short of the standard it
provides and his hate of himself for it. So there he is, imprisoned
with his disowned self and not able to get rid of it or to forget
it. He is like the lover who hates the beloved when she will not be
what he wants her to be in relation to him. For he has enough self
to love being a self and to know that being a self is the goal of
spirit, and yet he hates the self he finds himself to be, that self
which is so far from the ideal. This is the condition now called
introversion, "which is the direct opposite to immediacy and has
a great contempt for it, in the sphere of thought more especially"[61]

[59] *Sickness,* p. 98.
[60] *Sickness,* p. 100.
[61] *Sickness,* p. 101.

The Danish word Kierkegaard uses for this condition means more literally something like "close reserve" or "shut-up-ness-in-oneself," but Professor Lowrie has, I think correctly, rendered it in English by the anachronistic term "introversion." In the same spirit, we can, I think, use the term "extroversion" for the condition that Kierkegaard so often refers to as "immediacy," at least for that condition in its happier, more fortunate moments. That this modernization is probably permissible is confirmed by the most obvious characteristic of the introvert (quoted above), that he feels superior to the extrovert. His is the sad, slightly hypocritical superiority that grown-ups express toward children, when they pretend to be envious of the happiness of childhood while secretly secure in the knowledge of their superior wisdom. In fact, all adult extroversion strikes the introvert as a childishness which is hardly attractive in a grown man. The introvert need not be an unsociable person, but at the same time, "with respect to this thing of the self he initiates no one, not a soul, he feels no urge to do this, or he has learnt to suppress it. Hear how he talks about it. 'After all it's only the purely immediate men—who so far as spirit is concerned are about at the same point as the child in the first period of earliest infancy when with a thoroughly endearing nonchalance it lets everything pass out—it's the purely immediate men who can't retain anything.' "[62]

The introvert may try to do whatever is expected of him as a member of society and to be as much like the others as possible —but then he also has his times when solitude is his greatest need, and again he notes in passing that this is a sign of his "deeper" nature. And with what does he fill these times of solitude so necessary to him? With just that secret love for and secret chagrin about his self-relationship—how nice it would be to be a self in the ideal sense, and how sad that he cannot be the self he would like to be. But this is the despair of weakness, because he goes no further than that; he does not seek help, he doesn't want help, he prefers his lonely pride, prefers to lick the wounds of his pride in solitude.

Now if a potentially strong personality arrives at the impasse of introversion and sees through it—that is, understands why it

[62] *Sickness*, p. 101.

is he does not want to be himself and understands that this is the despair of weakness—he goes to the opposite extreme, and now, with all the strength of his will, he wills to be himself in spite of everything, though the heavens fall, and without the help of anyone but himself. In that case we have Kierkegaard's third form of despair, "the despair of willing despairingly to be oneself—defiance." A potentially strong personality cannot rest in the impotence of introversion. It would sooner or later commit suicide or throw itself into some self-obliterating fanaticism—for example, some political or religious totalitarianism. If it cannot get rid of itself it must assert itself—it is too strong to be able simply to ignore or forget itself.

But what is this self, this would-be self, but the negative, empty form of the *possibility* of the infinite self, the eternal self, which the defiantly desperate self now uses to help itself to assert itself? This defiant self-assertion, or self-making, is just what twentieth-century existentialism recommends that man should do, as the only noble or authentic response to the utter, unbelieving, unyielding despair which claims to be the correct post-scientific appraisal of man's estate. As Kierkegaard long ago noted, in order to defy the eternal a man must use the eternal in himself, usually without knowing quite what he is doing—and the more he *knows* what he is doing, the more his action approaches the limit which is the *demonic*.

In order to will in despair to be oneself there must be consciousness of the infinite self. This infinite self, however, is really only the abstractest form, the abstractest possibility of the self, and it is this self the man despairingly wills to be, detaching the self from every relation to the Power which posited it, or detaching it from the conception that there is such a Power in existence. By the aid of this infinite form the self despairingly wills to dispose of itself or to create itself, to make itself the self it wills to be, distinguishing in the concrete self what it will and what it will not accept. The man's concrete self, or his concretion, has in fact necessity and limitations, it is this perfectly definite thing, with these faculties, dispositions, etc.[63]

But he is not willing "to see his task in the self given him; by the aid of being the infinite form he wills to construct it himself."[64]

[63] *Sickness*, pp. 108-109.
[64] *Sickness*, p. 109.

He wants to be both God and the self in the self-creating process.
Sartre says this is the only thing to do, since there is no God to
give man his essence, his plan, his marching orders, so man can
be anything or nothing, whatever he wishes.

In this self-creating process there lie the possibilities of many
degrees and variations of activity or passivity, of ambitiousness
or of toleration, in relation to the self one is trying to become.
As an example of the more active type of self, it is easy to think
of the perennial young man in college who pigheadedly insists on
majoring in a subject for which he has no natural talent whatever,
hoping to make up for this lack with sheer will power and hard
work—all because he sees himself in a certain "role," and this
vision so fascinates him that he is quite blind to his actual apti-
tudes. He will not listen to his teachers or advisers; he simply
cannot believe that any goal whatever is beyond the grasp of
one who exerts enough will power. Or, there is the "I am the
captain of my soul" type of personality, who does not need anyone
to tell him what he should be and who recognizes no power, even
in the form of his most obvious (to others) limitations, that can
compel him. But it is just the absence of a compelling force, the
unwillingness to recognize the "must" in the very composition of
the self, that turns the self-creation into a misguided love's labor
lost. For in this manner one will never get a real self but only
a hypothetical self.

It is so far from being true that the self succeeds more and more in
becoming itself, that in fact it merely becomes more and more manifest that it is a hypothetical self. The self is its own lord and master,
so it is said, its own lord, and precisely this is despair, but so also is
what it regards as its pleasure and enjoyment. However, by closer
inspection one easily ascertains that this ruler is a king without a
country, he rules really over nothing; his condition, his dominion, is
subjected to the dialectic that every instant revolution is legitimate.[65]

Thus it holds in the realm of spiritual truth no less than in the
sphere of scientific truth that in any contest between hypothesis
and reality, it is reality that has the right of revolution. Reality
does not have to be understood of men in order to prove itself
real. This shows again how objectivity is reached through the

[65] *Sickness*, p. 111.

utmost subjectivity—but of course negatively here, by the revolt of the neglected.

So much for the ambitious, strong-minded, I-am-my-own mas-terpiece form of actively willing in despair to be oneself. But there is a more passive way of insisting on being oneself, and that is to discover some basic defect in oneself and then not be willing to hope that with the aid of the eternal, one might be delivered of it. A person in this form of despair complacently tolerates a weakness in himself which, if he understood himself as a task before God, he would have to take steps to overcome or to deal with constructively. At the outset this may not be despair, but simply ethical laziness. Nevertheless, carried beyond a certain point it does take on the form of insisting on being oneself, by passively overtolerating one's own weaknesses. We all know the type of person who asserts his "character" or "temperament" by imposing on everyone his irritating quirks and foibles, which he claims are "the way he is" but which he simply doesn't want to bother to overcome.

But suppose the difficulty is something deeper, something quite difficult to overcome—in fact, just the sort of thing for which divine assistance would seem to be indicated, "hardship of the sort that the Christian would call a cross. . . ."[66] This might be something psychological (like Kierkegaard's own melancholy) which sheer ethical resolution could not overcome, or something utterly beyond human control, such as being born crippled, or being born ugly when the career of one's choice demands being beautiful—or, in America at the present time, just being born a Negro. Now the question is: what basic attitude will the self take toward the irremovable source of its misery, whatever that may be? The more the element of despair is present, the more the sufferer will try to hold on to the torment, to refuse help from either man or God, to refuse to admit that existence has not done him an irremediable wrong. "Precisely upon this torment the man directs his whole passion, which at last becomes a demoniac rage."[67] He uses it as the platform from which to launch an attack against the whole of life, as if to say: see, this

---

[66] *Sickness*, p. 112.
[67] *Sickness*, p. 115.

is what life has dared to do to me! "He rages most of all at the thought that eternity might get it into its head to take his misery from him!"[68] Kierkegaard calls this the highest form of despair, the demonic despair, because it draws its strength from direct opposition to the good rather than from a wilfully mistaken notion as to how the good is to be attained.

The demoniac despair is the most potentiated form of the despair which despairingly wills to be itself. This despair does not will to be itself with Stoic doting upon itself, nor with self-deification, willing in this way, doubtless mendaciously, yet in a certain sense in terms of its perfection; no, with hatred for existence it wills to be itself, to be itself in terms of its misery; it does not even in defiance or defiantly will to be itself, but to be itself in spite; it does not even will in defiance to tear itself free from the Power which posited it, it wills to obtrude upon this Power in spite, to hold on to it out of malice. . . . Revolting against the whole of existence, it thinks it has hold of a proof against it, against its goodness. This proof the despairer thinks he himself is, and that is what he wills to be, therefore he wills to be himself, himself with his torment, in order with this torment to protest against the whole of existence. . . . It is (to describe it figuratively) as if an author were to make a slip of the pen, and that this clerical error became conscious of being such . . . it is then as if this clerical error would revolt against the author, out of hatred for him were to forbid him to correct it, and were to say, "No, I will not be erased, I will stand as a witness against thee, that thou art a very poor writer."[69]

So much for the symptomology of despair, the sickness in the spirit, the sickness which is unto death. To speak jokingly, despair is a little like certain childhood diseases, the measles or the mumps. The individual must get it in order to become immune to it. But it is no joke when the individual gets it and then does not allow himself to be cured, preferring instead to malinger in it, for then despair becomes the living death, the sickness that is death-in-life.

A modern psychologist or psychotherapist would not have too much trouble recognizing at least some of the forms of despair Kierkegaard has described for us, in some of the neurotic and schizophrenic tendencies he finds among his patients. The reason for the similarity, despite the difference of jargon, is that dynamic

[68] *Sickness*, p. 116.
[69] *Sickness*, pp. 117-119.

psychology (the kind that is able to make a difference in the lives of patients) is not so much a science of parts and their relations (instincts, drives, needs) as a description of how man comports himself and contorts himself in reaction to his own successes and failures in the situations life forces upon him. Depth psychology regarded as a science is more akin to gymnastics or acrobatics than to anatomy or physiology. The therapeutic session is a kind of gymnasium where one unlearns unrealistic ways and learns more hopeful and truth-grounded ways to struggle with present reality in order to win the boon of sanity, spiritual health. For this reason literature and mythology, legend and drama, provide the psychologist with such a magnificent array of "case histories." The descriptive devices change, the historical stage-settings change, and the philosophical notions change, but the actions—the soul's gymnastics and acrobatics in learning the dance of reality—these remain recognizably similar to those we observe in ourselves and in our contemporaries.

7. *Christianity as the Chance for Health*

Now comes the more controversial part of the investigation. So far, Kierkegaard has merely described the various forms of despair, as well as the inner, dialectical intensification of despair which occurs as the consciousness of self increases, along with the consciousness that the self's condition *is* despair. That is, the self, by thrashing about in the pains of its sickness, becomes more and more aware of what it is fighting and where it hurts. Looking at the thing medically, it would seem logical that the worse the pain, the more the patient would want to be cured. But as any psychotherapist knows, the more *his* patient is in the grip of a neurosis, the more he resists the cure. Oh yes, he wants to be cured, he tells the doctor, but by this he usually means he wants the doctor to do something about removing those more obvious and obnoxious symptoms which drove him to consult a doctor in the first place—his attacks of anxiety and depression, his unwarranted fears, compulsions, irritability, touchiness, etc. But actually he loves his neurotic strategy; it is after all his only defense, his castle in the world against the world. And when it comes to learning the awful truths about himself and facing the complete reorientation of attitudes that relinquishing the neurosis would involve, then the cure is a painful business, more painful, perhaps, than putting up with the neurotic symptoms. Kierkegaard however is not talking so much about the kind of clinical neurosis that reaches the doctor because, through an unusual combination of contributory factors, there has been an actual breakdown in livability. He is talking about that generalized, all-pervasive neurotic misrelationship of the self to itself which is the very nearly universal sickness of mankind. What is instructive in the analogy with clinical neurotic cases is the way in which the patient resists the cure. For mankind as a whole resists the radical cure of its despair, a cure that consists in becoming spirit with the help of faith. It would much rather dose its symptoms, try anything to deaden the pains, hire innumerable "doctors" to make the symptoms go away—anything rather than the radical cure.

Now from the standpoint of humanism, and of all purely humanistic psychology, what power, what argument, what incentive *is* there that can force a person to become healthy when he prefers to be sick? There is nothing. All that humanistic philosophy, psychology, and religion can do is point to the fact that there is this possibility in man of becoming spirit, and then rejoice, or shrug their shoulders, or wring their hands, over the fact that some people choose to develop this possibility and some do not, others only up to a certain point, and so forth. The vast majority obviously will have nothing to do with it, no matter how much it is presented to them as the ideal or the goal of life.

But what a different picture, as soon as Christianity steps in! While the self whose measure is man cannot rise above what man is willing or not willing to do, with Christianity "this self acquires a new quality or qualification in the fact that it is the self directly in the sight of God. This self is no longer the merely human self but is what I would call, hoping not to be misunderstood, the theological self, the self directly in the sight of God. And what an infinite reality this self acquires by being before God!"[70]

By the same token, however, the *failure* to become that self before God which God wills it to be, is also "infinitely potentiated." For you cannot have it both ways; either the self is a

---

[70] *Sickness*, pp. 126-127.

purely human self about which God does not care, whether it becomes this or that or nothing, or the self is a self before God, and God cares what it becomes, in which case the failure is a failure before God. "What we need to emphasize is that the self has the conception of God, and that then it does not will as He wills, and so is disobedient. Nor is it only now and then one sins before God; for every sin is before God, or rather it is this which properly makes human guilt to be sin."[71]

Humanism is helpless when it finds itself confronted by the reality of despair, the sickness in the self which the self *prefers* to health. But Christianity is forthright enough to give this a less neutral name than "sickness" and thus to reveal its true dimensions. This sickness is *disobedience*, therefore sin; not to wish to be healed of it is yet a further sin, a compounding of disobedience by disobedience. "Sin is: before God in despair not to will to be oneself, or before God in despair to will to be oneself."[72] And anticipating that people will object that this definition of sin is much too spiritual because it doesn't mention any *sins*, Kierkegaard hastens to add, "for sin is precisely a determinant of spirit. . . . Why should it [the definition] then be too spiritual? Because it does not talk about murder, theft, unchastity, etc.? But does it not talk of them? Is it not also self-assertion against God when one is disobedient and defies His commandment?"[73]

So then despair is sin, and the opposite of sin is not virtue but faith. "Faith is: that the self in being itself and in willing to be itself is grounded transparently in God."[74] The merely ethical interpretation that virtue is the opposite of sin is a partially pagan view, which has neither the idea of man existing directly before God nor the Christian view of sin. But for Christianity it is of the utmost importance that the opposite of sin be not virtue but faith, for as soon as the pagan view is admitted, work-righteousness appears, and with it the distortion of all the factors involved.

By erecting the opposition sin/faith instead of sin/virtue, Christianity has transformed all ethical concepts in a direction away from paganism and away from everything which the "natural man"

[71] *Sickness*, pp. 128-129.
[72] *Sickness*, p. 130.
[73] *Sickness*, pp. 130-131.
[74] *Sickness*, p. 132.

regards as the good life, or the moral life. Virtue all men can to some degree attain—by their own power, too, for they have only to get together and concoct a general definition of virtue that is within the bounds of what a man may reasonably be expected to attain. This general definition becomes the "ideal" or the Platonic Form, the higher reality under which particular men are subsumed as mere instances, some as worse and some as better approximations to the pattern, which is the essence. But the notion that each particular man exists directly before God turns this scheme upside down, so that the defined virtue is now merely an abstraction, while the *subject* of the several virtues, the self of the individual man in its struggles to become a self through the medium of existence—this entity, the self of man, is now the higher reality, far higher than any abstract definitions of virtue or the moral life. And just this reversal of the "natural" order of things is what gives rise to the possibility of *offense*, "in the fact that a man, as a particular individual, should have such a reality as is implied by existing directly in the sight of God; and then again, and as a consequence of this, that a man's sin should concern God. This notion of the particular man . . . before God speculative philosophy never gets into its head, it can only universalize the particular man fantastically."[75]

The real reason, then, that men are offended at Christianity is that it is too high for them, it proposes a relationship to God that is too close and too intimate, an honor that is uncomfortably inescapable:

Christianity teaches that this particular individual, and so every individual, whatever in other respects this individual may be, man, woman, serving-maid, minister of state, merchant, barber, student, etc.—this individual exists *before God* . . . , can talk with God any moment he will, sure to be heard by Him, in short, this man is invited to live on the most intimate terms with God! Furthermore, for this man's sake God came to the world, let himself be born, suffers and dies; and this suffering God almost begs and entreats this man to accept the help which is offered him! . . . Whosoever has not the humble courage to dare to believe it, must be offended at it.[76]

[75] *Sickness*, p. 133.
[76] *Sickness*, p. 137.

Such intimacy with God is really too much, and so many an individual politely begs to be excused from it, for the wisdom of the world consists of "nothing too much."

On the other hand, this intimacy must defend itself against being taken in vain, against forward persons who would exist before God without respect for the majesty in whose presence they are and without constantly being aware of what this majesty has the right at every moment to demand of them. Accordingly, the Christian concept of sin is so much stronger than the "natural" man's conception of it, or than the Socratic concept, that paganism cannot be said to have even approached it. Socratically, sin is ignorance, and a man never sins except through ignorance of what is right. This view can never be disproved, since any attempt to show that a man did what was wrong although he knew what was right can be rescued by a fresh appeal to ignorance: the man was deceived. "What determinant is it then that Socrates lacks in determining what sin is? It is will, defiant will. The Greek intellectualism was too happy, to naïve, too aesthetic, too ironical, too witty . . . to be able to get it sinfully into its head that a person knowingly could fail to do the good, or knowingly, with knowledge of what was right, do what was wrong. The Greek spirit proposes an intellectual categorical imperative."[77]

Yet the Socratic concept goes as far as the "natural" man can go, and this means that at bottom all of such a man's talk about sin reveals more and more his ignorance of what sin really is. "All his talk about sin is at bottom palliation for sin, an excuse, a sinful mitigation. Hence Christianity begins also in another way, by declaring that there must be a revelation from God in order to instruct man as to what sin is, that sin does not consist in the fact that man has not understood what is right, but in the fact that he will not understand it, and in the fact that he will not do it."[78]

"So then, Christianly understood, sin lies in the will, not in the intellect; and this corruption of the will goes well beyond the consciousness of the individual."[79] That is why in the early, mild

[77] *Sickness*, p. 145.
[78] *Sickness*, p. 153.
[79] *Sickness*, p. 155.

degrees of the graduations of despair the element of defiance seems absent, whereas actually it is only obscured by the weak-willed nature of the subject. A weak will can be a will against God as much as a strong will. The strength of the will determines the irruption of despair into consciousness, when finally the man himself cannot ignore the fact that he is in a state of despair and defiance. "The definition of sin which was given in the preceding chapter therefore still needs to be completed: sin is, after having been informed by a revelation from God what sin is, then before God in despair not to will to be oneself, or before God in despair to will to be oneself."[80]

By refusing to let sin be Socratically and pantheistically defined as a negation—"weakness, sensuality, finiteness, ignorance, etc."[81] —and by defining sin as a position, attitude, deed, or stand against God, Christianity is able to put the screws on humanity, thus overcoming the helplessness of humanism before the human preference for spiritual sickness over spiritual health. Bluntly put, this means simply that the final and only unshakeable reason for trying to achieve spiritual health is that this is what God wants for man; therefore, any preference for the easier solutions provided by the many varieties of neurotic strategy (the forms of despair) is simply disobedience to what God wants for man.

Here we encounter paradox upon paradox. It is as if God knew all about man's entanglement in the coils of his spiritual sickness and knew that man cannot simply be talked or argued out of it. He must be shaken out of it, grasped by the roots and torn out of the power of the sickness by a power stronger than himself and stronger than the sickness. That is why the attainment of spiritual health is a fight, a campaign, rather than the mere *receiving* of knowledge, even revealed knowledge about oneself, and that is why "the believer is a victor."[82] But the believer is a victor only because God is a victor, only because God has already shown the quality of his power over the sins of the world, a quality that reveals both what it means to be undefeatable and at what cost the sin-sickness can be cured. On top of this paradox, Christianity paradoxically raises the hopes of man as they have never been

[80] *Sickness*, pp. 155-156.
[81] *Sickness*, p. 156.
[82] *Sickness*, p. 140.

raised before and condemns his hopelessness, his sinful despair, as it has never been condemned before—then, on condition of his accepting the highest blessedness, proposes to do away with the guilt of this condemnation as it has never been done away with before. Christianity "works directly against itself when it establishes sin so securely as a position that it seems a perfect impossibility to do away with it again—and then it is precisely Christianity which, by the atonement, would do away with it so completely that it is as though drowned in the sea."[83]

The fact that sin is not a negation but a stand or position taken up against God, is shown by the law that governs the growth or development of sin, or perhaps one should say, the increase of its power over the individual. Not to wish to be cured of the sickness in the spirit, the sinful despair, is a new sin that adds itself to prior sin like compound interest, establishing a continuity with itself and automatically increasing itself as time passes. "And the law for the growth of this continuity is moreover different from the law which applies to a debt or to a negation. For a debt does not grow because it is not paid, it grows every time it is added to. But sin grows every instant one does not get out of it. . . . Christianly understood, the state of remaining in sin is really a greater sin."[84]

By acquiring continuity and thereby consistency with itself, sin also acquires power. In this way the believer and the demonic man can be seen as opposite numbers, the believer reposing in and having his strength in the consistency of the good, the demonic man allowing evil to become strong in him by virtue of its consistency with itself. Both of these types of man are different from the great mass of merely spiritless men, who have no consistency at all and merely flutter about from one thing to another. Thus, the *strength* of the spirit is seen to lie in consistency, an attribute which, however, may be oriented toward the good or toward the evil. The advanced demoniac finally fears the good for the same reason the believer fears evil—because it would spoil the consistency of his life. So, "the state of being in sin is that which, in the depth to which he has sunk, holds him [the

[83] *Sickness*, p. 163.
[84] *Sickness*, pp. 172-173.

demoniac] together, impiously strengthening him by consistency."[85]

Christianity proves itself to be the culmination of man's spiritual pilgrimage on this earth by providing the individual with just that factor which the sin in him does not want (and wants less and less as it increases in strength), namely, the forgiveness of sins. To draw a crude analogy from parasitology, forgiveness of sins is like the antibodies that form in the blood stream to attack and drive out the invading disease-organisms, but these, in turn, try to built up their resistance to the antibodies. The sin in a man defends itself against the threat to itself implied in the forgiveness of sins by refusing to believe in the forgiveness of sins. "When the sinner despairs of the forgiveness of sins it is almost as if he were directly picking a quarrel with God, it sounds in fact like a rejoinder when he says, 'No, there is not any forgiveness of sins, it is an impossibility'; this looks like a hand-to-hand scuffle."[86]

At this point Kierkegaard once again chides the romantic nine-teenth century for having so confused the religious with the aesthetic and metaphysical categories that the meaning of the forgiveness of sins was entirely obscured.

In real life the sin of despairing of the forgiveness of sins is generally misunderstood, especially now that they have done away with the ethical, so that one seldom or never hears a sound ethical word. Aesthetic-metaphysically it is honored as a sign of a deep nature that one despairs of the forgiveness of sins, pretty much as if one were to regard it as a sign of a deep nature in a child that it is naughty. On the whole it is unbelievable what confusion has invaded the religious sphere since in man's relationship to God there has been abolished the "Thou shalt," which is the only regulative principle. This "Thou shalt" ought to be a part of every definition of the religious; instead of which people have employed fantastically conceptions of God as an ingredient in human self-importance, so as to be self-important over against God. . . . And all that which in the old days was regarded with horror as the expression of impious insubordination has now become spirited, the sign of a deep nature. "Thou shalt *believe*," that is what was said in the old days, as soberly as possible and in so many words—now it is spirited and the sign of a deep nature not to be able to do so. "Thou shalt believe in the forgiveness of sins," was what they said, and as the only commentary to this text it was said, "It will go ill with thee if thou canst not, for what one shall do, one

[85] *Sickness*, p. 177.
[86] *Sickness*, p. 187.

can do"—now it is spirited and the sign of a deeper nature not to be able to believe it.[87]

"It will go ill with thee if thou canst not." When God himself has gone to the trouble to provide, at great cost to himself, the "antibody" for sin, and then the sinner refuses to take it, it will go ill with him simply because the disease is now stronger in him than the will to be cured or even the desire for his own good. We usually say about the spiritually sick person at this stage that he is "possessed"; he seems to be in the power of something stronger than himself that drives him to destruction, first of others, but eventually also of himself.

Christianity, then, as Kierkegaard conceives it, is the radical cure for the nearly universal spiritual sickness of mankind, but it is a cure that operates in a definite way—not in any which way that might suit the sick fancy of humanity in its efforts to get itself cured. First, Christianity undresses man of the spurious clothing of all the abstractions used in false cures—abstractions such as "mankind," and "the history of the human race" and "the concept of man"—in order to get down to the real, naked organ that is the actual locus of the disease: the individual selfhood of each individual man. Only the individual selves exist before God, because only the individual selves can obey or disobey, be faithful or faithless, decide for good or for evil. Mankind, the history of the race, the concept of man—these are summaries and collective expressions, a kind of abbreviated, shorthand way of speaking. *They* cannot exist before God, because abstractions do not believe or distrust, obey or disobey; abstractions are not humble nor can they be offended. "All these abstractions are before God nonexistent, before God in Christ there live only individual men (sinners)—yet God can well oversee the whole, he can care for the sparrows too."[88] We are misled by the very process of conceptualizing, of thinking in abbreviations or abstractions, to think wrongly about God. "His concept is not like that of man under which the individual is subsumed as a thing which is absorbed by the concept, His concept comprises everything, and in another sense He has no concept. God does not help Himself by an abbreviation, He comprehends

[87] *Sickness*, pp. 188-189.
[88] *Sickness*, p. 198.

(*comprehendit*) reality itself, all the individuals; for Him the individual is not subsumed under the concept."[89]

Christianity, in order to effect its radical cure, next proposes to bring together more closely than has ever even been imagined by thought, not the *concept of man* with the *concept of God* but the real, actual, unique man, who of course cannot be conceptualized, with the real, actual, unique God, who likewise cannot be contained in concepts. It is this unheard-of proximity, this divine-real rubbing directly on the human-real, that must be brought about if the radical cure is to be effected, for only then are all escape devices and buffers removed. Then there is no longer any question of not knowing, of not having had enough evidence presented, of not being responsible. "A man seated in a glass case is not put to such embarrassment as is a man in his transparency before God. This is the factor of conscience. By the aid of conscience things are so arranged that the judicial report follows at once upon every fault, and that the guilty one himself must write it. . . . Substantially everyone arrives in eternity bringing with him and delivering the most accurate account of every least insignificance which he has committed or has left undone."[90]

But precisely because the two realities (human and divine) must be brought so closely together to effect the radical cure, there is always the danger that the proximity will be misunderstood, misused, pantheistically dissolved, humanistically presumed upon, or frivolously taken in vain. This is the perennial precariousness of the Christian situation as between God and man. Take away the qualitative distinction between God and man and you take away the saving power of the proximity. And this is what all philosophy of religion tends to do when it moves away from the deep, rubbing reality of God to the distant, abbreviating abstractions, because at the misty distance of conceptual abstractions it is indeed true that the qualitative distinctions are hard to see. But Christianity, for the sake of the "patient," whose only hope for healing and health is at stake, must always maintain *both* the qualitative distinction *and* the proximity. The weapon with which Christianity defends itself against the danger of being taken in vain is the possibility of offense

[89] *Sickness*, pp. 198-199.
[90] *Sickness*, p. 203.

—where man takes offense at too close proximity to that which is qualitatively so superior. "The doctrine of Christianity is the doctrine of the God-Man, of kinship between God and men, but in such a way, be it noted, that the possibility of offense is, if I may dare to express it thus, the guarantee whereby God assures Himself that man cannot come too near to Him.[91]

The possibility of offense follows the Christian truth of the God-man relationship everywhere, like a shadow. It is the "shadow side" of the revelation, as Jung perhaps might say. In Kierkegaard's terms, it is the "seriousness" of the revelation.

That there is an infinite difference of quality between God and man is the possibility of offense which cannot be taken away. Out of love God becomes man; He says, "Look what it is to be a man"; but He adds, "O take heed, for at the same time I am God—blessed is he who shall not be offended in me." As man He assumes the lowly form of a servant. He expresses what it is to be a lowly man, to the intent that no one shall think himself excluded, or think that it is human prestige or prestige among men which brings one nearer to God. No, he is the lowly man. "Look hither," He says, "and learn what it is to be a man; O but take heed, for at the same time I am God—blessed is he who shall not be offended in me."[92]

Confronted by Christ, who is God showing man what it is to be man in the condition of health, the individual—the real, sinful, sick man—can only believe or be offended. If he is not offended, he worships, for that is the expression of faith which at the same time expresses the qualitative distinction. If he is offended, he does not worship, and his offense may take many forms or degrees, ranging from the mildest offense, which is a refusal to have any opinion on Christ one way or the other, to the strongest offense, which is to declare that Christianity is a lie, the form of offense that Kierkegaard calls the sin against the Holy Spirit. In between are all the various degrees of pretended indifference and paralyzing indecision—the flirting with, the backing away from, the procrastination, and so on—all of which witness to the reality of Christianity negatively, by showing that the question "What think ye of Christ?" is the most serious question of existence, one that will neither stop demanding an answer nor allow itself to be treated as a curiosity.

[91] *Sickness*, p. 206.
[92] *Sickness*, pp. 209-210.

XI

Concluding Remarks: Some Lessons for Today

1. Modern Psychology and the Concept of Self

Kierkegaard wrote to admonish the nineteenth century, in a role
that he himself styled as "the corrective." But the corrective must
not be mistaken for the whole, that is, for the body of experience
that is in need of correction. Rather, the corrective is the pinch
of spice that the cook adds to the dish when she sees that something
is missing.[1] However, the corrective is not merely another swing
of the pendulum in the opposite direction, in accordance with the
Hegelian zigzag march of the Idea through history. The corrective,
properly understood and applied, is the restoration and enrichment
of the understanding of a reality that has *always* been present to
human consciousness in various times, in various places, in various
degrees, but that now needs to be re-emphasized and reinterpreted
under a markedly new set of circumstances. It has been the object
of this book to trace and present Kierkegaard's "idea of the individual" as the corrective, as the restoration and enrichment of what
in various times and places has been called the "soul" of man,
under the markedly new circumstance of an era of thought that
was about to declare that no such thing as the "soul" of man existed.

Of course the "scientific" psychology of Kierkegaard's day, it is
true, had not yet come to the point of making such a declaration.
It was merely Kierkegaard's genius to be able to smell out in
the intellectual atmosphere of his day, the tendencies that were
already moving in that direction, and to warn what would happen
if a corrective were not applied. But the last years of Kierkegaard's
life coincided (probably without his knowledge) with the early
years of a group of pioneers in scientific psychology who felt more
and more that if psychology was to become an empirical science,
the concept of the self would either have to be deliberately avoided
or rendered unnecessary. These pioneers were in fact quite in agree-

---

[1] See *The Journals*, No. 1260, for an extension of this metaphor.

ment with Kierkegaard's statement that "when everything is explained by an X which is not explained, then nothing is explained," but *their* solution consisted in simply eliminating the X from the the discussion and in allowing a simple summation of parts and functions to bear the burden of explanation. Above all, the more positivistic among the experimental psychologists were in holy fear of introducing into the empirical data some kind of unobservable "thing"—an immaterial substance, a veritable homunculus—such as popular thought and some philosophical schools had usually meant by the "soul" of man. And, in so far as the soul of man is thought of as being a thing (and an unobservable thing at that), we must surely agree that the early empirical psychologists were justified in stating that no such *thing* as the soul of man existed.

So it was with the pioneers. But now, some hundred years later, let us listen to the description of the present situation in psychology by Gordon W. Allport, a psychologist of markedly balanced views:

Since the time of Wundt, the central objection of psychology to *self*, and also to *soul*, has been that the concept seems question-begging. It is temptingly easy to assign functions that are not fully understood to a mysterious central agency, and then to declare that "it" performs in such a way as to unify the personality and maintain its integrity. Wundt, aware of this peril, declared boldly for "a psychology without a soul." It was not that he necessarily denied philosophical or theological postulates, but that he felt psychology as science would be handicapped by the *petitio principii* implied in the concept. For half a century few psychologists other than Thomists have resisted Wundt's reasoning or his example. Indeed we may say that for two generations psychologists have tried every conceivable way of accounting for the integration, organization, and striving of the human person without having recourse to the postulate of a self.

In very recent years the tide has turned. Perhaps without being fully aware of the historical situation, many psychologists have commenced to embrace what two decades ago would have been considered a heresy. They have reintroduced self and ego unashamedly and, as if to make up for lost time, have employed ancillary concepts such as *self-image, self-actualization, self-affirmation, phenomenal-ego, ego-involvement, ego-striving,* and many other hyphenated elaborations which to experimental positivism still have a slight flavor of scientific obscenity.[2]

[2] Allport, *Becoming* (New Haven, Conn.: Yale University Press, 1955), pp. 36-37.

Professor Allport is not too sure that this new tendency is all to the good, because, unless it is made clear exactly what actions and states a self consists of, that little homunculus will creep in after all. He himself attempts to describe the self under the name of "the proprium" in terms that make growth conceivable, that is, terms that allow for real change in the passage from an infantile self to a mature self, stressing "the interlocking and emergent aspects of development rather than an unchanging nuclear self."[3]

With the word "emergent" we enter an atmosphere not at all uncongenial to Kierkegaard's way of thinking about the individual. An "emergent" view of process and of all becoming recognizes the fact that in any change from a simpler entity to a more complex entity, new qualities emerge which cannot be regarded as merely an increase, a reshuffling, or a rearrangement of the qualities already present in the simpler configurations. Kierkegaard claimed that all qualitative change involved a "leap" in order for real change to take place, regardless of how gradually, how "little by little," the change seemed to occur before the eyes of the quantizing intellect. We might compare such change with biological evolution: whether it took billions of years or five minutes, the change from the single-celled organism to the many-celled creature, once accomplished, was a qualitative change, a "leap," and with it there appeared qualities for which there had been no precedent in the single-celled organism (except as the mind supplied it after the fact with a mysterious, backward-extrapolated "capacity" for them). Analogously, as Kierkegaard claimed, the change in the individual from one central value orientation to another constituted a leap, regardless of how gradually the change took place in the life of the time-stretched individual. No sudden conversion, no dating of "the moment" was necessary; for even if the individual remembered such a moment, it would take time for the new value-orientation to permeate and penetrate the entire value-structure of the man and to change his way of life accordingly.

No matter what the vocabulary used—whether the term "self" or only some equivalent is employed—the tendency in recent depth psychology to regard the individual from the standpoint of

[3] *Ibid.*, p. 62.

his growth and development through various stages from the more infantile to the more mature is all to the good as far as an appreciation of Kierkegaard's idea of the individual is concerned. I have said that the reason I thought it valuable to select his idea of the individual for special study (as against the many other aspects of his work, whose importance is not denied) was that he described some characteristics of the inward struggle of selfhood in existence that modern psychology was also trying to grasp and understand, sometimes not succeeding as well. By that I do not mean to imply that Kierkegaard's is the only way of describing the growth of the individual personhood. There must be many, many ways of doing this, depending on the terms one selects for emphasis, and we should hope to learn something from all of them. Kierkegaard's description is in terms of the central value orientation, in terms of the "top value" of the individual's value system, and since these top values are fairly abstract (such as pleasure, the good, and the relation to the absolute) his description participates in the practical merit of all abstract thought, namely, that it covers a lot of ground. Many and varied cases can be subsumed under it. In this respect it differs from at least one other way of describing individual development, one which is interesting indeed but which is hardly conducive to schematization—the clinical case-history book. Admittedly, then, Kierkegaard's schema of the stages is highly abstract, and he himself apologizes for the abstract treatment resorted to in order to cover the ground.[4]

But while those psychologies which are interested in growth and development may be expected to learn something from Kierkegaard's description of the stages, the same could hardly be said for those psychologies which work under the assumption that all later stages are determined by the earliest stage, that character is fixed by the age of five. Such psychologies also have a variety of forms, depending on what factors are emphasized, but the upshot is the same: all later forms of striving must be regarded as either disguises or refinements of the earliest forms of striving. It is easy to see how we get the hedonistic reduction here, and also how we can never get beyond it. For as pleasure-seeking is obviously

---

[4] See the Preface to *The Sickness unto Death.*

a "top value" for the child, all the top values characterizing the later stages must be regarded as disguises or refinements of pleasure-seeking. So, here we run into the problem of the varieties of psychology, of how the different schools of psychology are predisposed and limited by the basic philosophies of the psychologists themselves.

2. *The Psychologists' Own "Top Values"*

At the end of Chapter VIII, following the description of the Kierkegaardian stages, the question was raised as to how the modern reader should interpret this "pilgrimage through existence," in what terms it is to be understood. Is it psychology, perhaps especially a psychology of individual becoming? Is it philosophy, perhaps especially a philosophy of the ordering of values? Or is it theology, perhaps especially a theology of paradox that leads from immanence to transcendence? To Kierkegaard it was all of these at once, and, though he would allow to each discipline its special province, he would not allow that they could be utterly independent of one another. However much one may wish, for the sake of "method," to restrict psychology to pure observation, the use to which one put these observations would still be determined by one's most inclusive view of reality, be it an ever so informal philosophy or theology. For the modern reader, then, the manner in which he can understand the Kierkegaardian stages will depend on *his* most inclusive view of reality. If he believes that the whole realm of religion is a delusion, he can follow the individual's development only as far as the ethical stage, under the assumption that ethical values are somehow independently valid and that any further religious grounding of them is a poetic elaboration and mythologization of these values, a compulsion that seems to be necessary to a certain type of temperament, a "religious" type of individual. In this view, making a distinction between "religiousness A" and "religiousness B" would be just as immaterial as making distinctions among all the known varieties of religious belief and practice. They would all be no more than different kinds of poetry, and, in this view, poetry has no cognitive relation to reality. Of course, if the reader believes that the whole realm of ethics is a delusion, he could not follow the individual's development beyond the aesthetic stage, from the standpoint of which all ethical values are merely prudential arrangements for the maximization of pleasure and the minimization of pain in a given society.

With whatever view we approach Kierkegaard's description of the individual's development in existence, we are forced to ask a question about our own most inclusive view of reality. Is this progress of the individual through the stages a movement from reality to delusion to still greater delusion? Or is it, as Kierkegaard thought, a progression from a superficial, childish understanding of existence to a deepening and more mature understanding, until finally, in Christianity, the absolute "depth" of the meaning of existence is reached? Here is a prickly "either/or" for the modern reader, predisposed as he is, perhaps, to having everything both ways!

But it is no different with the modern reader than with the various schools of psychology. The basic question is this: is it possible (not, is it *desirable*, for it may be desirable and still not be possible) to get a purely objective or descriptive, a purely non-normative, knowledge of what man is and what his "becoming" consists of? That psychology should be a nonnormative study, as much like physics as possible, merely recording facts without evaluating them, is no doubt an admirable methodological ideal, but is it possible? Physics, after all, knows of no abnormal atoms, no sick stars. Yet as soon as the words "abnormal" and "sick" are used, there has been an evaluation, some standard has been adopted as to what is normal and what is healthy. It matters not in the least whether this norm is perfectly obvious, whether the whole human race agrees upon it, or whether, on the other hand, a variety of norms or standards are held. As soon as psychology becomes psychotherapy (even if only indirectly, as in the case of what claims to be the psychology of "normal" people), we are in the realm of valuation, for therapy means healing, and healing means the restoration of a condition regarded as good, from which the patient has departed sufficiently to be in a condition regarded as bad.

Even the plant and animal worlds give us occasion for this kind of evaluation. It does not take a too practiced eye to detect a blighted tree or a mangy dog. In this case we know it is the *average* that provides the norm, that the appearance of the average tree and the average dog of their species enables us to declare these blighted or mangy specimens to be abnormal. But how is it with the human specimen? Here, if we use the average as the normal, we are making a specific "choice," an evaluation of what it means to be a human being, and we are also assuming that we know what an "average" human being consists of. A whole philosophy, a whole theory of human capacity and development is hidden behind this simple assumption that in the human case too, the average is the normal.

What is the solution? How are we most reasonably to deal with this impossibility of separating the human fact from the human evaluation? Well, one solution, as far as the various schools of psychology are concerned, would be for the psychologists to make their hidden assumptions manifest—and then let the buyer beware. Thus, in the future utopias of a more accurate nomenclature, we should expect that psychotherapists would advertise their basic philosophies alongside their professional skills when hanging out their shingles: as for example, Dr. Smith, evolutionary naturalist; Dr. Jones, rationalistic humanist; Dr. Brown, Zoroastrian religionist. Ludicrous as this stratagem may appear, it at least recognizes the situation that obtains. But the existence of this situation is not something for which the psychologists are to be blamed. It is not as if they were trying to deceive anyone. No, they try their utmost to be objective, and they try their best to restore the patient to a correct relationship with reality—but there is the rub: which reality? The psychologist can no more escape the implications of his own most inclusive view of reality than can anyone else. And this is exactly what Kierkegaard meant by saying that existence is, in this matter of values, so stubborn and so intractable that it will not allow a man to live nonvaluatively—like some god, with godlike detachment, on a plane above existence—but forces him to act, and action is already valuation. Beyond that it is only a matter of making these hidden values manifest, if self-knowledge is the goal.

Knowledge of norms is inseparable from knowledge of facts, where human nature and its "becoming" are under investigation.

That man is a creature who sets up norms and strives for them is a fact—the fact that is responsible for his becoming whatever he becomes—and as a fact it is no more "arbitrary" than any other fact that can be recorded about him. The psychologist, hugging his scientific objectivity and fearful of the supposed arbitrariness of values, would love to be exempt from this condition of existence, as if he himself had not become whatever he is because of norms he had set up for himself and striven for. To wish to be exempt from the conditions of existence is a desire that Kierkegaard roundly condemns. There is no nobility in it, as the scientist supposes, only vanity and self-delusion and even a little cruelty (as when the entomologist with his curiosity lords it over the impaled insect). Where knowledge of human nature and human becoming is concerned, seriousness consists of trying to be helpful, of always bearing in mind that which is edifying to the individual.

All Christian knowledge, however strict its form, ought to be anxiously concerned; but this concern is precisely the note of the edifying. Concern implies relationship to life, to the reality of personal existence, and thus in a Christian sense it is seriousness; the high aloofness of indifferent learning, is, from the Christian point of view, far from being seriousness, it is, from the Christian point of view, jest and vanity.[5]

In the case of the psychotherapist, of course, we must assume that he wants to be helpful, that his desire is his anxious concern about his patient, concern that he should use whatever knowledge he has to be able to discharge his patient as cured. But when is the patient considered cured? Erich Fromm, one of the more outspoken writers to recognize the philosopher-in-spite-of-himself role that is being forced upon the psychoanalyst, has this to say in answer to this question:

In the beginning of its development psychoanalysis was a branch of medicine and its aim was to cure sickness. The patients coming to the psychoanalyst suffered from symptoms which interfered with their functioning in everyday life; such symptoms were expressed in ritualistic compulsions, obsessional thoughts, phobias, paranoid thought systems, and so on. The only difference between these patients and those who went to a regular physician was that the causes of their symptoms were to be found not in the body but in the psyche, and the

[5] *Sickness*, p. 4.

therapy was therefore concerned not with somatic but with psychic phenomena. But the aim of the psychoanalytic therapy was not different from the therapeutic aim in medicine: the removal of the symptom. If the patient was freed from psychogenic vomiting or coughing, from his compulsive acts or obsessive thoughts, he was considered cured.

In the course of his work Freud and his collaborators became increasingly aware that the symptom was only the most conspicuous and, as it were, dramatic expression of the neurotic disturbance, and that in order to achieve lasting and not merely symptomatic relief one must analyze the person's character and help the patient in the process of character re-orientation. This development was furthered by a new trend among patients. Many people who came to psychoanalysts were not sick in the traditional sense of the word and had none of the overt symptoms mentioned above. They were not insane either. They often were not considered sick by their relatives and friends, and yet they suffered from "difficulties in living"—to use Harry Stack Sullivan's formulation of the psychiatric problem—which led them to seek help from a psychoanalyst. Such difficulties in living were of course nothing new. . . . What was new was the fact that Freud and his school offered for the first time a comprehensive theory of character, an explanation for the difficulties in living in so far as these are rooted in the character structure, and a hope for change. Thus, psychoanalysis shifted its emphasis more and more from therapy of the neurotic *symptoms* to therapy of difficulties in living rooted in the neurotic *character*.[6]

But of course just to the extent that character-change rather than symptom-disappearance is used to decide when the patient is cured, the therapist must apply his own idea of what human character should be and should include. Very different, and even contradictory, conclusions regarding the patient's state of health can be reached in this way, starting with the same symptoms:

We see that it is not easy to determine what we consider to be the sickness and what we consider to be the cure. The solution depends on what one considers to be the aim of psychoanalysis. We find that according to one conception *adjustment* is the aim of analytic cure. By adjustment is meant a person's ability to act like the majority of people in his culture. In this view those existing patterns of behavior which society and the culture approve provide the criteria for mental health. These criteria are not critically examined from the standpoint of universal human norms but rather express a social relativism which takes this "rightness" for granted and considers behavior deviant from them

---

[6] Fromm, *Psychoanalysis and Religion* (New Haven, Conn.: Yale University Press, 1950), pp. 65-67.

to be wrong, hence unhealthy. Therapy aiming at nothing but social adjustment can only reduce the excessive suffering of the neurotic to the average level of suffering inherent in conformity to these patterns.

In the second view the aim of therapy is not primarily adjustment but optimal development of a person's potentialities and the realization of his individuality. Here the psychoanalyst is not an "adjustment counselor" but, to use Plato's expression, the "physician of the soul." This view is based on the premise that there are immutable laws inherent in human nature and human functioning which operate in any given culture. These laws cannot be violated without serious damage to the personality. If someone violates his moral and intellectual integrity he weakens or even paralyzes his total personality. He is unhappy and suffers. If his way of living is approved by his culture the suffering may not be conscious or it may be felt as being related to things entirely separate from his real problem. But in spite of what he thinks, the problem of mental health cannot be separated from the basic human problem, that of achieving the aims of human life: independence, integrity, and the ability to love.[7]

Fromm here not only answers the question about when the patient should be considered cured, but, quite appropriately, gives us his own philosophy. He appears to be a humanist and an ethicist, with some religious sympathies. Kierkegaard would probably go along with him as far as he goes, having always in mind quite respectfully and unhurriedly "how much must be lived through," but then he would perhaps add that even this criterion of cure, so far superior to the "adjustment" view, is not radical enough. So perhaps the suggestion that the psychoanalyst announce his philosophy on his shingle is not so preposterous after all. *Much* is at stake!

3. Kierkegaard's Individual vs. "Other-Directed" Man

Respect for the individual is certainly the most disarming, the most ingratiating, of all American ideals. It almost seems as though our many national sins should be forgiven us for its sake. All those European and Asiatic countries that hate us for our materialistic boorishness, our political self-righteousness, and our success-obsessions—surely they would soften toward us if they knew that in this matter of respect for the individual we are sincere, and we do give it the old school try. Nor is our sincerity utterly devoid of knowledge. We have some idea of what an individual is. Our tradition

[7] *Ibid.*, pp. 73-74.

defines him for us, and our history provides us with many examples of the individual as cultural hero. Washington, Lincoln,
Boone, Edison—all different, yet all genuine individuals. Our constitution defines the individual as that entity which is endowed by
its creator with the right to life, liberty, and the pursuit of happiness—not such a bad definition, provided we do not immediately
identify the three items with what a child, or even with what the
average man, would mean by life, by liberty and by happiness.

Yet, when we compare this American idea of what an individual is with Kierkegaard's, we cannot help feeling that something
is lacking. A depth and a severity are lacking in the American version. It is all a matter of rights and privileges and rewards—very
little can be drawn out of it about responsibility, development,
obedience to truth, sacrifice. One might almost think that the
American individual, by the most fortunate accident of being born
or naturalized in this most fortunate of countries, had received a
huge, inexplicable holiday from the rigors of existence. And perhaps it is just this easiness and slothfulness in the American concept that has caused it to be taken in vain—especially in more
recent times, now that the famous "Puritan conscience" no longer
provides the elements of depth and severity, as it did in the earlier
days. Why bother to become an individual when the Constitution
says that you are an individual and moreover are endowed with
all these rights? And besides, you cannot even be certain, the way
things are tending now, that becoming an individual will make
you happy.

Respect for the individual in the American sense does, it is true,
provide the elbowroom, the working space, the opportunity to become an individual in the fullest possible meaning of the term, to
become the individual existing before God; at least no external
hindrance will be offered to anyone who wishes so to become. And
yet this very congeniality of the atmosphere, this very friendliness
of the conditions, may easily bring about a misunderstanding, and
therefore an internal hindrance, in regard to the accomplishment
of this goal. Surely one of the more obvious characteristics of
Kierkegaard's individual, as he makes his pilgrimage through the
various levels of existence, is that he gradually achieves an increasing independence of external conditions. From being abso-

lutely at the mercy of the fortunes and misfortunes of the passing flux of experience in the aesthetic stage, he passes, by stages of increasing selfhood, to being at the mercy of nothing and nobody except God. He fears nothing but the loss of God, or, to state it differently, he fears nothing but the loss of the kind of self which consciously exists before God. He does not become independent of psychosomatic conditions, he does not imagine himself to be disembodied—and yet, throughout the vicissitudes that these conditions provide, in patience he preserves his soul unto God. He has something that neither governments nor societies nor friends and relations can take away from him, any more than they could bestow it upon him in the first place—his relationship to God. And he knows that the loss of this self-before-God means only one thing, no matter what prizes the world offers him in exchange: it means despair, and despair is the sickness unto death. Losing the world is not despair, not because the world is worthless but because it is in the hands of God where sooner or later we all must leave it. But losing the self-before-God is despair, and despair more strictly is sin.

With this aspect of Kierkegaard's individual in mind, what are we to think of the apparently undeniable trend toward conformity and a host of allied conformity-ideals, that is supposed to be transforming American culture in the second half of the twentieth century? Of course we may not agree with Kierkegaard that the God-relationship produces the kind of independence that makes the Christian individual, by being bound only to God, the freest of men. We may believe that the God-relationship produces only conformity to the demands of a sect or denomination—but in that case it is obviously not the Kierkegaardian idea of the God-relationship that we are talking about, but already the religious variation of the conformity ideal.

The change that is taking place in our culture, sociologist David Riesman tells us in his writings and lectures, is from the predominance of the "inner-directed" individual to the predominance of the "other-directed" individual. The inner-directed individual is the man with the built-in gyroscope, while the other-directed individual is the man with the built-in radarscope, and the change from the dominance of the first to that of the second is to be correlated with the change from a producer-oriented economy to a consumer-oriented economy. Concurrently, this change is also to be correlated with the change from the explosion-phase of population growth to the incipient-decline phase and the general aging of the population.

In the producer-oriented economy, to produce is all, and the inner-directed individual is admirably suited to be a maker: with his built-in gyroscope undeviatingly pointing him to the self-set goal, he creates something—a commodity, an empire, a work of art, a personality, a service to the glory of God. In the consumer-oriented economy, to sell and to buy is all, and to be a successful seller and a successful buyer you have to be sensitive to the constantly shifting market value of everything and to the delicate marginal differentiation whereby, in an economy of abundance, the various items seek to recommend themselves. Whether it is a car or a personality you are selling, or buying, it must be just different enough from the others to have a selling point—perhaps even to start a fad—but not different enough to lose the market value of the class as a whole. For such skill in discrimination the other-directed individual is admirably suited, with his built-in radarscope continually supplying him with information from the peripheral centers of trade as to what the latest wrinkle, the latest craze, or the latest obsolescence in opinion or value is. The other-directed individual lives by and for the approval of the "others," especially of his "peer-group" but also of the more generalized "others" projected by the mass media. Thus a society in which other-directed individuals predominate has built into it (corresponding to the individual's radarscope) a kind of over-all self-correcting servo-mechanism, a thermostat, which permits small deviations but by and large stabilizes the society around the temperature set by the powers that be in the value market. One would expect such a society to hum along as smoothly as the most perfect dream of a machine and to do so without any external force or coercion being applied to it, operating simply by the willing conformity of all the parts to the approval of the other parts, allowing a reasonable margin for small deviations.

I cannot take time here to comment upon this *reductio ad absurdum* of "love thy neighbor" (or rather, "make him love you") that is about to overcome American civilization at mid-century. Nor must we take too seriously the pronouncements of today's sociologists when we know that tomorrow another avalanche of data will be handed in by the busy workers in the sociological vineyards. My only interest here is to compare the American idea of what an individual is with the Kierkegaardian idea; therefore, let us take just a brief second look at this other-directed man, at the nature of his selfhood. He seems to be quite an altruistic fellow, with his constant concern about the others, even if his main concern is about what the others think of him. He certainly is no naïvely self-centered pleasure seeker, who knows what he wants and goes after it. His sole pleasure would seem to be the good opinion of himself that he will be permitted to bask in when he has succeeded in winning the approval of the others. But this pleasure has now become so dispersed, so socialized, so thrown out to the periphery made up of the approvers, that it has passed utterly out of his control. What an embarrassing situation—even a fleshly gourmet can, with suitable effort, manage to buy himself a good dinner! But the other-directed man sits nervously at his radarscope, and he literally does not know where his next pat of approval is coming from.

Riesman permits himself the observation that the other-directed individual tends to suffer a certain amount of "diffuse anxiety." And well he might, for in the face of an unpredictable future that is both promising and threatening, all men experience "diffuse anxiety"; it is, as Kierkegaard pointed out, a condition of being human. Much more specifically, the other-directed man suffers from the despair of not having a self at all, for in refusing to choose his own values, including the value of his choosing self, and in allowing the "others" to make the choice for him, he has lost his selfhood by forfeit.

In Riesman's scheme the Kierkegaardian individual would of course be considered inner-directed, though his gyroscope would be set at different top values along the different stages of his development. If it is true that in America the other-directed individual is about to take over, and if is true (though hard to believe) that a predominant section of our culture is about to let itself be engulfed by the form of despair in which one has forfeited one's selfhood, then it looks as though becoming inner-directed will be more difficult than ever, with genuine selfhood gradually vanishing from the culture. Of course, the promise was never made to the inner-directed individual, least of all by Kierkegaard, that his way would be an easy one, only that the difficulties would bring with them their peculiar rewards, above all the boon of being a self and becoming more and more the unique self that one is. But now it would appear that in addition to the universal difficulties of picking one's way through existence from opaqueness to self-clarity, there will be in America the added disadvantages of doing so in a culture that positively favors the consumer-oriented, other-directed individual—if we can still call him an individual.

4. The Answer to "Arbitrariness of Values"

Kierkegaard raised respect for the individual above the plane of legal rights, above the plane of the average regarded as the normal, and above the plane of "what society expects," when he claimed that whereas in the natural world the species is above the specimen, in the human realm the individual is above the species. Not for what he is but for what he has it in himself to become must the individual be respected, for in him, and through his becoming, it will be decided, after the fact, what the human species is. Regarded simply as what he is, that is, what he finds himself to be when he becomes capable of self-reflection, the human individual might just as well consider himself to be the most wretched member of the creation as consider himself its crown and glory. Invidious, humiliating comparisons with plants and animals come easily to the romantic mind, while arrogant, prideful comparisons come easily to the classical mind. But when once the uniqueness of the human condition—and therefore the irrelevance of either kind of comparison—is realized, and when the inescapability of that condition is accepted, there remains after all only one question, the question which human existence in its variety of ways is trying to put to each individual: how far is "the human species" capable of reaching in you? How much of the human truth are you capable of becoming, or how far is the truth of life realizable in you? Yet not every individual hears this question, at least not in such a form.

Perhaps this is due to the fact that the individual is so noisy in putting his own demands and questions to life that he does not hear, or has no time to hear, deep down, the question that life is putting to him. In order for the individual to hear this question, or rather, to hear all questions in this form, it is necessary for him to have what Kierkegaard calls "seriousness," which is not pompous self-importance but is, rather, a primitive sense of accountability for the life he has been given, the life which he did not give himself and could not give to another.

This tendency (which is rather especially a tendency in all modern thinking) to believe that it is always man who puts the questions to life rather than life which puts the questions to man, gives rise to the ubiquitous problem of the supposed arbitrariness of values. For undoubtedly it would seem that if man is asking the questions, he is quite capable of giving an astonishing variety of answers, and the answers he gives are his "values." Now values, it is said, must be either absolute or relative. If absolute, they cannot show such variety as man's own answers to his own questions display; therefore they must be relative—and, if relative (not in relation to the absolute which has just been ruled out, but to other relativities), they must in the last analysis be arbitrary.

But suppose it *is* the other way around, suppose it is life that is putting the questions to man, and again it is life itself, in the nature of its qualitative possibilities, that is giving him the answers. In that case values cannot be considered either absolute or relative or arbitrary, but simply as structural interactions. Values, or, even more subjectively, valuations, are thus the tentative probes by means of which the individual tests the qualitative possibilities of human existence and, more exactly, of his own life. The valuating subject (and existence allows of no nonvaluating subjects), in order to be and to become a single person, chooses one of his values for the role of top value and orients his life around it. Everything then goes along swimmingly until the quality of his life changes from a plus to a minus, or until something happens to him that cannot be comprehended and dealt with by his present top valuation. This is the signal for a change at the throne. The new value which is then chosen for the throne must have the ability to change the quality of life back to a plus, it must make existence bearable, it must have hope in it. The value that was "dethroned" does not stop being a value; it is merely relegated to a subordinate position because of its proven incapacity for the sovereign position. This process of learning through valuation may be slow or may be fast, but it cannot be arbitrary. Anything arbitrary in it lies in the willingness or unwillingness, the teachableness or stubbornness, of the valuating subject in regard to what life is trying to teach him in this manner—the process itself is not arbitrary. And so we are brought back to the question of the individual's "seriousness," in the Kierkegaardian sense. Talk about the arbitrariness of values, and you are really talking about an individual who treats values arbitrarily because he does not wish to learn anything from his life and because he does not feel sufficiently accountable for his life.

Kierkegaard stressed the value-choosing nature of the individual, but nowhere did he imply that the choices an individual could make were either unlimited or arbitrary. They were not, first of all, unlimited, in spite of the apparent variety of choices. Just let a man choose not to die and see where this will get him. Finiteness, the givenness of certain conditions, hems him about, limiting the available choices—except perhaps in the realm of fantasy. And, secondly, given the requisite seriousness, the individual could only choose for his top value what he understood to be the "highest;" but what he understands, at a given point, to be the highest depends on what he has already lived through, on what values he had already dethroned because his own life convinced him that they could not be the highest. Regarded as a "philosophy of value," the spectrum of choices represented in the stages on life's way—pleasure-seeking, moral striving, religious abnegation, and finally Christian salvation —is anything but arbitrary. For the point is that the individual is led from one stage to the next not by a necessity of thought, but by a necessity of life. Each stage is abandoned only when it leads the individual into some form of despair, and the next stage is entered because it has an answer to the particular form of despair that led to the abandonment.[8] Despair is in every case the negative signal, the symptom that the "limits of the stage," to use Kierke-

---

[8] That is why Kierkegaard called the transition a "leap": because it is not determined by a necessity of thought, as the conclusion of a syllogism, or the Q.E.D. of a theorem, is determined, but by a necessity of life, by a life preserving, hope preserving necessity.

gaard's term, have been reached—and Christian salvation is the final stage because it alone finally drives out despair in the relationship of faith.

Because a small child is unconscious of, or has incorrect notions of, the relationships of space and time, we do not say, when he learns the correct relationships, that he has invented them. Because the individual in existence is at the start unconscious of, or has incorrect notions of, the ordering of values, we should not say, when his own life has taught him some ordering, that he has invented it. He has discovered it, and his further learning in this direction, however far it may reach, will be further discovery, not more imaginative invention.

Kierkegaard claims that the individual exists before God whether he is conscious of this fact or not, and whether he has the most erroneous conception of what God might be or has a pretty good idea of God. The fact that it is not until he reaches the religious stage that the individual exists *consciously* before God (though still perhaps with an inadequate conception of God) does not mean that in the previous stages he existed before something other than God. It only means that he existed before God in ignorance and misapprehension and possibly also alienation. "God" appeared to him under various guises or masks that he could not, or did not wish to, penetrate—guises such as sheer vitality, the urge to survival, fortune and misfortune, purposiveness, creativity, the question about the meaning of existence, the eternally valid aspect of himself, and so forth. Kierkegaard's doctrine that subjectivity is the truth is thus poles apart from the subjectivism in modern thinking that leads automatically to the arbitrariness of values, wherein the subject not only invents his own values but, by implication, also invents his own universe. Subjectivity, personhood, is the truth because it is the "locus" where the truth-learning and the truth-living take place. "Through subjectivity to the genuine objectivity" is the path the individual must take if he would not be forever shadow-boxing with himself, and in the depths of subjectivity he encounters that which everywhere stands over against him as "the Other," that which he himself never invented or made to his order, and against which he beats his self-willed head in vain, existentially smashing himself to pieces.

It could be, of course, that modern thinking—and especially all technical philosophical talk about ethics and values—is simply impatient with the fact that value-learning is such a long-drawn-out, precarious, and agonizing process as compared with the toddling infant's learning of correct space and time relations. If only we could get everybody to agree on some really sound and unassailable definition of the terms we use—then our ethical and religious problems would be solved, or would in time solve themselves! More and more sophisticated semantic analyses of terms like "good" and "ought"; more and more accurate observations about man as "the symbol-using animal"; more and more discriminating distinctions between the "cognitive" and the "emotive" meaning, or intention, in the words and signs we use—such are the goals of the technical philosophers at the present time. Meanwhile, where is the existing individual, the person who is to beware of, or benefit from, the ill- or well-defined terms? He may be participating in this discussion as a philosopher, but his own nature as an individual (in the sense described in this book) is not allowed to enter into the discussion at all. His own nature is considered to be much too subjective and even "emotive" a matter for philosophical discourse, therefore a thing that can safely be entrusted only to the psychologists, thus completing the buck-passing circle. We should not be surprised if this truncated discourse, semantic refinements and all, leads nowhere else but to the familiar impasse of the famed arbitrariness of values.

5. Gentleness or Severity

If the individual is above the race and it not just a "sample man" of which billions of copies can be found, he cannot be judged, and cannot judge himself, by the average regarded as the normal. Strictly speaking there is no average man; the "average" is itself an illusion promoted by outward appearances and large numbers. Every individual is not only different from every other individual in hereditary and environmental make-up, but, on top of that, every individual, with his particular make-up, is in a different stage of becoming. The "normal" for each individual must be the highest that he can comprehend at a given point, which nevertheless draws him out and beyond that point. The normal for whoever would be an individual, and not just a sample man, must be the self-transcending self-ideal.

Yet we know that when man sets up his own self-ideals and strives after them, it results in all sorts of distortions, fanaticisms, neurotic defense strategies, self-deceits, and hypocrisies. For the "becoming" to take place in the proper way, each individual needs a combination of severity and gentleness that is a personal prescription for him. But no man is wise enough, and no philosophy is concrete enough, to deal out to every man his proper and unique combination of severity and gentleness. Man needs God for this, and therefore his highest perfection from the purely human side is to recognize this need. Besides, who other than God could be severe or gentle in any ultimate sense, that is, with absolute authority?

Thus, if both severity and gentleness in proper proportion are needed by the individual for his proper becoming, it is obviously no kindness to an individual to offer him severity when what he needs is gentleness; far less obviously, it is equally no kindness to an individual to offer him gentleness when what he needs is severity, in order to bring out what is in him, and to get on with it. Severity is as much a part of God's love as is gentleness, but it is not nearly as easy to see in that light.

Do you want to be an important man?
Yes, who does not want to be one? Well, then, enter into communion with God, but directly, without having millions between you and him —and you will see, you are such an important man that even the slightest mistake is punished as though it were an atrocious crime.

'How is that,' you say, 'is that what it means to be an important man?' My friend, do you not understand that it cannot possibly mean anything but that you are an extremely important person, since you are so severely treated.[9]

In Christianity, Kierkegaard claims, or rather, in the Christ, God as it were turns to man and says, "See what it is to be man!" But Christ is at the same time Model and Redeemer, at the same time severity and gentleness. As Model, as the Lord, he is all severity, keeping the standard at the highest, so that no one need worry about exhausting this ideal. As Redeemer he is all gentleness, for he knows our weakness, how we faint without forgiveness and grace. So Christianity is quite capable of giving man all the

[9] *Journals*, No. 1347, pp. 521-522.

severity and all the gentleness he needs. And what about man, of what is he capable? Well, as it turns out, he is quite capable, precisely as a Christian, of taking both the severity and the gentleness in vain. In Medieval monasticism, he took the severity in vain, making God out to be an Oriental tyrant who relishes flagellations. Then came the Reformation and then Protestantism, and then it seemed to Kierkegaard that, particularly in Denmark, man was busily taking the gentleness in vain. All the preaching about forgiveness and justification by faith for the purpose of easing the "anxious conscience" when not a single individual was being sufficiently severe with himself to suspect even remotely what an "anxious conscience" might be! Furthermore, it was not really possible to preach the gentleness as a general proclamation—that was a misunderstanding of gentleness. For Christ as the highest was the same for all, namely, the Model in all its severity, but Christ as the Redeemer, as grace and as gentleness, could only be a private matter between each individual and Christ.

The Requirement—Indulgence

The requirement is the universal, that which applies to all, and is the scale by which everyone shall be measured. The requirement, therefore is the thing that must be proclaimed; the teacher has to proclaim the requirement and thus provoke uneasiness; he dare not reduce the requirement.

Indulgence must not be proclaimed, neither can it be proclaimed, for it is completely different for the various individuals, and it is their inmost private understanding with God.

The proclamation of the requirement must drive men to God and Christ with the intent of finding what indulgence they need, what they dare pray for in the sight of God by way of indulgence, while the proclamation of the requirement at the same time holds them to God.

But the relation has been inverted. The teachers (the parsons) do not proclaim the requirement, but indulgence. Instead of regarding the indulgence as the profoundest secret of the conscience before God, in the face of the requirement, they have inverted the relation and proclaim, with mutual contentment and edification, indulgence simply and solely; they entirely omit the requirement, or even say that it was only for the Apostles; and so one man enthusiastically proclaims indulgence to the others—indulgence which, however, is one of the prerogatives of God's glory, so that it can only be bestowed by him upon the individual, that is, upon every individual, but quite separately and individually.[10]

[10] *Journals*, No. 1097, pp. 391-392.

All this preaching of gentleness and indulgence, Kierkegaard saw, was not only a misunderstanding but was actually no kindness at all to the individual. On the contrary, it was a monstrous cruelty ignorantly masquerading as kindness, for it arrested the individual at the stage of paganism and worldliness, yet with enough of the Christian trimmings to delude him into thinking that this refined paganism and worldliness was Christianity—even Christianity in its more "advanced" form. So he took it upon himself as his providential task to reintroduce the element of severity. Yet he knew that the task of a reformer would always run him into the risk of misrepresenting the total quality of Christianity, because of the necessity of emphasizing the neglected factor out of all proportion just to get people to listen, or even to pay a modicum of their attention. People, in spite of their protestations of reasonableness, do not listen to temperate and reasonable statements. You had to goad them, make them angry, even attack them, just to get their attention, and in the literary medium this meant satire, ridicule, exaggeration. But in all this there lay the true danger of misrepresenting Christianity to *genuine* pagans who were looking toward it to find their hope and their salvation. So Kierkegaard tried to counteract this danger in various places in his writings, especially in *The Journals.* "It is my firm conviction (and I have never understood Christianity differently) that severe as it is, it is equally gentle."[11] And, in fact, the whole idea of the stages, that man is not required to become what God wants him to be at a stroke but by steps—this to him was another evidence of God's gentleness, a gentleness which, alas, could also be taken in vain.

. . . God is infinite love in this too, that he does not suddenly and all at once fall upon a man and demand that he should be spirit—for then a man must perish. No, he takes hold so gently, it is a long operation, an education; sometimes there is a breathing space, when God strengthens the patient in finite ways—but then on again. And one thing God demands unconditionally at every moment: honesty, not to reverse the position and prove his relationship with God, or the truth of his concern, from good fortune, success, etc. but *contrariwise* to admit that this is so because of his weakness, one of God's adjustments, something which perhaps at a later date he must dispense with —in order to go further.[12]

[11] *Journals,* No. 1113, p. 397.
[12] *Journals,* No. 1242, p. 456.

As far as our own spiritual condition is concerned, things are a little different here and now from what they were in Kierkegaard's Denmark—and yet, not so radically different. We in America have been spared by our history some of the pitfalls that come with an established Church, the stifling atmosphere in which it is assumed that all are Chrisitians and where the officialdom of the clergy is paid by the state. And technical philosophy has become more humble than in Kierkegaard's day. People no longer look to it for salvation because it disclaims to offer any. People now look to science, to various forms of the organization of society, and to art and culture for their salvation. These are the true inheritors of the Hegelian dream. The sad thing is that under such conditions as these so many do not become individuals—they have even lost the idea of what an individual is, in spite of our tradition of respect for the individual. One follows the line of least resistance today in suppressing any lurking desire to be and to become an individual. And yet, all of us *are* individuals: an incipient individual is what each person finds himself to be when he first discovers himself at all, and from this condition no one can escape.

And of course the problem of severity and gentleness is perennial, and is to be found wherever the Church is. The Church prays for "all sorts and conditions of men," and Kierkegaard surely teaches us how varied these sorts and conditions are—not only by outward circumstance, but by the inward qualifications of the stage they are in—and how, whether they are "inside" or "outside" the Church, they nevertheless always "understand" Christianity according to the stage they are in. The Church's problem here is to get the person from a childish understanding of Christianity, where the individual sees God as the giver of candy, to a mature understanding of Christianity, where the individual sees God as the giver, in Christ, of life everlasting.

Kierkegaard addressed all of his religious discourses to "the individual" and he also wrote many beautiful prayers for the consolation and strengthening of the individual, especially the obscure, humble individual who counted for nothing in the eyes of the world.[13] But I do not wish to end this book on quite such a serious note. For Kierkegaard also had the light touch, and wrote many

[13] *The Prayers of Kierkegaard,* ed. Perry D. LeFevre (Chicago: University of Chicago Press, 1956).

instructive parables which not only made a moral or spiritual point but also made people see how comical they were letting themselves become. So I will end on such a parable, one that has the particular merit of bringing together the whole idea of the individual becoming what God wants him to be, in the particular situation in Christendom in which Kierkegaard saw it as his providential task to reintroduce severity:

THE DOMESTIC GOOSE
a moral tale

Try to imagine for a moment that geese could talk—that they had so arranged things that they too had their divine worship and their church-going.

Every Sunday they would meet together and a gander would preach. The sermon was essentially the same each time—it told of the glorious destiny of geese, of the noble end for which their maker had created them—and every time his name was mentioned all the geese curtsied and all the ganders bowed their heads. They were to use their wings to fly away to the distant pastures to which they really belonged; for they were only pilgrims on this earth.

The same thing happened each Sunday. Thereupon the meeting broke up and they all waddled home, only to meet again next Sunday for divine worship and waddle off home again—but that was as far as they ever got. They throve and grew fat, plump and delicious—and at Michaelmas they were eaten—and that was as far as they ever got. It never came to anything. For while their conversation on Sundays was all high-sounding, on Mondays they would tell each other what had happened to the goose who had taken the end set before them quite seriously, and in spite of many tribulations had tried to use the wings its creator had bestowed upon it.

All that was indeed common knowledge among the geese, but of course no one mentioned the subject on Sundays, for as they observed, it would then have been obvious that to attend divine service would have been to fool both God and themselves.

Among the geese were several who looked ill and wan, and all the other geese said—there, you see what comes of taking flying seriously. It is all because they go about meditating on flying that they get thin and wan and are not blessed by the grace of God as we are; for that is why we grow fat, plump, and delicious.

And so next Sunday off they went to divine service, and the old gander preached of the glorious end for which their Maker (and at that point all the geese curtsied and the ganders bowed their heads) had created them, and of why they were given wings.

And the same is true of divine worship in Christianity.[14]

[14] *Journals,* No. 1392, pp. 541-542.

Type used in this book
Body, 10 on 12 and 9 on 10 Times Roman
Display, Lydian
Paper: "R" Standard White Antique